The Closest Thing to Crazy

The Closest Thing to Crazy

My Life of Musical Adventures

Mike Batt

NEB 032

First published in the UK in 2024 by Nine Eight Books
An imprint of Black & White Publishing Group
A Bonnier Books UK company
4th Floor, Victoria House, Bloomsbury Square, London, WC1B 4DA
Owned by Bonnier Books, Sveavägen 56, Stockholm, Sweden

✕ @nineeightbooks

◉ @nineeightbooks

Hardback ISBN: 978-1-7851-2084-8
eBook ISBN: 978-1-7851-2085-5
Audio ISBN: 978-1-7851-2260-6

All rights reserved. No part of this publication may be reproduced, stored in a retrieval system, or transmitted in any form or by any means, without the prior permission in writing of the publisher, nor be otherwise circulated in any form of binding or cover other than that in which it is published and without a similar condition including this condition being imposed on the subsequent purchaser.

A CIP catalogue record for this book is available from the British Library.

Publishing director: Pete Selby
Editor: James Lilford

Cover design by Bonnier Books UK art dept
Typeset by IDSUK (Data Connection) Ltd
Printed and bound in Great Britain by Clays Ltd, Elcograf S.p.A

1 3 5 7 9 10 8 6 4 2

Text copyright © Mike Batt, 2024

The right of Mike Batt to be identified as the author of this work has been asserted in accordance with the Copyright, Designs and Patents Act 1988.

Every reasonable effort has been made to trace copyright-holders of material reproduced in this book. If any have been inadvertently overlooked, the publisher would be glad to hear from them.

Nine Eight Books is an imprint of Bonnier Books UK
www.bonnierbooks.co.uk

In memory of my extraordinary parents, Norman and Elaine Batt

'Far better is it to dare mighty things, to win glorious triumphs, even though checkered by failure . . . than to rank with those poor spirits who neither enjoy nor suffer much, because they live in a gray twilight that knows not victory nor defeat.'

Theodore Roosevelt

Contents

Prelude ix

PART ONE
1. A Brush with Death 3
2. Breaking into the Music Business 17
3. Learning the Ropes 31
4. Out on a Limb 47
5. 'Breaking' the Wombles 63
6. Busy and Hot 81
7. Let's Get Serious Again 95
8. Films and Family 109

PART TWO
9. Making Waves 127
10. Atlantic Crossing and Caribbean Adventures ... 139
11. 'Shittin' in High Cotton' 145
12. The Mighty Pacific 155
13. Sydney 165

PART THREE
14. A Winter's Tale: The Heartache Hits 173
15. The Hunting of the Snark – My Mad, Onward Journey ... 187

16.	The Phantom of the Opera	199
17.	I Watch You Sleeping	211
18.	The Mounting of the Snark	223
19.	The Roaring '90s	233
20.	Ewshot Hall	251
21.	Small Girl, Brown Hair	267
22.	The Difficult Second Album	283
23.	The House and the Palace	291
24.	I Will Be There	301
25.	The Shape of Things to Come	307

Acknowledgements 319
Index 321

Prelude

It struck me recently that an artist's work can often unconsciously resonate with what is actually happening in real life. A number of years ago I was commissioned by a film director to write the song that became 'Caravan Song' – about a girl who wants to break away ('I don't know where I'm going, but I'm going'). It did not occur to me until much later that although my lyric was solely written to express the emotional position of the girl in the movie, it exactly represented my own position at that time in my life.

When I began to write the first lyrics that kick-started my lifelong project, 'The Hunting of the Snark', based on Lewis Carroll's epic nonsense poem, these were my first words:

> Out in the deserts of darkness and dreams
> Out through the oceans of sadness we sailed.
> Venturing onwards through mystical scenes,
> Blown on the whim of the wind that prevailed.
> We had no reason to doubt the truth
> Driven by danger and discontent
> And the drums of youth.

When I wrote those lyrics I had just returned from a two-year, trans-global sea voyage of my own. They were intended to be the words of fictitious characters created by Lewis Carroll and yet they fitted my own life as if they had been completely autobiographical. The family had just completed a literal sea voyage that had indeed involved the realisation of dreams, but also sadness, danger, discontent, mystical scenes, drums and adventure:

> Don't let the memory die
> Children of the sky, heroes of the sea;
> And as your life passes by,
> Remember how it feels to be
> Children of the sky.

It never crossed my mind that these words might have been born from real-life feelings and experiences. I was just trying to write a treatment of a nonsensical adventure story created by a literary genius who had died many years earlier.

As I studied the Snark poem I began to examine the characters. Carroll left us to decide for ourselves what might be the meaning of the poem and the essence of each character. I saw the Bellman (the captain) as being someone who bravely blasts onwards through life and dismisses any thought of danger – and thus he encounters little or none of it. In my mental picture, if the Bellman were to be walking through a forest full of snakes, his confidence would drive them away and he wouldn't even know they had been there in the undergrowth. Conversely, the Baker tells the crew that his uncle once warned him that if he were to find an ordinary, everyday snark, that would be fine, but if he were to encounter a boojum snark, he would vanish away and never be met with again. This describes the timid Baker – in a general sense, as the antithesis of the Bellman. Hence, I used the conflicting characters of the bold, sometimes ignorant

PRELUDE

Bellman and the sensitive, cautious Baker as my pivotal rationale for what happens in my treatment of the work: the only one who is afraid of finding the boojum is the only one who finds it.

Just as I have found with my own lyrics, works of fiction can sometimes have a focusing effect on reality, rather in the same way that tarot cards, in my view, contain no genuine arcane magic but provide a fascinating point of focus for our thoughts and contemplation about who we are and what we do.

I believe that, simplistically, we are all, to varying extents, a mixture of the Bellman and the Baker. Starting with myself; yes, I often behave like the Bellman. Confident, strong and resolute. But does my appetite for risk drive me and my loved ones towards or away from danger and pain? And sometimes I am the sensitive Baker. Too cautious? Too scared? I am both characters at the same time. Which will it be from moment to moment? And it's not just those two-dimensional analyses that apply – it is, in real life, completely three-dimensional and constantly changing in all of us to different degrees.

Forgive me if during this autobiography you will find Snark or other references that try to explain my actions, emotions and philosophical observations. I have added this note to explain clearly why I've done that. As a writer, usually of songs, it's almost uncanny how often I notice how real life and art are running along together as if bound to each other like partners in a three-legged race.

Mike Batt
May 2024

PART ONE

CHAPTER 1

A Brush with Death

Sixty miles an hour into a concrete block on a lonely Spanish mountain road early one dark morning was not the way I had planned to leave this world – not that you plan to go any particular way – but as I looked up from the back seat of the people carrier to see that it was plunging off the road, the probability that these would be my last moments flashed through my mind. I shall always remember the heavy, final crunch, the jolt, the sensation of stopping instantly, the violence of it, the shocking pain in my neck. Someone was screaming with agony in a deep, rhythmical, unworldly voice and I suddenly realised it was me.

Damn. Shit.

I suppose you don't think straight. You don't think you have a broken neck. You don't think you are so close to instant death if that last remaining millimetre of your C2 vertebra snaps because of a sudden movement. You just focus on what's foremost in your mind – the video shoot we were travelling to and which I should be directing would now be cancelled.

Bollocks.

And they are taking you to hospital in a bus with the word 'ambulance' written on the side, because they haven't got actual ambulances in the mountains of Spain, or at least they don't on that particular morning. There are other people hurt, too. The oboist in the band is knocked unconscious and has injuries to her face and legs. Our cameraman, Roger McDonald, has three broken ribs and a punctured lung.

Later, I'm lying in the local hospital and they've finally sussed that I'll die if I move, so my wife Julianne is whispering in my ear about how there is a negotiation going on with the health insurance people and that my doctor in London is insisting I should not be moved under any circumstances. But eventually, with his approval, I am taken by a spinal unit ambulance to Madrid. I'm hanging in a sort of floating stretcher and being cuddled by an attractive nurse as I am rather precariously transported to Madrid, a journey of about ninety minutes. Ultimately, they will fit me with a halo brace by screwing it into my skull at four points. It's a contraption I'll have to wear for four months, twenty-four hours a day.

That was twenty-three years ago and I didn't die. People ask if the near-death experience changed my life. I don't know. It probably did, but it wasn't the road to Damascus. I've always been aware of our transient existence, always been grateful for each moment. Life's like a party where your dad's going to come and take you home but you don't want him to come just yet.

The Wandering Batts

It's a life that started in Southampton, seventy-five years ago in 1949. My dad was Norman Frederick Batt, my mum was Elaine Jennings, and two more different people you couldn't hope to meet.

A BRUSH WITH DEATH

He was an ex-wartime army officer (but stayed in the Reserve after the Second World War) – athletic, talented in all things mechanical and electrical, a professional civil engineer. A brilliant man, he died in 1997 and I miss him every single day. He always did his own electrical and plumbing work, had a hell of a temper but a great sense of humour. Mum was an eccentric former athletic PE and art teacher with a superb theatrical streak and the ability to make fantastic toys, clothes, dressing-up outfits and, eventually, Womble costumes. From this odd couple, I learned to be whoever I am.

Our family of six lived happily for the most part in many different towns as Dad got different jobs in local government civil engineering. Having finished the war as a 24-year-old acting major in charge of the rebuilding of Tobruk harbour in Libya, he took a contrastingly humble civilian job for 250 quid a year as a junior assistant in the municipal engineering department at Southampton. He had met my mum when, as a dashing Boy Scout, five years her senior, he had been supervising a party for young people in Winchester. They had kept in touch and took up their romance just as the war began. They were married in early 1946 at the Southampton Civic Centre Registry Office. Ration books and the post-wartime mentality of frugality prevailed. My dad was a motor-car nut and his dad and his two uncles had an Esso garage in Totton, near Southampton. Their sisters – my dad's aunts – ran the general store. To this day, there is still a bus stop called Batts Corner in Totton, just near where the old general store stands. It's a vape supplies store now.

My brother John was the first to arrive and I followed him two years later. I was born where we all lived, in the remaining two-bedroomed half of a bombed house in Gordon Avenue, Southampton. Six months later, we were on the road again and moved to York, where Dad had moved up to be a slightly less junior assistant. Dick was born there, two years after me. Two years later, we were back down South again, this time in Eastbourne, where Dad was a tiny bit less junior and Paula, our only sister, joined us.

In Eastbourne, there was always a little red speedboat moored to the pier and the lamp posts had crowns and flowers left over from the Queen's Coronation in 1953. I wasn't at school yet so I used to spend afternoons with my mum on the promenade by the sea. There was a bloke called Uncle Bertie who used to do Punch and Judy and conjuring tricks on the seafront. I worshipped him. It was my first experience of the magic of show business.

We still have a photo taken on my first day at junior school, aged five. I look quite happy — even cheeky — in the picture, sporting a ridiculous combination of tartan shirt and regulation striped school tie. I know my mum made all my clothes in those days so it can't have been my own fashion sense that prevailed, but friends say it pre-empted my entire attitude to — and taste in — clothes. I never know whether to take that as a compliment or not. Probably not.

Nevertheless, I cried and had to be taken out of school on that first day. It was the daunting experience of all the new things — the smell of the floor wax, the feeling of being lost and overwhelmed. I also remember a few days later not being allowed to leave the classroom to go for a wee and the inevitable feeling of warm piss running down my legs, out of my grey shorts, over my socks and shoes and into the aisle between the desks in the classroom.

The teacher slapped my legs really hard in front of the whole class for pissing on the floor. I still remember the humiliation.

When I was five my mum and dad, who were such great parents, stayed up all night to make me a fantastic puppet theatre and some magic tricks, including a top hat with a false bottom, from which I could produce a stuffed pink toy rabbit. It was the spark that was lit by Uncle Bertie on the seafront. I jumped at it and was soon giving shows to all the neighbours. I even gave a show to my class. There was a script for the puppet show, which came with it. It said 'Enter Punch', 'Enter Judy', 'Enter Policeman' and other such stage directions. I didn't know you just had to obey the stage directions; I thought you had to read them out, so I'd yell out 'Enter Punch!' and then I'd make him enter. Then I'd say the lines. I suppose it gave it a certain something.

I had a little money box when I was about seven. It was shaped like a red post box, with a slot for the coins. This made me aware that post boxes were, clearly, for putting money in. So every week, for about six weeks, when I passed the local red post box in the street, I would put my sixpence pocket money into the real, big post box to save it. I could just reach the slot. When my mum found out, she told me that you only put money in toy post boxes, not real ones, but by then I'd posted six weeks' pocket money. What kind of kid does that? I must have been uniquely naive.

Our next stop was Coventry, where we joined the Cubs. *I promise to do my best, to do my duty to God and the Queen, to keep the law of the wolf cub pack and to do a good turn to somebody every day.* One night I remember being on my own, walking home and there weren't any street lights. Terrified that some 'rough boys' were going to jump out of an alleyway and attack me, I decided to walk down the middle of the dark street. At least that way if they jumped out I'd have a three-yard start. I began talking in three different, deep voices, saying things like, 'Okay, Charlie, get that baseball bat ready' and 'Yeah, Jim, okay. How was your karate class tonight?' to give the impression that a really tough gang of lads was walking down the street. With my eight-year-old voice doing all the voices it must have sounded hilarious, but I never got jumped out on, so it clearly worked.

When I was about nine, Dad's work took us to Bradford. By now he was chief assistant at the Engineering Department. Which meant he was a chief, but also that he was still an assistant. He had a trench coat and wellies and would often be called out in the night to go walking through sewers, which basically meant walking through shit. I took the 11 plus exam in Bradford and apparently surprised my parents by passing it.

I got to go to Belle Vue Grammar School on Manningham Lane, where John had already been for two years. It was a Victorian-style school building, noted for the fact that J.B. Priestley had gone there. Not that we kids knew who the fuck he was. Corporal punishment went on all the time. If you forgot your homework, you were hauled out in front of the class, bent over a desk and whacked. Bradford was quite a rough place, back then. If you saw a group of lads walking towards you down the road, you'd cross over and walk down the other side. Having posh southern accents only made things worse, so we soon learned the flat vowel sounds of the Bradford accent in an attempt to fit in.

Money was always tight. With four kids, most of our clothes and toys were handmade or hand-me-downs. Dad made me a fantastic pair of wooden stilts and I stilt-walked the 4 miles from Bradford to Shipley and back, and pogo-sticked it one way only, without ever falling off. I thought marathon stilt-walking and one-way pogo-sticking had some value to the world. My parents also scrimped to buy me a second-hand Whitaker and Mapplebeck racing bike. At thirteen, they let me go off alone on it to visit a 'girlfriend' in Bolton, all the way across the Moors, staying in youth hostels (one shilling and ninepence a night) over a four-day period, during which I didn't contact them once. They seemed to give all four of us a lot of freedom to be independent.

We played war games, killing the enemy in the park with hockey sticks as machine guns, shouting, '*ak-ak-ak-ak-ak*'. We learned to roller-skate at what seemed to us like 40 miles an hour down the steep hill that was called Emm Lane and just save ourselves from falling under the wheels of lorries and buses by doing a rapid ninety-degree turn on busy Manningham Lane. The Bay of Pigs crisis happened while we were in Bradford and we all really thought we were about to be wiped out by a nuclear war.

Kennedy and Khrushchev faced each other across the world stage and played the ultimate game of brinksmanship as Russian warships headed towards Cuba under threat of nuclear retaliation from America. My thirteen-year-old brother John worked out that the nearest target town would probably be Leeds and that the blast would come from there. Without telling Mum and Dad, we took over the cellar of our house, hoarding blankets, torches, maps, clothing, food, a radio and tinned food, borrowed tin by tin from the larder. We were ready so that if it happened, we would be able to offer our parents a solution.

I was annoyed that I was probably going to die before ever having sex, preferably with either Janet or Allison from school, neither of whom had ever been particularly nice to me.

Playing It by Ear

At Belle Vue Grammar School there was a Polish kid called Kazak Novakowski, who taught me to play the accordion. I hadn't shown much of a talent or interest in music until I was about eleven, when

THE CLOSEST THING TO CRAZY

I started picking tunes up by ear, tinkling on an upright piano my dad bought in a junk shop. He was always buying things in *Exchange & Mart* magazine, or in junk shops, and doing them up. The piano was just another of those items. He never claimed to be musical, but he could vamp about three songs on the piano, all on the black keys, with a tremendous, rhythmical feel. I thought it sounded brilliant. One of those songs was 'In Eleven More Months and Ten More Days I'll Be Out of the Caraboose' and another was 'The Still of the Night'. I tried to emulate him and gradually picked up tunes I would hear on the radio. When Kaz taught me the basic chord structure of the left-hand buttons of the accordion, the whole pattern of harmonic structure clicked into place. On an accordion you play a single button and get a whole chord (like chord organs), but I worked out that if I could play those chords as three-note chords on the left hand of the piano, I would have cracked it. That's when the penny dropped and I soon found myself able to play pretty much anything on the piano by ear.

I joined Concert Hall Record Club by responding to an offer on a leaflet that came through the door. You got six classical EPs for nothing if you promised to buy three proper albums for twenty-six shillings each. The first album I bought was Schubert's 'Symphony No. 9' conducted by Carl Schuricht. I played it over and over again until I knew every entry of every instrument and would hum it through from top to bottom. When the family went out shopping on Saturdays, I would stay behind and build an orchestra using the dining room furniture, putting little cards out to mark where the violins, violas, trumpets and woodwinds were. Then I'd put Schubert's Ninth on the gramophone and conduct my orchestra of furniture all afternoon, using my right hand to beat the rhythm and my left hand and facial expressions to coax a more passionate performance from the dining-chair violin section.

I also learned all these classical pieces on the piano, but not from the sheet music (as they were correctly written); I got what I could get by ear, from listening to the records. My versions of the classics were often in a different key from the original and very flamboyant. I don't know if I impressed anyone else, but I certainly impressed myself!

A Bedroom Full of Piano

I was thirteen when we moved to Winchester. It was like moving from darkness to light. We went to Peter Symonds' School, where my dad had gone when he was young, and my sister Paula went to the County High School, where Mum had been when she had met him – so the family really was coming home. Dad's new job was actually in Bracknell new town, 40 miles north of Winchester, so his long drive to work each day was his sacrifice to enable us to go to those schools. We walked to school from our nearby house and there were no gangs of lads looking for a fight. Bradford had given us some great experiences and memories, but coming to Winchester was life-changing. Our house was a nice, small, detached one in a leafy suburb, but it only had three bedrooms. I was therefore allocated the front sitting room as my bedroom and this coincided with my noticing an ad in the paper asking for someone to take away a Broadwood grand piano, for free. We collected our free grand piano and it lived in my downstairs bedroom. Dominated it, in fact. You couldn't get into the bedroom by walking in; you had to crawl under the piano, which was quite good for privacy. It was huge. The pointed end was rammed right up against the door and

THE CLOSEST THING TO CRAZY

the keyboard end was so close to the fireplace at the other end of the room that I had to put the piano stool on the hearth in order to be able to squeeze myself in to play it. It was a full-length concert grand in a tiny suburban front room. The only other thing in the room was my small bed, squashed into the corner almost as an afterthought. As I progressed into adolescence, I would sit at my grand piano with all the windows open just as the girls all came out of the nearby County High School and I'd play my dodgy versions of the classics as loudly as possible in the hope that some gorgeous girl would hear the music and fall in love with me. If any of them ever did, they kept it to themselves.

Those were the exciting years during which I learned about my talent and about what was driving me. I loved all records. I played Frank Ifield's 'I Remember You' till it wore out, bought the Springfields' 'Island of Dreams', delved into classics, flamenco and pop. Rock didn't really exist yet, but it was ultra-cool to be into Leadbelly, Howlin' Wolf and Josh White, whose album *Empty Bed Blues* was a favourite of mine. The Beatles had just started and were putting out singles regularly all throughout my adolescence. The Stones were laying down a regular barrage of great white R&B. I copied them – I wanted to be Mick Jagger, John Lennon, Paul McCartney, Brian Wilson and probably John Sebastian of the Lovin' Spoonful as well. And then it was all Jimi Hendrix, the Animals, the Yardbirds and the Move, and suddenly rock did exist.

There were other great bands, lesser-known ones like the Downliners Sect and Geno Washington's Ram Jam Band. I went to see Geno at Southampton Civic Centre in December 1966 with Jimi Hendrix supporting! By now, the Dining Room Furniture Symphony Orchestra had been disbanded and my role-playing was epitomised by my buying the double A-side 'Ruby Tuesday' and 'Let's Spend the Night Together' and leaping around the sitting room being Mick, with all the actions and the vocals. Very embarrassing if anyone walks in while you're in the middle of a full, aerial Mick Jagger impression!

I played piano in a pub in town when I was fourteen. It was the only way to get into the pub, under-age. I would always have a few free pints on top of the piano and some drunk hanging off me, trying to sing 'Slow Boat to China'. It taught me that the piano was a good way to be welcomed socially and it was indeed a good way of making friends, even if the County High girls hadn't taken the hint yet.

I answered an advertisement in the paper and joined a Southampton rhythm and blues band called Phase Four. The other guys were printers during the day and all of them were nineteen; I was fifteen. We'd get the odd gig, but not much. Most of our gigs were in youth clubs, but we played the Park Ballroom a couple of times. When I joined, I knew next to nothing about blues, but I soon picked it up. We played a lot of Chuck Berry songs. His songs showed me the importance of lyrics. The tunes were all pretty much the same, but the lyrics were chunks of urban poetry, completely original, totally unique. Many kids at school got to be the singer in a band for one of two reasons. Either they owned a microphone and a PA system or they could remember lots of Chuck Berry lyrics. In Phase Four, when we ran out of songs, one of us would shout, 'Twelve-bar blues in G' and we'd be off again.

I started singing lead vocals, even though I didn't own the PA system. My voice was still a fifteen-year-old voice and must've sounded pretty squeaky, but it was good practice. Shortly after that I teamed up with a kid at school called Andy Renton, who was, at fourteen, a damn good drummer. He worshipped Keith Moon of the Who. We called our duo That Lady's Twins because we were all sitting down to lunch one time, trying to think of a name for me and Andy and my mum said, 'What do they call that lady's twins?' – referring to pop-star twins Paul and Barry Ryan (sons of TV singer Marion Ryan), so that's what we called ourselves. We were still at school, but we managed to get work as a duo. I sang and played a Watkins Telstar organ – very loudly – and Andy went mad on the drums. We were only a duo, but we made as much noise as a four-piece group. One of the songs I sang was John Mayall's 'Crawling Up a Hill', which I would record forty years later with Katie Melua.

Trying to Impress Girls

I always thought music was there for one main reason – to impress girls. It became a sort of lifetime habit, trying to impress women. When I first crossed that line from thinking girls were nuisances to trying to persuade them to take their shirts off, I was about fourteen. It was being near County High School that was pivotal to my jumping that gap as I grew older. I started going to ballroom dancing classes to meet girls. They were held at Highclere School of Dancing in Winchester. The boys lined the walls at one end of the long room, the girls at the other. When we had to choose a partner we would walk gingerly down the room and go up to a girl. It was excruciatingly painful and embarrassing, and required a great deal of courage. All the girls danced with stiff backs and held you as far away as possible, but you did get to brush up against their school jumpers and they all smelled wonderful.

The girl I did connect with at ballroom dancing was slim, pretty Kathy Stocks. She had a way of looking at you through half-closed

A BRUSH WITH DEATH

eyes that was mysterious and totally sexy. I plucked up the courage to ask her out and we spent some time thinking we were an item, though at the age of fifteen I didn't have the nerve to do very much even if she'd wanted me to, which I'll never know.

My brothers used to sail at Hamble River Sailing Club. I had the tie, but never went there to sail our Albacore dinghy – I didn't like the way Dad yelled at people in a boat. I thought I'd rather not learn. My brothers both put up with Dad's loud instructions and became proficient sailors. In fact, Dick eventually became British champion of several different classes, is now one of the best-known racing sail makers in Britain and was chief measurer (technical judge) for three Olympic Games in succession. When they went to Hamble River I'd go along with them anyway, with Kathy, and we would sit in a corner of the dark little coffee bar listening to 'The House of the Rising Sun' by the Animals and what must have been circular-breathing kissing. 'The House of the Rising Sun' was the most popular song on the jukebox because it was the longest for the money. I think it was about five minutes long and still only cost sixpence to hear.

One day, Kathy started acting strangely and not returning my calls. I waited for an hour outside the cinema before I realised she had stood me up and trudged home miserably. I bought 'It's Over' by Roy Orbison and played it endlessly in my bedroom. I thought life itself, not just my relationship with Kathy, was over. Her perfume hung in the air and each line of lyrics cut into me: 'Golden days before they end/whisper secrets to the wind/your baby won't be near you any more'. With hindsight, I suppose I was all the time subconsciously learning about the power of lyrics and the importance of love in our lives.

CHAPTER TWO

Breaking into the Music Business

At school, I had joined the Army Cadets and was so keen, going to every available camp, every available course, that they promoted me to company sergeant major. As a career choice, my musical leanings fought this. I did look at the music side of the army, but they don't let you go in as an officer. Also, even if you get to the top in army music, the highest rank you can reach is lieutenant colonel. My competitive streak won the day and I decided the army wasn't for me, not when some of my contemporaries might become brigadiers and generals.

When I was seventeen, I told my headmaster Mr Ashurst I was going to be a songwriter. He wasn't amused. In fact, he was horrified. Knowing I was making a bit from playing in the pub and in local bands, he said, 'Ten pounds a week might seem a lot now, Batt, but when your friends come out of university in three years' time you'll be laughing on the other side of your face.' He himself never laughed on either side of his face!

I left school with two Es in Music and Art, and an A in English Literature as my three A-levels. Terrible grades seen in the context of the fact that I was unusually good at art, the best in my year by miles, and I was the only Music A-level pupil, with a teacher to myself. I feel no guilt in blaming the school, whose art and music faculties were almost non-existent. In fact, I was only told the syllabus of A-level music three months before the exam. But my A in English Literature showed I wasn't a complete idiot.

I told my dad that I wanted him to understand that I needed a year to try to break into the music business – I didn't want him to support me financially, I just wanted him to understand. Which he did. If I didn't get to a position where I could make a living at it within a year, I would go to art school or university, if they would have me. But I had no real intention of going to university: I was going to break into the music business, whether the music business liked it or not.

I got a job playing the organ in a strip club. Well, it wasn't actually a strip club *every* night, just a drinking and dancing establishment called the Paradise Club. I used to borrow my mum's Austin 1100 and drive the 12 miles from Winchester to Southampton. The band was me, a sad little bloke called Johnny, who was the drummer and band leader, and the bass player, who was a milkman. At 4 a.m. he went straight from the club to the dairy to do his rounds. Occasionally we were joined by a sexy girl singer who sang 'Moon River' and a rather less convincing 'A Whiter Shade of Pale'. I don't know if it would have interested her to know that I fancied her – she was about thirty-five to my eighteen – but in any case I didn't have the nerve to make a move. Apart from anything, I think she was almost certainly shagging the milkman/bass player. On Thursdays and Saturdays the club did indeed become a strip club and several ladies of sparsely clothed potential would descend on us. Those were the best nights. As the band, we were upstage of the girls so whenever their modesty needed protection from the audience, they turned upstage and we got the good news.

During the days, I went 'up to London' on the train (two quid return) to try to get signed as a writer and artist. I would make appointments with junior A&R men, talent scouts and record producers. I never sent my tape in; I was always very insistent that I had to meet them, and they usually relented. My very basic demos were made in my bedroom using an old Ferrograph reel-to-reel tape recorder that my dad had found in (yes!) a junk shop.

The Beatles had made *Sgt. Pepper*, Jimi Hendrix was in his prime. The long, Flower Power summer of 1967 formed the backdrop to my visits to London. The Kinks' 'Waterloo Sunset' was in the charts and I would walk in the sunshine from Waterloo Station to 9 Albert Embankment, where Decca Records had their headquarters. There, I met Peter Shelley, a young guy but still older than me, whose job was to scout for talent and to assist the record producers. He worked for Dick Rowe, the man who famously turned down the Beatles but signed the Stones. Peter was very friendly, and liked what I played him, but said he didn't hear a hit. It was to take two or three more visits before he announced that he wanted to do a test demo with me as an artist.

Peter loved the gimmicky side of the business. He even said he thought I ought to wear a Noddy hat as part of my 'image'. I said I'd rather eat an anchovy sandwich than do that. 'For a hundred thousand quid a year, I'd go round with my dick hanging out,' he told me. It shocked me a bit, innocent eighteen-year-old that I was, but funnily enough, Peter's obsession with gimmickry was very rock 'n' roll. He liked the ridiculousness of it.

THE CLOSEST THING TO CRAZY

Nothing came of my recording test – Peter's bosses rejected it, but they had also rejected the Beatles, so I reckoned I was in good company. Nevertheless, Peter and I eventually became good friends. Years later, he 'created' the name Alvin Stardust and found Shane Fenton to 'be' Alvin, writing 'My Coo Ca Choo' and producing a string of other big hits. So, his gimmickry made him rich. Unfortunately, he didn't really have the fighting spirit in business matters and made a few decisions that allowed his wealth to slip away. His accountant, Michael Levy – later to become Lord Levy, Tony Blair's chief fundraiser – was the one who made most of the money out of Peter's hits, seizing the opportunity to form Magnet Records, with Peter taking more of a back seat and concentrating on production for the label.

Meanwhile, back in that summer of 1967, killing an hour between appointments at record companies, I lay down on the grass outside Westminster Abbey. The sun shone and the Beatles' 'Baby You're a Rich Man' was playing on somebody's transistor radio. I had seen Peter Shelley in the morning and was to see Dick Leahy that afternoon, so I walked across St James's Park and up Park Lane to Dick's office at Philips Records in Bayswater. He was another junior A&R man, assistant to Jack Baverstock, a well-known recording manager as we called producers in those days. Dick always liked my stuff, saying, as Pete had, that he couldn't hear the hit in my work yet but he always asked me to come back and see him again. I never got anywhere with Philips, but Dick played his part in my development by encouraging me. He went on to become a very successful label chief at Bell Records, where his nose for a hit was legendary. Later on, he guided George Michael's career and was his music publisher.

BREAKING INTO THE MUSIC BUSINESS

Liberty Wants Talent

One day, while riding in a bus in Southampton, I read an ad in the *New Musical Express*. It said 'LIBERTY WANTS TALENT'. It had been placed by a talent scout/A&R manager called Ray Williams, who had just started working for Liberty Records – quite a successful US label that had opened a UK office. It was unusual to see a record company advertising for talent – they usually told you to get lost. Anyway, I replied and got an appointment with Ray. I went to see him at Liberty's smart offices in the Mayfair area of London.

Ray Williams was the epitome of Swinging London as it was called then. Twenty years old, he wore a sharp, dead-cool suit with flared trousers, blue shirt, kipper tie and had the looks of a slightly more handsome version of Robert Redford. I played him my best song, 'Mr Poem', which includes the line, 'Hello, they say, your fame has made you gay'. Ray thought that he had found the next bisexual or gay pop star. Back then I didn't even know what the word 'gay' meant. He asked me what the line was about and I said it just described the guy as happy and bright.

Ray suggested there and then that I should sign to Liberty's music publishing company as a songwriter. He wanted me to meet Alan Keen, the head of publishing, who had just joined them after being programme controller at the legendary pirate radio station, Radio London. The UK government had recently legislated against pirate radio and when many of the pirate DJs joined Radio 1, Alan got the job as managing director of Metric Music, Liberty's publishing company. He was an advertising man, a salesman at heart. When he was younger, he had sold advertising space for girlie magazines. Now he was a forward-thinking music executive with a great sense of humour and a love of jazz, particularly singer Blossom Dearie and the piano virtuoso Bill Evans, to whom he would introduce me at Ronnie Scott's jazz club in Soho. Not long after our first meeting, we went to see them perform a set.

So, I was ushered into Alan's plush office the next day. We liked each other and got on ridiculously well. He signed me to an exclusive contract with Metric Music. I was elated because SOMEONE had shown an interest in me and just so pleased to be signed that I agreed to all the terms. No advance money – just a low royalty percentage – and the copyrights to all my songs exclusively to remain with the publisher until seventy years after my death. Now that's what I call an unfair contract. Luckily, because the law is on the side of the young creator rather than the big exploiter, as I was soon to discover, it afforded me such terrible terms that it was unenforceable. It wasn't Alan's fault, but it was great for me because I was able to walk away the following year.

The fascinating thing about the first day I met Ray Williams was that I didn't find out until months later that two other guys who answered Liberty's advertisement were Reg Dwight (soon to become Elton John) and Bernie Taupin (the renowned lyricist of Elton's songs). Elton and Bernie didn't meet until Ray teamed them up. In his attic office with red chairs with raffia seats, Ray met Reg Dwight and separately discovered Bernie's lyrics. He didn't sign Reg/Elton to Liberty, but he did act as the catalyst for one of the most formidable songwriting teams ever to work together. When Ray eventually left Liberty a few months later to pursue his own projects and eventually to manage Elton, in association with Beatles' publisher Dick James's record company, DJM, he vacated a job at Liberty which would soon be offered to me.

Having signed to Liberty as an artist and songwriter, I was obviously keen on developing my writing, but I needed to make a living – Liberty's enthusiasm for my work didn't pay the bills. Meanwhile I was living on people's floors and sofas, sometimes commuting from my parents' home in Winchester, and looking for a flat-share opportunity.

Because he paid me no money as a writer, Alan Keen offered me work writing out 'lead sheets' or 'top lines' for songs in the Liberty catalogue. A songwriter would deliver a song to the company on tape, but for copyright reasons and in order to have simple sheet music to offer producers who might be interested in recording the song, they needed the tune, lyrics and chords to be worked out and written down. I did it for one pound, ten shillings (£1.50) a song. So, if I did ten songs a week, I made £15 – almost enough to live on in 1968. I wanted to be the best top line writer in London so I spent extra time making sure I got the tunes down accurately and then spent ages writing them out with a music stave pen, adding the titles with Letraset, which was the only way to get a printed-looking title in those pre-computer days.

Family: Music in a Doll's House

One morning in February I was in Alan Keen's office when John Gilbert came in. The son of film director Lewis Gilbert, John was managing the hottest band in town – Family. Featuring Roger Chapman on vocals, this was the band that everyone – including the Beatles – thought would be the next Beatles. The talk of the rock social scene, they had agreed to sign to Liberty. The demos had blown me away when I had been asked by Liberty to write out their top lines. Fantastic songs, brilliantly recorded. We played those superb, weird, creative records loudly in the office and declared them to be more exciting than drugs – not that I knew the first thing about drugs!

THE CLOSEST THING TO CRAZY

Seeing that I had done the lead sheets, John asked if I arranged strings. Being passionate about arranging, but never having done a string arrangement for a record in my entire life, I said yes. He hired me on the spot to write the string and brass arrangements for Family's debut album, *Music in a Doll's House*, to be recorded at a session at Olympic Studios in Barnes, the following week. The deal was that I would get £5 per arrangement, plus a credit on the cover.

The next day, Roger Chapman, John (Charlie) Whitney and the rest of the band came in and we met in Alan Keen's office – where there was an upright piano – and talked through the material. They had specific ideas about which songs needed strings and brass, where the climaxes should begin and peak, and where they just wanted 'something'.

The song that interested me the most was one called 'The Chase'. It was already fantastic without strings or brass, with a kind of hunting rhythm and about the thrill of the chase to get the girl. With Roger's rasping, almost angry vocals, it was a great track. I thought it would be good with a couple of French horns imitating hunting horns and a string section chugging along to add excitement.

There was another song called 'Old Songs, New Songs'. I couldn't see how it could be improved. The band said they wanted a jazzy brass section to build slowly through the track, but before the track started I should add four big major chords as a kind of fanfare to start it off. At the end of the meeting, the band left, and Alan Keen came over to me. 'Ooh dear, they smelled a bit, didn't they?' he said. He was right, but they actually smelled of patchouli oil. Everyone wore it in those days, at least everyone who was part of the hippie culture. It smelled a bit like you'd slept in your clothes for a week and/or had been chain-smoking joints. Family probably slept in their clothes, smoked joints *and* wore patchouli oil!

BREAKING INTO THE MUSIC BUSINESS

One of the floors I sometimes slept on was a flat in Carlton Hill, St John's Wood, where a group of recently-graduated Cambridge students lived. I can't remember where I met them, but I was impressed that one of them had been on *University Challenge*. I wrote the Family string and brass arrangements while lying on the floor of someone else's bedroom because as a temporary visitor to the flat, I didn't actually have a bedroom of my own. I used textbooks to tell me how high and how low the instruments went (the 'compass' of the instrument). Then, back at my parents' house in Winchester, I checked them on my grand piano, which was still there in my downstairs 'bedroom' blocking the way in – unless you got down on your hands and knees and crawled under it.

On the way to the session at the famous Olympic Studios in Barnes, southwest London, I bought a baton so that I could conduct the orchestra. I was quite nervous, having only had a week to do five arrangements, and had no idea whether it would end up a disaster, a triumph or anything in between.

As I entered the huge studio, the strings were tuning up. I was taken into the control room to meet the album's producer, Dave Mason, the star of Traffic – the band who had recently made one of my favourite albums, *Mr. Fantasy*, containing the brilliant hit, 'Hole in My Shoe' – despite it featuring the annoying spoken-word section about climbing on the back of a giant albatross.

There were various members of the group around, plus a few girlfriends, people rolling spliffs. Quite a community. I felt like a schoolboy in contrast to all these cool people smelling of patchouli and looking beautiful, which all of them did. Luckily, I had with me for moral support my indescribably attractive girlfriend, Michele Green.

I made my way to the studio floor and stepped onto the podium. Big studios like this usually have quite an elaborate conductor's podium with a hook for your headphones, a phone to the control room and sometimes a small table behind you for your scores. I tried to look nonchalant, as if I did this often, but I'm sure the musicians had me sussed from the start. We began with a song called 'Mellowing Grey', which just needed strings (we would overdub the brass separately as soon as we'd recorded the strings).

I raised my baton at the fateful moment and brought it down crisply to bring the strings in at the right place as the rhythm track played in our headphones. To my surprise it sounded great. Strings, even if you make errors of judgement, have a way of sounding good. They find their own balance. Obviously they sound better if you arrange them brilliantly, but as long as the notes you write fit the chords of the song, you can't really make a complete bollocks of it.

Encouraged by how well the first three tracks had gone with the strings, we moved on to the brass. The string players went home and the brass section came into the room. I was a little awestruck by the fact that the section was led by the great jazz legend Tubby Hayes on tenor sax. I gave out the parts – two trumpets, two tenor saxes, a baritone sax, a tenor trombone and a bass trombone. The first song to be recorded was 'Old Songs, New Songs', the one that the band wanted to have four big chords at the beginning. The backing track had clicks over which the brass chords were to be recorded before the entry of the band's rhythm section. As these clicks clicked in my headphones, I brought my baton down again and a horrendous noise came blasting from the brass section. It was avant-garde to say the least.

I stopped the band; I just wanted the floor to develop a huge hole right under the conductor's podium and suck me out of sight. I imagined all those cool people in the control room laughing or rolling their eyes in disbelief. I had forgotten to transpose the Bb instruments in the brass section (trumpets and tenor saxes play a D when they mean a C), with the result that it sounded like a complete and utter cacophony. Just as I thought I was going to be sacked, Dave Mason came bounding towards me and started shaking my hand – even though it was shaking all by itself anyway.

'Brilliant, man!' he exclaimed. 'Totally fucking original. How old are you? Eighteen? Bloody hell, this is great! Let's record the rest of it.'

The brass section and I knew that it wasn't quite that simple. Where my ineptly arranged brass chords had sounded avant-garde on their own without accompaniment, as soon as the rhythm section came in, the game would be up. The odd, discordant tonality wouldn't match the backing track and I would be exposed as an incompetent teenager rather than the brilliant new bohemian genius that I had been for about four minutes. It was Tubby Hayes and the brass section who came to my rescue. Realising (as you would) that this was my first gig and taking pity on me, the brass section transposed the erroneous parts by ear so that they sounded right. So when the sound of Family came crashing into our headphones, playing the phenomenal rhythm, with harmonica riff grinding away throughout, my beautiful brass section sailed on through the track, building, building, soloing and sounding like stars, with me pumping my new baton up and down, like an expert.

The people in the control room all thought it was brilliant. I have never been more grateful to a group of musicians in my life. They really did save me from looking like a complete twat. This was a real lesson: be prepared, be careful, don't be afraid of making an idiot of yourself, but most of all, if you want to make discordant noises like Schoenberg or Stravinsky, do so.

THE CLOSEST THING TO CRAZY

Although Family were delighted with my arrangements, I was never paid for them or credited on the album – a credit that would have done me a hell of a lot of good. But those four chords taught me to be brave and take chances.

In 1968, everything was happening so quickly. Liberty signed me as an artist before the summer was over. My activities as an artist entailed – initially – the recording of three of my songs: 'Mr Poem' (the song I had initially played Ray Williams), 'Fading Yellow' and 'Mary Goes Round'. Of these, only 'Fading Yellow' stands up as a remotely presentable song now, but at the time I thought all three would have sounded fine on my hero Cat Stevens' first album, *Matthew & Son*. The brilliant title track had been a big hit, and other tracks like 'Portobello Road' and 'Granny' impressed me with their originality and wit. My attitude to the recordings was totally influenced by that album.

Bob Reisdorff, the managing director of Liberty Records, produced my first sessions as an artist. I wanted that 'Cat Stevens' sound, so he hired Richard Hewson, a brilliant young arranger who had worked with Paul McCartney, to provide the scores and conduct. Despite Richard's brilliance, the exciting session at Wessex Studios yielded three very 'nice'-sounding records, which would only get 'nicer' when I overdubbed my 'nice' voice onto them. At that age my voice was a bit like that of Herman of Herman's Hermits. I really would have liked a rockier, raunchier voice, but you get what you get. On a good day, one *Melody Maker* critic later described it as a perfect halfway point between Lennon and McCartney, so I suppose it's all in the ear of the beholder, but it was a rare compliment among the more usual brickbats or apathy. As I got more experienced and a little older, my voice began to sound more acceptable to me.

BREAKING INTO THE MUSIC BUSINESS

From Artist to A&R Man

'Mr Poem' (with 'Fading Yellow' as the B-side) came out in 1968 and sank without trace, as did my second single, an ill-advised release of 'Mary Goes Round', which was memorable only for the fact that it was even worse than 'Mr Poem' and was really only released because it was left over from the first session. Its B-side, however, was the first of my own productions – a song of mine called 'I See Wonderful Things in You', rather Bee Gees-esque in its cloying emotional vulnerability – but my first chance to arrange a track of my own as well as produce it. I was pleased with the production, done on a shoestring budget written on the back of a tape box. The whole thing, including studios and orchestral musicians, came to nearly £60.

Something about my production of this B-side impressed Bob Reisdorff. I don't know whether it was the quality of the sound or the fact that I'd stayed within my allotted sixty quid budget that impressed him most, but I didn't really care because the result was that he called me into his office shortly afterwards and offered me Ray's job as head of A&R. I was nineteen years old and hadn't a clue how to run a production department, but now I was a signed writer, artist and A&R executive, which gave me a huge buzz as a teenage bluffer with talent but not much idea of who was supposed to do what to whom and for how much. The salary was pitiful, but I had a small royalty percentage of every record I produced, a secretary and a huge office (not Ray's attic, but Alan Keen's recently vacated plush office) with Picasso lithographs on the walls and, more importantly, a piano. Even better, I had a business card with 'Mike Batt, Head of A&R, Liberty Records' on it. It was great for getting me into clubs and would have been great for pulling girls if I hadn't got the most amazing girlfriend already.

THE CLOSEST THING TO CRAZY

I'd met Michele Green at a party in Winchester when we were both eighteen, just about to leave school. She had a beautiful face, short blonde hair and wore paper knickers – only three of the many great reasons for me to be attracted to her! She and I became inseparable during the summer of 1968 and we were both bursting to get it together. I still hadn't actually 'done it' with anyone, but Michele lived with her parents in Winchester and wasn't on the pill so our repertoire of moves and activities did not include going 'all the way'. It was only when she left Winchester to live and work as a TV production assistant in London that I followed, often visiting the lovely, one-bedroom Kensington flat she shared with her friend Jenny.

One morning while the rest of the world went to work, I got a cab back over to Michele's place from Liberty Records and she and I finally took the ultimate step. I don't think she knew then or even knows to this day that it was my first time. After that, we would spend many evenings in that flat, sleeping on a mattress on the kitchen floor, smoking cigarettes in the glow of the pilot light under the gas stove, while Leonard Cohen's 'Suzanne' droned magically in the background.

CHAPTER THREE

Learning the Ropes

Because I write both music and lyrics, people often ask me which I think is the most important. Of course, the answer is that they are equally important, but I'd also have to say that if I don't write what I consider to be a great lyric, the song will never be a great song. You can almost get away with a slightly boring tune, but with a dull or inept lyric you are dead in the water. The first rhyme I ever remember writing was in Mr Field's English class at St Barnabas' Junior School in Bradford when I was eight. It went like this:

> A man from Armada was searching his larder,
> A jam tart for to find,
> He saw someone coming and was very cunning,
> And hid it behind his behind.

Not exactly poetry (and where on Earth is 'Armada'?), but at least it showed the beginning of a fascination with words and their meanings which has stayed with me all my life. When I was in my teens and developing the musical side of my personality, I was – perhaps without realising it quite as much – simultaneously reacting with fascination to great poetry by Keats, Browning, even Pope and Shakespeare, along with the lyrics of everyone in the pop culture of my time and a few oddballs like George Formby.

The one thing that had absorbed me during my teens had been the quest to educate myself as a conductor and arranger. I had been the wrong kind of musician to get into music school. Although I had taught myself to play piano, I hadn't done grades. I could write music down quite easily, but had difficulty reading piano music, where you had to instantly recognise and play handfuls of notes one after another. I have since realised that mild dyspraxia was probably the reason for my initial slowness in keyboard sight-reading. I could understand and follow through the score of a classical piece – analyse it, discuss it, pull it to pieces – and after much untutored study and practice I could write a full orchestral score to quite a high standard, but for some reason I was destined to be a loner when it came to acquiring an advanced musical education because I didn't speak the language or, for some reason, just wasn't the right kind of musician to fit into the education system. Hence when first directing sessions as a very young conductor and producer, I learned all my lessons on the job.

I had all sorts of learning experiences, many of them embarrassing, some of them exhilarating and encouraging. Staying up all night writing a piece that I would then have to conduct at 10 a.m. the next day was a regular occurrence. I would chain-smoke and drink coffee all night, nodding off occasionally before calling my copyist at about 6 a.m. He and his team of other copyists would then tear my handwritten orchestral score into several pieces and copy out the individual parts in time for the 10 a.m. session.

LEARNING THE ROPES

In those days the Musicians' Union allowed you to record up to six pieces in a three-hour session and so I often did. Taking into account a fifteen-minute union tea break, plus let's say fifteen minutes for the engineer to get a sound on the whole orchestra, that leaves twenty minutes for each song, during which the band would sight-read each one as I conducted a run-through for the engineer and we would then do a couple of takes. It was the best training you could ever get, simultaneously requiring alertness, application, meticulousness, guile, diplomacy and musicianship. The latter, in my case, was the quality that needed the most work. If a musician queried a note – 'Is the fourth beat of bar 463 a G sharp or an F sharp?' – you'd have to come up with the answer immediately, for two reasons. First, you'd look like an idiot in front of the whole band if you didn't and, second, the clock was ticking and you had to get the piece right and get it in the can, or you wouldn't have a record to release.

If I had my time again and someone were to offer me the chance to run that gauntlet on a regular basis, or to have a conservatoire education as a conductor or composer, I'd pick the real-life version any day. It was thrilling, scary, exciting and totally full of joy and energy.

Life at Liberty

While recording as an artist for Liberty, I was also doing my job as an A&R man. This meant listening to hopeful artists who, as I myself had done only months earlier, managed to get an appointment rather than just send their tapes in. It also meant meeting with managers and producers who wanted to sell or lease finished tapes of their artists to Liberty and going to see bands and artists playing in clubs and other venues. But mainly, to me, it meant producing records. I signed a duo of London boys called Thoughts and Words and we made a very good album of their songs – just acoustic, with about three of the songs accompanied by a string quartet, which I arranged. It didn't sell well, but was, as we say by way of consolation, 'critically acclaimed'. I also signed a soul band called the Soul Committee and made a single called 'The Hard Way', which actually wasn't very good and died the usual death. Then I started getting involved with blues artists, which, because I was a blues piano player, felt like going back to my own roots.

Andrew Lauder was a colleague of mine at Liberty, whose job as production manager was to get all the tapes to the factory and all the records pressed, printed and catalogued. He knew the catalogue number of every release in Liberty's catalogue and was a real music buff, even more so than me. It was Andrew's and my job to keep a lookout for good stuff coming in from Liberty's head office in the States, and each week, he and I went through piles of new records which came at us from the US. Of course we couldn't possibly release them all, so we had to be selective. We picked out Creedence Clearwater Revival's 'Proud Mary', which broke the band in the UK, and then one night we found Canned Heat in the pile, which led to them becoming huge in the UK, with songs like 'On the Road Again' and 'Going Up the Country'.

I met the band at Heathrow with Andrew and took them to their hotel, the Royal Garden in Kensington. In his bedroom there, Al Wilson, the high-voiced singer of the group, played us a cassette of the freshly-finished master of 'Going Up the Country' with its characteristic flute intro and we all knew it was going to be a huge hit.

Long-haired, hippie bluesman Al was thrilled with England. For some reason he needed a small electrical item, like a British plug adaptor or something, so we went across the road to look for it in Derry & Toms department store. As we walked through the shop he remarked on how fantastically free he thought England was. This was in contrast to America, where the cops were rude to long-haired people, there was a high level of violence and you never really felt safe walking in the street.

A couple of years later, after I'd moved on from Liberty, I was devastated to read that the thoughtful, gentle Al Wilson had died of a drug overdose.

Andrew Lauder introduced me to Roy Fisher, manager of the Groundhogs, who were led by the brilliant bottleneck blues guitar player Tony (TS) McPhee. We agreed to make an album and that I would produce it. We made the record at Marquee Studios, just behind the legendary club of the same name. The band played and I just sat there and watched the engineer record it, really. I guess I must have done a bit more than that, but in those days as long as you sat next to the engineer, you'd produced the record.

I loved the Groundhogs, but the fashion back in 1968 was for quite long tracks with lengthy solos in them. On one occasion, after a particularly tiring day's recording, the band started up a new track. We put the machine into record and listened as they played. It seemed interminable. When the band had finished, they came back into the control room to find both me and the engineer slumped fast asleep across the recording desk, the tape flicking round and round, having come off the end of the spool. Luckily, they all thought it was quite funny rather than being offended.

The album, *Scratching the Surface*, was a medium-sized hit and sold enough copies for us to have made a profit and to feel we had broken the band in the UK. I didn't produce their second album – perhaps something to do with having fallen asleep during the first one – but they went on to record a series of very successful albums for us over the next few years.

Other bands we had at the time were the Bonzo Dog Doo-Dah Band (who were very successful for us under the guidance of producer Gus Dudgeon, who would shortly afterwards produce Elton John's albums) and the Idle Race, not very successful for *us*, but their frontman, Jeff Lynne, was later to have huge success with the Move, ELO and the Traveling Wilburys.

There were several other blues albums which I produced around that time in the Groundhog Series. Some of those albums really were at the centre of the UK blues movement back then. One was an album featuring a mix of artists such as Jo Ann Kelly and another was the cheapest album I ever made. Unlike the B-side of my second single, which cost sixty quid, this whole *album* cost the same! It was a recording by the old blues legend, Big Joe Williams, who came into my office one day, having been introduced via the Groundhogs. He didn't want to sign a contract, just wanted to make the album. We insisted he at least give us the rights. Big Joe just signed the letter with a cross. He didn't want royalties (didn't trust us to pay them), but instead asked for $150 and a bottle of Scotch. I took him round the corner to Spot Studios in South Molton Street, Mayfair, which used to cost £30 an hour. He was so fat, he could hardly get up the narrow stairs. As he climbed them, he leaned heavily on a walking stick covered in notches. He told us that he carved a notch every time he did a gig and on the day the stick broke under his weight, he would retire. I silently expected that he probably would retire soon if those were indeed the conditions of his decision.

LEARNING THE ROPES

I sat Big Joe in the middle of the studio with his beaten-up, twelve-string guitar and just let him play. He recorded the whole album straight through with little chatty bits between the songs. At the end of it, I gave him $150 cash and the bottle of Scotch, helped him downstairs onto the street and never saw him again. The album – *Hand Me Down My Old Walking Stick* – sold 5,000 copies.

Hapshash and the Coloured Coat (Featuring the Rock 'n' Roll Women, the Human Host and the Heavy Metal Kids)

Another little adventure I had around that time was to become a member of an acid rock group called Hapshash and the Coloured Coat – or to give them their full title, Hapshash and the Coloured Coat Featuring the Rock 'n' Roll Women, the Human Host and the Heavy Metal Kids, a name that perfectly fitted their psychedelic image. Like most of the things that happened to me around that time, I sort of lucked into Hapshash. Before I came along, they had released a very experimental album on Liberty, pressed on red vinyl – unheard of in those days. It caused quite a stir with the Underground fans. If a thing was 'progressive', it was 'Underground'.

Brian Jones of the Stones had been involved in the first album, which was very much a bash-through, musically, but had an insistent, druggy quality that caught the moment. The Hapshash members themselves weren't really musician s at all, but were brilliant designers of all the psychedelic, hippie posters and album covers of the time. Former art student types, they were leading players in the pop culture social set. One of the founders of the 'group' had had the misfortune to be detained at one of Her Majesty's penal establishments for an offence related to the partaking of naughty substances and so they were down to two.

THE CLOSEST THING TO CRAZY

Michael Mayhew and Nigel Waymouth were designers and painters who still had a lot of musical ideas even though they couldn't play anything, so I stepped into the breach as the musician who would guide and co-write the next album. I should point out that, at nineteen, I was a would-be clone of Ray Williams in an Austin Reed suit bought on credit, and a kipper tie – not quite the image of the others, who were cool bohemians with bits of leather hanging off them and smelling of patchouli. However, we got our ideas together and came up with some interesting stuff.

Nigel had an old tape of a mayor from the bayou giving a speech, with which he wanted to open the album, and so we followed it up with a French Cajun song which was part traditional and part made up, called 'Colinda'. Then with the help of an Australian singer called Michael Ramsden, we launched into a series of doomy and/or euphoric songs with me on piano, a very non-hippyish but excellent bass player called Eddie Tripp on bowed double bass and Andy Renton – he of That Lady's Twins – on drums. I got Tony McPhee to come along and play guitars and over two days, we cut the rhythm tracks for the album at Marquee Studios.

They were really atmospheric, wild-sounding performances with McPhee's wailing bottleneck and me trying to play piano like Richard Manuel of the Band, on 'Music from Big Pink'. In those days, everything was four-track. Marquee Studios were state-of-the-art four-track but just along the road in St Anne's Court (where a young lad like me would often be harangued from above by sex workers calling from upstairs windows), there was a new studio called Trident that had – gasp! – EIGHT-track. It was the coolest studio in town, not least because the Beatles had recently recorded 'Hey Jude' there and you could actually play the piano they played it on.

LEARNING THE ROPES

I'd seen Paul McCartney walking down St Anne's Court several times although, strangely, no girls shouted 'Hello, sailor' to him, as they did to me.

Being 'players' in the Underground movement, Nigel and Michael were ultra-cool. One day, they rocked up at my office, secretively announcing that they had 'something special'. At first I thought perhaps they meant some new strain of cannabis, but it turned out to be a pre-release cassette of the Beatles' *White* album, obtained from George Harrison's girlfriend, Pattie Boyd, at a party the night before. As we sat on the floor in my office and listened to it all the way through, it blew me away.

I had booked Trident so that I could copy my four tracks of the Hapshash rhythm section onto four of their eight tracks, leaving four *whole* tracks to do vocals, percussion and general weird stuff. I wanted the overdub sessions at Trident to be a sort of controlled 'happening', where we would invite various friends and 'beautiful people' to come along and bang something or sing. Consequently, on the evening of the first session, Mickey Finn (later to be the second half of T. Rex with Marc Bolan) turned up with a set of bongos. Also there were three girls who seemed to be able to sing – one of whom was called Nicole, who I think later married Steve Winwood. So, I put Michael, our Australian lead vocalist, right in the middle of the studio, the three girl singers over to one side and Mickey and his bongos opposite them at the other side. Various other beautiful, Underground, bead-wearing people turned up and were positioned at different points across the stereo image. I worked out hand signals so that the girls (later dubbed the Rock 'n' Roll Women) would know when and what to sing. My right hand up meant they had to shout 'Ha!' as aggressively as possible each time I stabbed the air.

A wafty arm movement meant they had to sing 'Ooh!' in whatever notes they felt like singing, and so on. People were encouraged to move across the stereo image, shaking wind chimes and finger cymbals. Then we lit some candles, put the lights out and started recording.

The result was the album *Western Flier*. Released in the UK and the States in 1969, it got quite a lot of attention and did reasonably well. It wasn't a work of genius but it was great fun to make and was a document of a moment in time. Nigel and Mike, the other two Hapshash guys, insisted that we three be photographed for the album cover, although I kept to my Austin Reed suit and held a cigar (as all nineteen-year-old heads of A&R should) so as to contrast as much as possible with my hairier cohorts.

Another Beatle thrill happened due to Andrew Lauder's and my friendship with Wayne Bardell, the twenty-year-old music publisher at the Beatles' Savile Row offices. One day, Wayne told us about the impending concert on the roof and invited us to be there. His small office was actually adjacent to the roof access doors. I was, of course, very excited. Sadly, on the day, Wayne was unwell and didn't come in to work. Nevertheless, I walked over and witnessed it all from street level. Not that you could see much, just the odd head bobbing up occasionally, but the music was loud and it was a terrific buzz. I couldn't have known, then, how iconic a moment it would become.

Meanwhile, all sorts of artists used to come in and see me in the office. One was a guy who said nothing, but walked right up to my desk and started singing an Elvis song without accompaniment. I let him finish and was just searching for the right diplomatic words to tell him not to give up his day job when he launched into another song with all the actions, arms out wide. After that song, I opened my mouth to give him the bad news and he launched into a third one, all the way through with actions. Eventually I did manage to tell him I didn't have a vacancy on my artist roster for an artist of his 'type'. (The rubbish type.) I could never tell people they were terrible. That's rude. I always had to let them down lightly, but at the same time you did have to be careful not to give off the wrong signals or they would just come back another day and give you three more Elvis songs.

Wendy and the Raconteurs

One morning in September 1968, an agent called Cyril Black sent a trio of performers to see me in the office. They had just come second to Mary Hopkin ('Those Were the Days') on the *Opportunity Knocks* TV talent show – no shame, considering that Mary was on a huge long run of six weeks as the winner. They were called Wendy and the Raconteurs. It was a terrible name and yet when I passed them on the stairs before our meeting, I did a double take. 'Wendy' was absolutely mind-blowing. She had golden hair in a kind of beehive style and wore a black jumpsuit, which wasn't really of the time. In fact, it was slightly old-fashioned and cabaret-ish – all held together by a Girl Guide belt. The whole effect was riveting.

The three of them stood in the office and did a couple of songs. There were two guys who stood either side of Wendy, playing guitar, but I hardly noticed them. The songs were a bit trite. 'Froggy Went a-Courtin'' was one of them, and the other was possibly something like 'Hang Down Your Head, Tom Dooley'. I didn't think they stood a chance as an act, but the girl was magnetic.

THE CLOSEST THING TO CRAZY

She was twenty-four and I was a young-looking nineteen. She was nervously flirting with me, which was exciting. Here I was in my great big office in my Austin Reed suit, talking about whether or not there was a market for another Peter, Paul and Mary. At the end of the meeting I took their phone numbers, mysteriously 'losing' the two blokes' numbers somewhere around the waste paper basket area of my office, but called Wendy a couple of days later and told her the only chance I thought she had was as a solo artist. I was honest and said that I had no idea whether she had what it took to be a solo artist, but I didn't give the group, as a trio, many out of ten. They were competent enough, sang in tune and all that, but the time had passed for that kind of act, in my opinion. However, I was also honest about another thing – the fact that I fancied the hell out of her and would like to take her out to dinner.

I took her to the Golden Egg in Trafalgar Square, a franchised, egg and chips version of McDonald's. My exalted position as head of A&R for Liberty Records had not, it seemed, imbued me with any class or style. Not only that, but after ordering whatever we had, I ate mine at rapid pace and ordered the same again before she was even on to the grilled tomato. We got on extremely well, although it was a bit like that scene in *The Jungle Book* where Kaa the snake hypnotises Mowgli – I, as Mowgli, was helpless.

Having dinner with Wendy was an act of treachery to Michele, who I was still seeing. Worse still, I learned that Wendy was married but that this relationship was already on the rocks as she was having an affair with one of the two guys in the Raconteurs. At least if I was being sneaky, I wasn't the only one. I was sorry for the husband who had lost her and for the boyfriend, who, I hoped, was just about to. Nothing much happened that night other than a walk along the Embankment and some hand-holding, but the way was clear, the map open. I dropped Wendy back at her hotel and arranged to see her again soon, then I got a cab back to Michele and Leonard Cohen.

So began the first long-term relationship of my life. It lasted thirteen tempestuous years, blessed us with our two daughters, Samantha and Robin, and ultimately ended in an acrimonious and long-overdue parting, which damaged all concerned. Our marriage was full of happiness, passion, despair, humour, euphoria and misery. What people choose to write about each other in their memoirs is always subject to a battle within the conscience, between diplomacy and honesty. There are two sides to every story and in every relationship a thousand stories.

Wendy was enormously supportive of me and my work, and had a very 'rock 'n' roll' attitude to life, which I found hugely attractive. A larger-than-life character, who dressed all day long as if she was out for the evening, she loved attention and got it from every man she ever met or passed in the street. She could make friends with other women, with her jolly, North-of-England bonhomie, but it was not unusual for them to see her as a threat or to be alienated by her flirty personality. Her moods could – and would – change by the minute and she was either your best friend or your worst enemy, whether you worked for her or were married to her. She was inherently very loving and kind, but could turn on me angrily or go into a huge stroppy mood if I said anything she didn't like. There wasn't a week in all those thirteen years when I didn't consider leaving her or when I concluded that I never could.

Meanwhile, back in 1968, we knew nothing of the future. I only knew there was this woman who occupied my every thinking moment and one night at the Revolution Club just off Berkeley Square in Mayfair, I unchivalrously put Michele in a cab home so that I could stay and be with Wendy. Michele was a charming, beautiful girl who I re-met later in life when she was married with two teenage daughters. Our close relationship ended that night at the Revolution Club in 1968 and I acted like a schmuck, but the attraction for Wendy was too strong. They say there's no fool like a fool in love. I wasn't necessarily in love with Wendy at that time, but I was deeply in lust. To a rampant nineteen-year-old, there wasn't much difference between the two.

Although I tried to record Wendy as an artist, it really didn't get very far. We recorded a demo, but it was clear that it wasn't going to happen. My bosses at United Artists (who had merged with Liberty to become Liberty/UA Records) didn't think I should sign her and of course they were right. I think they knew my judgement was temporarily impaired by the fact that I fancied the crap out of her.

She lived in Leamington Spa, near Coventry, and our relationship was conducted by my commuting from London to Coventry by rail every night for weeks. She would pick me up from the station in a green TR4A sports car and take me to her home, then in the morning she would cook me breakfast and I'd be at work by 11 a.m. in London. My secretary used to cover for me by saying I was in meetings or out somewhere. It was exciting and clandestine, but it was the worst thing possible for concentrating on my job. I don't really think I was that good as an A&R man back then – I was too intent on my own career as a writer and artist, but I was a good producer, learning to become a good arranger. An A&R man ideally has to have a good, detached judgement of other people's music and some idea of the nature of deals in the industry. I sup-

LEARNING THE ROPES

pose I was just inexperienced. My knowledge of deal-making came quickly, but not quickly enough for it to have helped my early days in A&R. I just didn't have the experience to look for – and sign – really strong acts, apart from which, I was commuting to Coventry at night and thinking about sex most of the day. I did enjoy my time working for Liberty/United Artists and I knew that one day I would love to run a record company, if ever I got the chance.

CHAPTER FOUR

Out on a Limb

After a couple of months, Wendy and I moved into a flat above a solicitor's office at 26 Warwick Road, Earl's Court. It had a big living room, an appalling kitchen with old red lino and a tiny bedroom, which we decorated with a huge poster of Jimi Hendrix. When it rained, water used to drip down the lighting cable and off the light bulb in the centre of the living room ceiling so we would put a bucket there until it stopped raining and complain to the landlord the following morning.

Earl's Court was a funky place to live. We would walk down Penywern Road to Earl's Court Road, where, just opposite the Tube station was a restaurant in a cellar called the Pot, where you could eat really cheaply. Once a month we would blow the budget on a visit to a great little Italian called Il Palio de Sienna, but we really had to watch the pennies because I wasn't earning much at the record company and Wendy had got a job as a teacher.

There was a rocky-looking character I used to run into quite often at the Tube station with long, unkempt hair and a rough appearance. He said he was a singer. In fact, I did get him to sing on a rather naff pop record – 'Fairyland' – produced by my friend Ben Findon. Luckily, the vocal wasn't used. The singer was Lemmy. We kept in touch and in the '90s, he sang 'Eve of Destruction' for me on my *Philharmania* album with the London Philharmonic.

In the spring of 1971, Wendy was suddenly pregnant. There had been no mutual decision for this to happen, but at least outwardly I said I was pleased. Inside, I was in turmoil. My mother put a lot of pressure on me to tie the knot. I think she was just excited about being a granny, but it was her enthusiasm and her argument that the child should have married parents that finally led me to relent. I was twenty-one and Wendy was twenty-six when we married at Kensington Registry Office. We said to each other the morning of the ceremony, 'Let's just not do it', but we did because our parents were there, all dressed up and everything. She said to me, 'If either of us ever wants to walk away from this, the other will just let it happen, no regrets, no problems.'

We were both young enough to believe it. Or at least I was.

The Mike Batt Orchestra

Married and with a newborn baby, Wendy and I moved to West Byfleet in Surrey, purchasing a 60-foot canal narrowboat as our home for £1,250. Samantha, our eldest daughter, spent the first eighteen months of her life at *Pooh Corner*, the name we gave the houseboat. It was a tough life on the canal. You rowed your groceries up the quarter of a mile of water from the car park at the bridge and emptied the contents of your chemical toilet into a soakaway dug into the ground on the other side of the canal, necessitating a trip by rowing boat that occasionally ended in tears when the bucketful of shit spilled on the way across. I had an especially small

OUT ON A LIMB

'ship's piano' that I worked on in the boat. Its keyboard folded up into the body of the piano so that you could walk past it in the narrow space that was our floating abode.

While we had been living in the flat at Earl's Court, I had resigned from my job at Liberty/UA after a year and a half, to concentrate on furthering my skills and reputation as an arranger and producer (while still signed to Liberty as an artist). Essentially, I still made my living by writing lead sheets of songs for publishers. When we moved to the canal boat, my new publisher, Shapiro Bernstein, offered me the chance to arrange six orchestral albums for a record deal they had made with various record company partners in Japan and America. The idea was to create a series called *Portrait of . . .* (Cat Stevens, Simon & Garfunkel, etc.), but just orchestral instrumental versions. I jumped at the chance. To arrange these albums for a twenty-seven-piece orchestra would be like having a university course in arranging and conducting, but using live ammunition instead of blanks. There were to be twelve instrumental tracks on each album, meaning that I would have to write seventy-two arrangements for the whole series.

With hindsight, perhaps I should have seen that these instrumental albums would inevitably sound like cheesy elevator music, but I had just turned freelance and had a wife and family to support so I needed the money. I was also idealistic enough to think I could make the arrangements sound cooler and hipper than your average orchestral album. Most of all, I loved the art and the technique of arranging and orchestrating and I wanted to give myself the challenge of learning as I went along.

In order to meet the deadline set by my publishers, I had to do three to four arrangements per *day*, so I set myself a four-hour time

THE CLOSEST THING TO CRAZY

period per arrangement, resulting in a nine- to twelve-hour working day. In each four-hour period I had to plan and mark out the score, using twenty-four stave orchestration paper and a 2B pencil, listing all the rhythm and orchestra instruments down the left-hand side. I then had to decide the structure of the arrangement, how many verses and choruses there would be and which instrument or instruments would take the lead tune at each point. Finally, I had to write the tune and harmonies in, usually adding an intro at the front which would, I thought, give the arrangement some individuality. Exhausting though it was, there was a certain exhilaration to it all and a tremendous feeling of achievement when I came out of my little music room on the boat with three finished orchestral scores each day to add to the growing pile.

When all seventy-two arrangements were complete, I put them in several boxes, drove to my publisher's office in London and struggled up the stairs with them. That very day, the bottom had fallen out of the deal with the Japanese record company. The managing director looked me in the eye and denied ever having commissioned me to do the arrangements and said he wasn't going to pay me for them. I had worked for many hours a day, six days a week for five weeks, writing to an impossible deadline, with my publishers sending me the sheet music to work from and encouraging me along. They now owed me something like seventy-two times £50, but here was the boss of the company – my own publisher – denying he ever told me to proceed.

Because I hadn't done any other work during all this time, I was in huge debt. I was gobsmacked. Without this album series deal, the arrangements were of no value. I don't know how I managed to remain in control of myself long enough to find the necessary negotiating power and diplomacy, but over the next few days, I got my publishers to hand over the tattered remnants of the deal to me and fly me out to the forthcoming Midem (Marché International du Disque et de l'Édition Musicale) conference in Cannes, France, so that I could at least try to sell the series to other record companies.

Midem is an annual music business convention attended by music publishers and record companies from all over the world, which has been going for years but was then in its infancy. I did manage to stitch the deal back together by leasing the UK rights to Dick James's record company and the overseas rights to a variety of other companies. This gave me enough cash per album to pay myself the fee that I would otherwise have been paid and enough to record the albums so long as I recorded six pieces in each three-hour session. It had also taught me something about not trusting people quite so readily.

I made the six albums, including *Portrait of Cat Stevens* and *Portrait of George Harrison*, in two sessions per album at Wessex Studios in north London. They were busy sessions, always with the last of the six pieces sight-read by the orchestra and played straight to tape without rehearsal. In a recording session, Musicians' Union rules don't allow you to go overtime even by one minute (unless you pay, which I couldn't afford to do). Consequently, the albums are a rag-bag combination of cleverness and middle-of-the-road awfulness. My biggest mistake was to allow them to be issued under my own name – as the Mike Batt Orchestra – and they had terrible cover designs by DJM's art department. I cringe whenever I see one of them, usually in a box in the attic. I would rather they had disappeared without trace, but that doesn't mean I didn't gain a lot of good experience making them. Sometimes a journalist in some far-flung land will raise them as an admired example of my body of work, but I don't share that view. They were not my finest moments. I would have been better off doing more string arrangements for bands like Family.

While at Midem, trying to resuscitate the *Portrait* deal, I met a very nice couple called Stuart and Patsy Reid. Stuart was head of Chappell music publishers (now Warner Chappell Music). I signed a deal with him, giving me my own music publishing company, Batt-Songs Ltd., an office owned by Chappell in Maddox Street, Mayfair, and they took a percentage of my publishing income. It was the perfect set-up for me, once again back in the West End, near to where I had been at Liberty/UA but this time as a totally independent company. In those days, people who fancied themselves as cool often had very dark offices. I splashed out on some snazzy office furniture, had the blue velvet curtains drawn all day and a lamp on my desk gave the whole thing a dark, nightclubby look. The small, outer office was manned by Wendy, who by now had given up singing and teaching. She could only type with one finger but she looked the part. She was good on the phone, good at booking musicians and good at chatting people up.

Around this time, we moved out of the houseboat and bought a house in Surbiton, Surrey, for £14,500, an absolute fortune to us. It was our first mortgage and we had to go through a special mortgage broker who could get mortgages for musicians. At a time when rising prices were making us all fearful that homes would soon become unaffordable, at least we were on the 'property ladder'.

Soon after finding work writing jingles and TV music, I sold my first car – a beach buggy deemed too frivolous by Midland Bank's Mr Skinner when refusing my request for a loan – and bought an even more frivolous one, a Mustang Mach 1, which just fitted onto the drive of our tiny home.

Meeting the Wombles

Those were good days. We weren't by any means rich, indeed we lurched from one cash-flow crisis to another, but it was a time of youth, energy, ambition. I signed to DJM as an artist, my Liberty/United Artists contract having expired. In doing so, I found myself, coincidentally, a label-mate of Elton John, who was just breaking as an artist around that time. I did some paid work as an arranger, some songwriting, produced a record by the Troggs, signed an artist called Vaughan Thomas and wrote some jingles and TV commercial soundtracks. Guinness, Smarties, Harmony Hair Spray . . . anything to make a living and keep learning my craft.

Just before we moved from the houseboat, when our daughter Sam was about one, my agent for jingles – a girl called Liz Channon – fixed up a meeting with 'some people who are making a TV show called *The Wombles* for the BBC'. I thought it might be a bit of a laugh and so I went to the meeting at FilmFair Productions, at their offices near Manchester Square in London. The director and designer Ivor Wood was in charge of the project. Ivor had had a lot of experience on things like *The Magic Roundabout* and after *The Wombles*, he would go on to create Postman Pat and many other successful characters. He had redesigned the look of the characters from a children's novel by Elisabeth Beresford. Whereas in the book they had looked like teddy bears, now they resembled big fat mice with hats, scarves and other accessories. For those who somehow missed it, I should say that the Wombles lived under Wimbledon Common in burrows and, ahead of their time, enhanced their lifestyle by upcycling garbage and litter into things which were useful to themselves. The films were being shot in stop-frame animation, using character puppets about 8 inches tall, on sets about 12 by 6 feet. Ivor would shoot one frame, move the character a little, shoot another frame and so on until the film was laboriously but meticulously created.

I suggested to Ivor and his team that perhaps instead of a signature tune, a song might be a way of gaining the attention of children. The films were to be five minutes long and would be shown in the coveted 'cult animation' spot previously occupied by *The Magic Roundabout*, just before the BBC *Six O'Clock News*.

So, back at the houseboat, I bashed away on my little 'ship's piano' and came up with the jazzy intro with the descending bassline, followed by the tune and the words, 'Underground, Overground, Wombling Free, the Wombles of Wimbledon Common are we'. I thought it was quite cute. The rest of the lyrics were written on the train on the way to meet again with Ivor. I remember seeing a small child playing on the opposite seat bench and thinking to myself, *I wonder if this child will ever hear the song I'm writing now?*

> Underground, Overground, Wombling Free,
> The Wombles of Wimbledon Common are we
> Making good use of the things that we find,
> Things that the everyday folks leave behind.

The FilmFair people liked the song and offered me £200 for it. I said I'd prefer to have the character rights for music-related activities. They were delighted – it saved them £200, and the musical character rights weren't worth anything at the time.

In those days, several of us budding record producers used to make what we called 'rent' records. All it meant was that you made a record for, say, £300, using money which should really have been used to pay your rent or mortgage and tried to sell it to a record company for £500 before the landlord noticed. I would often try to record three A-sides in one session, enabling me to sell three records to three different record companies, then go out and make B-sides – more cheaply – to fit them. I'd do the rounds of young A&R men in London and sometimes get lucky, selling or leasing my 'product' to a record company.

Having a hit was many stages beyond that. One record which I recorded on such a hopefully multi-A-side recording session at Wessex Studios was 'The Wombling Song'. When I had finished it, having arranged it, produced it and sung all the voices, I took it to Frank Rogers, a young guy who worked in A&R for Decca. He loved the record and convinced his bosses that they should license it from me. My deal would have been a £500 advance and about 18 per cent of the retail price. Royalties were better then, funnily enough. It was after the rip-off days of the '50s and '60s, but before record companies got wise and started basing royalties on the price to the dealer – a price 30 per cent lower – as they do today.

But I wanted to make an album, a Wombles album. I had already written several other songs about these funny little characters and I wanted a budget of £2,000 to make a longer record. Frank's bosses, including Dick Rowe, thought I was mad. They turned me down and offered me a singles deal only, which I refused. Frustratingly, I lost out on the five hundred quid I could have taken.

The Big Revolt

Around the same time in my life, I had another experience which was seismic in both a positive and a negative way. One weekend I had been fantasising about making a great rock album, using heavy metal rhythm section and a huge orchestra. I would call the album *The Big Revolt* and it would be about war. The Vietnam War was raging at the time and I wanted to write an angry, powerful piece that could be a 'concept' album but possibly a musical about the war itself and the effect it has on the characters in the songs. I was bemoaning the fact that it would cost about £11,000 to record just one twenty-minute album side. For context, this was around the time I had just raised a mortgage to buy a three-bedroomed semi-detached house near London for £14,500, so £11,000 was a vast sum.

But the next day – and this is still hard to believe – I opened the door to my Maddox Street office and inside there was an envelope from the Performing Rights Society (PRS). Inside was a cheque for £11,000. Not £10,000 or £12,000, but £11,000 – the exact amount I had yearned for the day before. I rang Wendy. I told her to sit down, then I told her about the cheque. 'Count the noughts again,' she said. I counted them. I couldn't believe it myself. Then I ran to the bank to deposit the money before I woke up from the dream. But I didn't wake up. The money was real.

Some months earlier, I had recorded the music for my first ever commissioned TV series – *Yoga for Health* – as a composer. There were only three musicians involved in the recording, plus me on piano. I had paid the union scale rate of £18 per musician for a three-hour session. At the time I had been threatened with legal action by the Musicians' Union (MU) because the music I recorded and delivered innocently to the production company had been dubbed onto fifty-six American TV half-hours without my knowledge. This low spot in my life was marked by the fact that the Union representative, Don Smith – or 'Doctor Death' as he was widely known – had, according to a cellist in the orchestra, stood up at a Paul McCartney session at Abbey Road Studios and told them that Mike Batt was blacklisted and they were not allowed to work for him until he had paid each musician a large extra payment because of the wider use of the music. I note that things at the MU are more reasonably managed today, but at twenty-two years of age, with a small child to feed and a union member myself, did they help? Did they ask me how it had happened? Did they give me time to pay? No, they just blacklisted me and so deprived me of my means of making a living. Shoot first and ask questions later. I was 'bailed out' of my trouble on this occasion and consequently un-blacklisted by obtaining a commitment that the TV production company would make the extra payments to the musicians (up from £18 per person to £625 per person). It was an unpleasant experience and coloured my relationship with my own union for some years.

The upside to that story was my receipt, a few months later, of the cheque for £11,000. As a composer or songwriter, you join the Performing Rights Society (PRS). In each country there is a similar society dedicated to the negotiating with broadcasters and the collecting of fees for the composers and publishers whenever a song is played on the radio or TV. It isn't very much per minute, but it can add up if you have a big success. In America there are two main societies in competition with each other, the American Society of Composers, Authors, and Publishers (ASCAP) and BMI. ASCAP had collected this money, sent it to PRS and they had sent it on to me. Because there were so many episodes, and they had been played across America and repeated several times, my £11,000 had accumulated and here it was.

I was so excited that I began writing my piece about war. I booked the sessions first. I've always done that and still do it to this day – I think if you book the sessions, it gives you a strong incentive to finish the music and lyrics on time. I worked for several weeks, writing the music and lyrics straight onto blank manuscript paper, fully orchestrating as I went.

Artistically, the war concept album was much more the serious 'me' that wanted to say something, something with substance. It contained influences ranging from Prokofiev to Led Zeppelin. The writing was stylistically adventurous, with guitar riffs, unusual flute and oboe lines and angry vocals sung by a friend of mine called Tony Rees.

After I had spent the £11,000 recording only half of it, I set about trying to get a deal with a record company. I decided to think big. I wanted to score a massive record deal that would set me up for life. I hired the most recommended US attorney, a top-dollar lawyer called Richard Roemer. US music business attorneys aren't just lawyers, they are deal-makers and relationship facilitators. I made the trip out to New York, figuring this was a US deal, not a British deal. At the time I had never been to the States. I was twenty-two years old and a bit scared of New York and its violent reputation. I had asked a friend what might be the best hotel for me in New York. 'The Americana,' he told me. But it wasn't. It *definitely* wasn't. However, that's where I stayed, and I arrived during the American Meat Institute Convention, so it took me an hour to check in. Everybody had badges with 'AMERICAN MEAT INSTITUTE CONVENTION, Hi, I'm (GEORGE, FRANK, CINDY, etc.)'.

Clive Davis was just ending his days at the helm of CBS Records before he got fired. I met him briefly but my meeting was with his head of A&R, Kip Cohen. Kip played my twenty-minute tape all the way through at high volume, proclaimed it to be a masterpiece, told me he would get back to me, eagerly took my contact details and I never heard from him again. As I left his office, I was elated. Apart from Kip, Dick Roemer had earned his vast fee by getting me in to see the presidents of most of the major companies on my trip to the US, including Jac Holzman – a charming and erudite man who ran his company, Elektra Records, from a skyscraper office building high above Columbus Circle – and the legendary Jerry Wexler at Atlantic, situated in the same building. Those were really positive meetings for me. I had a great record, I was young, these were the top people in the business and tough talkers who would tell me if they didn't want to waste their time with me. All of them raved about my record.

I didn't know that I would never see any of them again for years. Or indeed ever.

My scheduled trip was to include LA as well. Once again, I had asked where the best place was, and the Hyatt House on Sunset Boulevard had been recommended. In those days it really was a rock 'n' roll hotel. On my first evening in the bar, Marc Bolan and Mickey Finn came in and we spent the night trading stories and getting drunk. I'd known Mickey from Hapshash and the Coloured Coat, and Marc just from being around the business. As for the subsequent meetings, I got to see all the big shots that Richard Roemer had set me up with, including Joe Smith, who ran Universal Records, some top guys at Motown, and most importantly for me, Jerry Moss, the 'M' of A&M, the company he owned with his partner, Herb Alpert.

Moss's office was in Charlie Chaplin's vast old dressing room, the record company having bought Chaplin's old studio just off Sunset Boulevard as its base. His office reeked of success and good taste, and he was a charismatic and polite character. He listened intently and loudly to *The Big Revolt* and then spent quite a long time raving about its uniqueness, vision, commercial appeal and artistic originality. He asked what deal I was looking for. I said I wanted a three-album deal at $100,000 per record.

This was at a time when my income was £25,000 a year even with TV jingles. It was a lot of money I was asking for, but not unheard of in the States — and to be honest, that's why I was there instead of the UK. Moss didn't blink, said the deal sounded fair and asked for some time to think about it, explaining that he had a sales convention starting in Chicago the next day and asked how long I would be in town. I had planned to leave the next day. He told me that he wouldn't be able to let me know for sure for about three days but it would be a quick deal to close on his return if we were both willing. Of course, I said, no problem, I'd hang around.

So I hung expensively by the pool on top of the Hyatt House where I was staying for the next three days, waiting for his phone call. The New Seekers were staying in the hotel — it was at the height of their fame — and I got to know them as they spent a lot of time in and around the pool. After four or five days I managed to get Jerry on the phone. He was still at his convention and would be back the following Monday, could I wait another few days? I said no problem, went back to the pool and waited. When the call did not happen on Monday, I finally left for the UK. I had hoped we might close the deal while I was in LA — that's how keen Jerry had seemed. When I got home, I called him. He explained that he had just acquired the rights to the orchestral version of *Tommy* by the Who, which he — incorrectly — saw as similar in that it combined rock material and instrumentation with a symphony orchestra. He didn't feel he could take on both projects; he was sorry.

Crestfallen, I had now exhausted all my high-level contacts in the States — all of whom had raved about my 'innovative' music and production, but with no commitment. I had run out of money and was into overdraft at the West Byfleet branch of the Midland Bank. Nobody wanted my record. So I turned to the UK record business and in particular to Purple Records, the label run by Deep Purple, who were in their prime as one of the world's top rock bands and sympathetic to symphonic work since Jon Lord was their keyboard player and he himself had classical, compositional experience and aspirations.

I met with one of their managers, Tony Edwards. He loved the record and asked if he could keep a copy. By now, the deal I was looking for was more along 'British' lines, something like £10,000 to £25,000 – just enough to get me out of the hole I was in and to recoup some of my costs. A week later, I called Tony and he said he was very interested indeed. We had another meeting, during which he said he had played the record to Ian Gillan, Deep Purple's lead singer, and that Ian would be interested in replacing Tony Rees's vocals with his own.

I swallowed and agreed – my arse was on the line, Tony's wasn't. Edwards then said that Ian Gillan also wanted to re-write my lyrics. In other words, it would become Ian's project. This is my recollection of the meeting, so it may not be true in every detail, but it is what Tony told me. It was such a different concept from the one that Jerry Moss had come within a hair's breadth of taking that I refused to compromise. I thanked Tony politely and that was the end of the matter, but now I was in deep shit financially. Instead of paying off my mortgage and giving myself some creative headroom to work on my next project, I had blown the lot on the big gamble and failed. Uncomfortable calls were coming from the bank every day.

CHAPTER FIVE

'Breaking' the Wombles

Just after I returned from the States, I made an appointment with Dan Loggins (brother of Kenny Loggins, the American singing star). Dan was the newly appointed head of A&R for CBS Records, who had set up a medium-sized UK office in Theobalds Road, London, under the leadership of Dick Asher, a lawyer who had previously run the business affairs department for Clive Davis at the New York HQ of CBS. I played Dan a few records I had. He was underwhelmed by them. Finally, I played him 'The Wombling Song', which had remained 'unplaced' since I had stubbornly refused to take less than an album deal from Decca. By now the TV show was on air in the *Magic Roundabout* slot just before the BBC's *Six O'Clock News*. It wasn't exactly a well-known thing and hadn't by then been particularly successful, but it was on air, which I pointed out.

Dan asked if he could take it home and play it to his young son. The next day, he rang me: 'My boy liked it, how much did you say you wanted for it?' he said. 'Five hundred pounds, but I want to make a whole album of Womble songs and I'd need £2,000 for that,' I said. Loggins couldn't understand why I'd want to make an album – I just thought it would be fun and I'd get £2,000 instead of £500. But he offered me free studio time and some money to make the album – I think it might even have been the full £2,000.

With things at the bank a little more comfortable, I set about making the first Womble album at CBS's Whitfield Street studios, using a rhythm section and a small orchestra of strings and woodwinds. First, I wrote a song about Madame Cholet, the Womble cook: 'Madame Cholet/What's cooking for you today?' it went. Then I wrote an exercising song for Tomsk, the keep-fit Womble: 'Standing on your tiptoes, running on the spot/Exercise is good for you, laziness is not'.

It was a far cry from my angry, heavy *Big Revolt*, but looking back, it was just as creatively stimulating. I had always admired humorous and witty songs like those of the comedy duo Flanders and Swann, Gilbert and Sullivan and George Formby. This was just me being light-hearted. God forbid that my first bit of success would have come from being a member of a scowling rock band so that I would have had to have kept up the scowl (and worn leather trousers) for the rest of my life to retain my credibility. Not caring what people think has always been equally my strength and my weakness. Contrarily, of course, like most people who say they don't care, underneath it all I care very much what they think, if I would only admit it more often.

The Womble single was released in late 1973, but nobody noticed. I had tried to get an appointment with Clive Selwood, CBS's marketing director, but to him, I wasn't an artist or the manager of an artist, so why would he give me any time? In fact, technically I was an artist on the label because I had sung the vocals on the Womble song, but it didn't get me through Selwood's door. Why weren't

'BREAKING' THE WOMBLES

CBS interested in trying to help me make this record a hit? Later, I was told that Dan Loggins had picked up the deal only because it might give the company some spin-off sales by association with the TV programme, but at that time I was convinced that I could make it into a hit. How could I convince them? Then I realised that record companies want to sign artists, not projects. They want to *meet* the artist and be able to say they *work* with the artist, that they *know* the artist. So I rang my mother – she who had made all the fancy-dress costumes when we were kids, she who was inspirational and energetic, she who had a sense of fun and joy.

'Could you make me a Womble costume?' I asked her.

The following week, wearing an ingenious costume which had two inflatable beach balls (one at the front, another at the back) to create custom-made adjustable fatness for the wearer and a face made from a rolled-up plastic washing-up mat and a black-painted ping-pong ball for a nose, I presented myself, unannounced, outside the office of Dick Asher, managing director of CBS.

'Who shall I say it is?' asked his bemused secretary, maybe thinking I was one of his American bosses playing a joke.

'Just say it's Orinoco Womble,' I said.

Dick came out of his office, laughing. The visit was a huge success. He took me *down* to see Clive Selwood and the promotion team and all the girls in the secretarial area (yes, it was like that in those days) gathered round to hug me and have pictures taken. The 'Wombles' were born on that day. CBS had an act, an artist, and *I* had their attention.

With Prime Minister Edward Heath in charge, Britain was in the grip of powerful and aggressive unions. In 1973, NUM President Arthur Scargill was organising the miners' strike, there was an energy shortage and businesses were operating on a three-day week by early 1974 because of it. There was also a shortage of raw material to make vinyl for records. We were seriously worried about this from a selfish point of view. Even if we could persuade the public that the record was a hit, in a financial depression they might not have the Wombles' record on their list of priorities. And if they did, was there enough vinyl to press enough copies to make it a hit?

Now that I had a Womble costume, I decided not to waste it and indeed to wear it ALL DAY LONG, every day, wherever I went. I wore it on the train, on the Tube, in taxis; I wore it on unannounced trips to Birmingham and Manchester. I walked, without invitation, past the receptionists and into the on-air studios of regional radio stations. I stood behind the DJ on *Top of the Pops* and waved to try to get on camera. At every town I visited, a hundred or so records would be sold that day in the local record shops. I figured that if I went to a town a day, we would sell a hundred records a day and CBS would notice this sales pattern back at HQ. And that is exactly what happened.

Five hundred records a week was a signal. It wasn't enough to get you into the top thirty, but it was sales activity that a record company could not ignore. Tony Blackburn began playing the record on his influential Radio 1 breakfast show because he liked its 'silliness', not having a clue what it was about, never having heard of the kids' TV show. We had been hoping for a Christmas hit, but Christmas came and went without chart action. On 5 January 1974, actor-comedian Bernard Cribbins, who narrated the show, had been booked as a guest on BBC's *Cilla*. He kindly took me with him, as Orinoco, and I joined in what would otherwise have been a duet with Bernard and Cilla. It was the first time a musical Womble had been seen on television. We sang a little bit of the theme tune, but I also remember Bernard, Cilla and me singing and dancing to 'Exercise is Good for

'BREAKING' THE WOMBLES

You (Laziness is Not)' from the album *Wombling Songs*. There was a great reaction to this unusual TV moment. Perhaps because of this, and with CBS now fully engaged, their regional promotion people managed to get me onto the lunchtime magazine show *Pebble Mill at One* in early January. The show went out live daily from their Pebble Mill studios in Birmingham. I would play the piano, as Orinoco, and sing the full song using a radio microphone inside my Womble head. It was the first proper Womble TV performance of the song, albeit by a *single womble playing the womble single!* I wasn't bothered by playing the piano with my womble gloves on – they were loose enough to feel through – but I was terrified of forgetting the words. So at the last minute, I scribbled them onto a piece of paper and shoved it into the empty, pointy nose of my Orinoco head. When the time came and the cameras swung around to come to me live, I performed it without mishap, and nobody could have imagined that inside that Womble costume was a nervous young man squinting with crossed eyes at the crib sheet, only inches from his face.

All of this excitement had created a sales pattern that was growing strong enough for us to hope for a low chart entry towards the end of January. Tuesday was chart day – the day you found out whether you were in the chart and at what position. At ten o'clock, pacing the promotion team's office, I learned that we had entered the chart at number thirty-six. This was sensational in the days when you entered low and climbed slowly. The chart would be announced that weekend, officially going to number thirty-six on 26 January 1974. More radio stations would surely pick up the record now, things would start happening. I ordered a crate of champagne to be delivered and distributed throughout the building. This was huge for me, the first hit I'd ever had, the beginning of something, whatever it was. I was determined to keep it going rather than let it drop.

As I descended the stairs of the CBS offices that Tuesday, I ran into head of A&R Dan Loggins, the man who had signed the Wombles, coming up.

'Mike,' he said, 'don't be too disappointed if it falls next week. It probably will.' He had signed the record as a novelty, and to him, that's what it was.

'Don't worry,' I insisted, 'it's going to be a big hit.'

He forced a sympathetic, almost pitiful smile. It was the first time I learned the lesson about the way record companies work. Often you have to drag them, kicking and screaming, against their will towards success.

However, as luck would have it, not everyone at CBS was as pessimistic as Dan. Later on the same day, I had a call from Paddy Fleming, the head of TV promotions for CBS – a wonderful, polite Irishman who had seen much action in the RAF in the war and who had ditched into the English Channel at least once. 'I've been speaking to Robin Nash, producer of *Top of the Pops*,' said Paddy, 'and he wants to know, is there just ONE Womble or a whole group? The group is *called* the Wombles, but you only have one costume, don't you? Robin says he won't book just *one* Womble as "the Wombles" on the show.'

'Oh, there's a whole group,' I lied, desperately. 'There's a drummer, a guitarist, a bass player . . .'

'Great!' said Paddy. 'You're on *Top of the Pops* the day after tomorrow.'

This placed me in a position, shall we say, somewhere between heaven and hell. My 'band' was going to be on *Top of the Pops* – everybody's dream, particularly after five years of trying to have a successful record, and yet I didn't have three other band members or any other costumes and literally thirty-six hours before I had to have a band together, rehearsed and costumed.

'BREAKING' THE WOMBLES

It was time for another call to my mum: 'Any chance of three more costumes in one day?' I asked. My dad, brothers and sister rallied round, helping to make the costumes in an overnight session of manic sewing and gluing at my parents' house in Bracknell, and I rang three pals who I knew had a band, one of whom was 22-year-old Andy Renton, the drummer of Hapshash and, prior to that, of That Lady's Twins, my duo at school. They turned up at the BBC TV Centre on Thursday afternoon, 31 January, and tried on the costumes. We rehearsed briefly in the dressing room, then suddenly we were called to the stage and it was all happening. The strange new band in furry outfits surprised and delighted the live audience. 1974 was soon to become a hectic and thrilling year of TV appearances, press articles and hits. The following week we jumped ten places to number twenty-six in the chart, then enjoyed our weekly escalations to nineteen, then seven, finally reaching number four on 23 February, where we remained for two weeks.

As the record had entered the chart, Wendy had been in hospital in Wimbledon (by coincidence) having our second child, another girl, who we called Robin Jennings Batt. Rob was not only a joy to behold and a great delight for all of us, but she also presented a photo opportunity to help the new record on its way. A few days after the birth, I sat on the bed dressed as Orinoco, next to her proud mother, and 'Womble Has Baby' or some such headline provided a much-needed bit of national tabloid press. Of course, all this Womble image-building was great at the time, but it was to be a nail in the coffin of my perceived musical credibility in the UK in later years. Nevertheless, it had been a busy week: a baby *and* a hit record.

It was the beginning of a string of nine top-forty hits for the Wombles, and although Elisabeth Beresford had created the characters, my songs and pop group had elevated them as an act and presented them to the mainstream family audience via regular appearances on *Top of the Pops* alongside artists like Stevie Wonder, ABBA and Roxy Music. Also, unlike even those artists, we made regular appearances on younger-targeted shows such as *Blue Peter*, *Crackerjack!* and other peak-time family favourites. Contrary to some journalistic accounts, the Wombles' records were being bought by teenagers and adults alike. It wasn't just kid-pop, it was silly fun. We began to get letters from people like the RAF warrant officer who told me he was the Great Uncle Bulgaria of his squadron – in the UK, we take our silliness very seriously.

Following Up 'The Wombling Song'

I'd always said that as soon as I had a hit, I would do all I could to follow it up quickly and successfully to keep the momentum going. For years I'd studied the art of following up hit singles. I'd seen successful follow-ups and failed follow-ups. If ever I had a hit, I was not going to let it stop at one: I was ready. If *The Big Revolt* album had been a hit, I would have followed that up and become known as the creator of that, and its follow-ups. As it happened, my first hit was with the Wombles and so I became known for the rest of my career – in Britain at least – as the 'Wombles Man'. Is that good or bad? In balance, a bit of both. I'm happy about the fun I had and pleased with the songs and the quality of what we did, but I'm sad that I have often been seen since then as a lightweight by many people in the business.

Thankfully, the Wombles only became a big phenomenon in Britain. Elsewhere, I have a life as an artist – I am just Mike Batt, the singer-songwriter, or Mike Batt, the producer or conductor or whatever it is I am doing. As time has passed, there are now many people, even in Britain, who see the bigger picture. Overall, I'm enormously grateful for all of it.

'BREAKING' THE WOMBLES

The task of following up 'The Wombling Song' with its rather jolly-but-nonsensical lyrics and French horn 'jazz' intro was a huge challenge. Why would radio stations play a second Womble song when they (except for Tony Blackburn, bless him) hadn't bothered to play the first? Did the world need another Womble song? I didn't care what the world needed; *I* needed another. So I sat at the piano in the garage of my small house in Surbiton and analysed what it had been that had made the first song a hit. It was not unmusical, with an instrumental intro, which was quite complicated, but it was a simple song with 'whimsical', good-natured lyrics.

After a day's grafting, I emerged from the garage with 'Remember You're a Womble'. The simplest chorus – just 'Remember You're a Womble', repeated several times on the three-chord trick often used in pop songs – was almost a rip-off of something by Gene Vincent or Carl Perkins or anyone else who had written three-chord pop songs in the early days of rock 'n' roll. To balance this simplicity with musicality and memorability, I added an intro for two violins in counterpoint that might have been (but wasn't) taken from a Vivaldi piece or, if you looked at it differently, an Irish jig:

When the sun doesn't shine and it's cloudy and grey
And it's only the beginning of the Wombling day
And you've got to do the washing up for Madame Cholet. . .
Remember, remember, remember, remember
Remember, remember, remember

Remember you're a Womble (remember you're a Womble)
Remember you're a Womble (remember you're a Womble)
Remember you're a Womble (remember you're a Womble)
Remember you're a Womble (remember you're a Womble)

THE CLOSEST THING TO CRAZY

>Remember, member, member
>What a Womble, Womble, Womble you are.

Okay, not exactly Shakespeare.

As soon as I'd written it we went back into Wessex Studios and recorded it with my usual team; Chris Spedding on guitars, Clem Cattini on drums and Les Hurdle on bass guitar. Jack Rothstein played the first fiddle. Paddy Fleming at CBS managed to get it featured as the 'entertainment' during the judging break at the Eurovision Song Contest, which happened to be hosted in Brighton that year by the BBC.

They made a film of all of us Wombles pratting about in Rottingdean, the village just outside Brighton, and I had to go on the programme 'live' as Orinoco to wave and give a rose to the vivacious presenter Katie Boyle. For the film, the BBC used my specially recorded vocals but replaced the music backing track with an awful orchestral arrangement of the song, played 'live' to a click track and conducted by Ronnie Hazlehurst, the BBC's light entertainment musical director. Artistically, it spoiled the whole thing for me, but still made it available to an audience of millions of people – enough to make the record a huge hit. It went to number three in the UK charts.

Backstage at the Eurovision Song Contest, there were a couple of rather attractive girls to whom I thought it would be churlish not to chat. I introduced myself – not in my Womble costume – and they in turn introduced me to their husbands, Björn and Benny. I spent the day getting to know them all, wishing them luck. I gave Agnetha and Björn a Womble badge each – and they pinned them onto their now famous costumes. I even stayed backstage while the votes came in, watching their faces, and sharing a drink as they won. Actually, we had a drink each.

'BREAKING' THE WOMBLES

Famously now, ABBA and their song 'Waterloo' wiped the board, both as a Eurovision song and as the launch pad for the band's incredible career. I stayed in touch and often ran into them backstage at various European TV shows we all performed on. Because we were both on CBS, I experienced their career growing alongside mine, saw each single go out, enjoyed their success vicariously and was often around the CBS offices when ABBA strategy decisions were being made.

* * *

Soon afterwards, I got a phone call from a man called Paul Russell. Dick Asher had hired him as head of Business Affairs for CBS. His first brief was to secure a contractual relationship with me that would ensure I did not leave CBS and go with another company for a better offer. Dan Loggins' lack of long-term faith in me and CBS's subsequent shock at my success had left them in a difficult position: they only had the rights to one single and one album. Even the follow-up, 'Remember You're a Womble', had been recorded and delivered out of contract in good faith. Russell wanted my music publishing rights, a producer deal which would prevent me from working with other labels, a solo artist contract with me and a further five options for more Wombles' albums. I was flattered, and delighted to discuss it.

We set up a meeting.

'How much money do you want?' he asked.

'£50,000,' I said.

Looking back, I could have asked for (and would have got) more, but I had seen a house down the road in Surbiton – a nine-bedroom pile in very bad shape, but in a lovely avenue. It had previously been the headquarters of the Transport and General Workers' Union.

I had set my heart on it. Property was going through a slump and I knew I could get this house for £35,000 and do it up royally for £15,000. It seems a low figure now but it was more than £500,000 in today's money.

'Okay,' said Russell. 'I'll put together a schedule of what we'd like you to commit to for a fifty-thousand advance.'

Over the next couple of days, we negotiated like two men with fencing foils. I came out of it with a cheque for £50,000, a solo album deal, the Wombles signed to CBS for four albums and a non-exclusive producer contract that did not prevent me from working for other labels. I've now known Russell all my life and he is a brilliant man. Our friendship has wavered on occasion because of business differences, but we are abiding friends. His technique was simple: ask your 'opponents' what they want *and agree to give it to them*. Then make it cost them as much as possible by balancing up your list of demands so that they get what they want and so do you. Simple.

After cashing my £50K cheque, I found out that £36K of it was owed to me by CBS already from records already sold (known in the business as 'pipeline money') so Russell had nailed me to the floor for £14K. I would have got the £36K of it in three months' time anyway. It would have been helpful to have known that before the negotiation! But we were both happy – his first deal went well and I got my house.

Life at Langley Avenue

This was the beginning of a whirlwind adventure for me, Wendy and the kids. The house in Langley Avenue, Surbiton, was gutted and redecorated from top to bottom and my tasteless-but-I-don't-bloody-care bright electric blue Rolls-Royce Silver Shadow parked

'BREAKING' THE WOMBLES

alongside Wendy's rather more classy silver Mercedes 450SLC. Some workmen came and dug a pool into the back lawn. We were now rich. Policemen visiting the house, perhaps to offer crime prevention advice, would call you 'sir' and talk up to you rather than down.

I was twenty-three years old and after five years of no hits I was now officially an interesting business proposition and not just an aspiring scruff with a recurring cash-flow problem. To be fair, I had been doing jingles and other similar work prior to all this since leaving United Artists, plus my work as a budding arranger and producer made sure I wasn't doing as badly as some of my fellow scruffs who were also struggling for hits. When we'd lived in the little three-bedroom house down the road, I had my Mustang sitting in the tiny driveway. Despite my reasonably good business sense, which put money into my hands, my cash-flow problems were due to a flamboyant attitude to spending, which made sure the outgoings were always high, both personal and business.

Nine-bedroom house in Langley Avenue or not, this was to continue to be the pattern of my business ups and downs. I was good at making money but world class at spending it! We had been given a chance, an opportunity. Our thrills and spills became my education in deal-making and positive thinking and the ability to capitalise on my growing track record is what saved us from disaster many times.

The Wombles had now become more than a book, more than a TV series, more than a pop group; they were a national phenomenon and they were probably at that time regarded by most people as a pop group first and foremost. This was not my fault; I did not want to steal the limelight from Elisabeth Beresford's books and characters, but most people in England thought of the

THE CLOSEST THING TO CRAZY

Wombles as a wacky new pop group and me as their creator. I *was* indeed the creator of the group and the songs, but I was not the creator of the characters. I did not hold the underlying character copyright – that was held by Wombles Limited, a company owned 25 per cent by Elisabeth Beresford and 25 per cent by her husband, Max Robertson, who just prior to that moment had been a popular TV presenter, commenting on tennis and hosting a BBC antiques quiz programme called *Going For a Song*.

The other 50 per cent of the company was owned by John Hanson, a sports agent, and Terry Flounders, who was more orientated towards merchandising. The latter two gentlemen had earned their shareholding by persuading the production company FilmFair to make – and ultimately, the BBC to broadcast – the TV series. This company, presided over by Max Robertson as chairman, was a nightmare to deal with. Terry and John were supposedly the 'good guys' who I liaised with most. Max was grumpy and suspicious, and plainly resented the fact that a creative person other than his wife had become involved. Instead of just book and merchandising rights (not involving me), there were now music rights and the appearance rights to the all-powerful pop group, whose costumes had been designed by yet another creative person – my mother. I owned these rights, much to the irritation of Wombles Limited, even though, without the hit records, the Wombles would perhaps have remained a charming but smaller-scale affair.

Wombles Limited's attitude to character merchandising was interesting. They were determined to put Wombles onto any product possible and to make as much money as they could. Not a crime by any means, but there was a rather tacky urgency attached to the way they did everything. They succeeded in getting the images of

'BREAKING' THE WOMBLES

Great Uncle Bulgaria, Orinoco and their pals onto bubble bath, sweets, hot-water bottles, bed linen and everything else you could think of. It must be said that they did a great job in this respect, although the word 'overkill' comes to mind. The trouble was, however much money they made, none of them were ever going to get rich from it. The BBC took a chunky percentage off the top and remitted the rest to FilmFair, who took half and paid the rest to Wombles Limited, which split its receipts four ways: between Elizabeth, Max, John and Terry. There were just too many participants. I gave them a percentage – 12.5 per cent – of my music publishing receipts and I'm sure they made as much, if not more, from this than from the character merchandising rights. In return, they refused to let me participate in character merchandising income.

Wombles Limited wanted to make money from the Wombles pop group characters opening fetes and garden centres. But I didn't. I didn't want my precious, original costumes being schlepped around England when they should have been kept pristine for professional TV engagements. More than that, I didn't want to downgrade the status of the pop group (pop groups don't open garden centres). The Wombles were by now thought of as a top pop band, and it was essential that the status of an entertainment act be maintained. Wombles Limited were insistent, though, and for a while, I succumbed.

My elder brother John ran that side of the business. He would book the Wombles into the openings of a new chain of stores called Topshop and always accompanied by a DJ – usually Annie Nightingale or Tony Blackburn – from BBC Radio 1. These visits were coordinated by a young marketing man called Ralph Halpern, who was on the phone to John all the time, telling him about a new store opening and the need for two Wombles to be there at fifty quid a go, or something like that. Years later, we realised that the 'young hustler' from marketing was actually the founder of Topshop, becoming the famous tycoon Sir Ralph Halpern.

I personally wore my Orinoco costume on one occasion to a record store opening in Bath. I did feel that a record store opening was okay for 'pop stars' to do – and the Wombles really were pop stars – but not garden centres and clothes shops. Eventually, I explained to Ms Beresford's company that I couldn't keep on doing this. But they insisted that if I wouldn't do these gigs, they would. They demanded that I should allow them the right to send their own costume-wearing 'actors' around the UK, making appearances in different Womble costumes, which they themselves would commission to be made by a costumier. My fatal error was to agree to this. I did insist that at least their characters would not be seen to be dancing or 'performing' to my music but it still wasn't protection enough.

The Wombles received the Music Week Award for Best Selling Singles Group of the Year for 1974. In eighteen months we clocked up eight top-thirty hits and four gold albums. The albums were packed with songs about Wombles in every conceivable character and situation. Whereas I thought the first album was rather twee, it had its moments and, in hindsight, I can see its value. As I progressed through albums two, three and four, the ideas became more ambitious and the production standard grew stronger. There was a James Bond Womble (00W), a cowboy Womble ('The Orinoco Kid') and even a piss-take of Rick Wakeman's 'Journey to the Centre of the Earth' and 'King Arthur' projects. My version was called 'The Myths and Legends of King Merton Womble and His Journey to the Centre of the Earth' and was recorded in 1975 using the London Symphony

'BREAKING' THE WOMBLES

Orchestra at Olympic Studios in Barnes – the studio where I had first done the string overdubs for Family, a few years earlier.

In those days I used to work quickly, often staying up all night to do an arrangement for the session in the morning. My training making orchestral albums and recording six songs per three-hour session a few years earlier was now paying off. For the third album, I remember Dick Asher, the genial and pragmatic boss of CBS records, ringing me up and saying, in his delightful New York drawl, 'Mike, we need a new Womble album.' 'When do you need it?' I said. He said, 'In six weeks' time!' I had to write, arrange, sing and mix the whole album in that time period. Looking back, it was madness, but I suppose that's about the length of time you get to compose and record a film score even to this day, so it was all part of being a professional – the object being to meet the deadline without compromising on quality.

The Wombles' singles kept coming, one after the other. To maintain the momentum, I would put a new one out just as the previous one was dropping in the charts. Consequently, in the summer of 1974 we became the first act since the Beatles to have three singles in the top fifty simultaneously with 'The Wombling Song', 'Remember You're a Womble' and 'Banana Rock'. Throughout 1974 and 1975 the hits continued with 'Minuetto Allegretto', 'Wombling Merry Christmas', 'Wombling White Tie and Tails', 'Superwomble' and 'The Womble Shuffle'. The Wombles even cracked America in a small way when my Beach Boy tribute, 'Wombling Summer Party', made it to number fifty-five in the Hot 100 singles chart.

When 'Wombling White Tie and Tails' was a hit in 1975, Fred Astaire happened to be in London. He called CBS from his hotel room at the Savoy and asked if a copy might be sent over for him.

THE CLOSEST THING TO CRAZY

Needless to say, one was biked over immediately. I would love to have met the great man. He was a big hero to me and he had told my record company folks that he loved the record. That was phenomenal for me to hear. I so much admired him, and it had been a season of his old black-and-white films on the BBC that had been the inspiration for me to write a song about him dancing with the Wombles . . . albeit in Orinoco's imagination.

CHAPTER SIX

Busy and Hot

At the request of CBS Records, we headed to the States in August 1974 to try to break the Wombles there. We were under the care of their head of promotions, a big, solid guy called Steve Popovich, a legend in the US music business. As well as appearing on TV shows like *The Captain Kangaroo Show*, he had us Wombles on a Womble Wagon, like a carnival float, being driven through the streets of New York, sponsored (without our prior knowledge or permission) by a chain of new fast-food restaurants called Zum Zum. Our duty was to jump off the Womble Wagon and amuse the people in the restaurants and sign autographs in full Womble regalia. Needless to say, it's very hot and humid in a Womble costume in New York in August! Put the two together – and add the fact that there was nowhere to hide and take your 'head' off in the Womble Wagon – and you can imagine the ordeal. Sweat ran into our eyes and covered our bodies. We only had one set of costumes with us, not having foreseen this problem, so the suits soon got very sticky and smelly indeed. Each night we kept them in the sitting room of my suite at the Hilton on 6th Avenue and each morning (when

THE CLOSEST THING TO CRAZY

sometimes we'd be up at 5 a.m. to do morning TV), we'd gather in my bedroom, hold our breath, rush into the sitting room and – trying not to inhale too much of the stench – we'd put on these horrible, smelly costumes which were coated on the inside with a claggy layer of the previous day's cold sweat.

The layer of sweat grew thicker each morning; it was like cold, putrid jelly. On the last day of our five-day stay, I was joined in the hotel lift by a small boy and his mother. Dressed as Orinoco, I was trying to amuse the kid with some silly miming when he turned to his mum and announced, 'Hey, Mom, that Womble stinks!'

Not a lot you can say back, really.

* * *

Back in England, I was still turning out new songs one after the other. It was exhilarating. Of course I got plenty of stick from *New Musical Express* and some of the other music weeklies, but for the first time in my life I was making shed-loads of money and getting the chance to try all different arranging styles from classical to rock 'n' roll, even a military band song called 'Wombles on Parade', partly fulfilling my youthful military band ambitions.

One of the downsides to this fast pace of writing and producing was that all lyrics had to be approved by Wombles Limited chairman Max Robertson, a dour and self-important man. I'd sometimes call him the night before a session.

'Our contract says I have to have ten days to approve lyrics, Mike,' he'd say.

I'd reply, 'Max, if you want the next single to go out with no vocal, let's stick to the contract, but if you want a hit, can I please have approval by tomorrow morning!'

BUSY AND HOT

He made the strangest objections to certain lyrics. One song, about the Wombles in the jungle, started:

Drums in the jungle,
They make the monkeys run,
Tell the animals in the undergrowth
The Wombling has begun.

Harmless enough, I thought.

'Ooh, I'm not sure about that,' said Max. 'I don't think the Wombles should be seen to be scaring the other little animals away.' I thought for a minute.

'How about "Drums in the jungle, They make the monkeys *come*?"' I said. 'That way, the Wombles are *inviting* the other animals towards them rather than chasing them away.'

'Brilliant!' said Max. 'Let's have that.'

So that's how it remains to this day. Max never noticed the double meaning, or if he did, he must have refrained from pointing it out in case I thought he had a dirty mind. Another time, I called him for approval of a song containing the lines 'There's a light in the corner where the jukebox stands/It was made by a Womble out of old tin cans'. Not exactly a perfect rhyme, but hey, it was rock 'n' roll.

'Oh, we can't have that,' said Max. 'A jukebox is seedy and gives a very low impression of the Wombles.'

'Haven't you been to tea at the Ritz lately?' I improvised. 'There's a jukebox there – the Ritz wouldn't have one if they are a symbol of anything unpleasant.'

Of course there wasn't a jukebox at the Ritz but Max believed me and the lyric got through. More often than not, it was like talking to someone from a different planet. I felt I had to treat him with kid gloves and used to get so wound up when he wouldn't take a point, or when he would block a perfectly good lyric. Now that he was no longer a TV tennis commentary star and, worse still, his wife Elisabeth had become the breadwinner of the family, it seemed he took his job as chairman of Wombles Limited very seriously indeed.

* * *

Life at Langley Avenue was a mixture of elation and unhappiness. Wendy was unpredictable. One minute she was my best mate, almost gushing with support, love and fun, and the next she'd be yelling at me and locking herself in the bedroom. She was a good mother to our girls, but often too strict with them for my liking. There were blazing rows and periods of time when I would go for a walk round the block, caught in a dilemma; vowing to leave but knowing I couldn't. We had two kids who were terrific girls and they were enjoying life most of the time. Their mother loved them, just as she loved me, but she expected to have her way and never to be thwarted.

I obviously have my faults too and knowing how blind other people can be to their own faults, maybe more blame lay with me than I knew about at the time or know about now. I tried to be – and thought I succeeded in being – generally caring and supportive. And I loved Wendy, or at least I loved one of the two Wendys. Living with them both was, in a way, exciting. Rather in the way that walking through a minefield must be exciting.

All the while we Wombles were busy doing lots of TV appearances. The rule was, if you had a record going UP the top thirty,

BUSY AND HOT

you were booked for *Top of the Pops* every other week, but never for two weeks in a row and not if your record was going down the charts. Because through 1974 and 1975, we seemed almost always to have a single going up the chart, we were on the show pretty well every other week. We'd turn up with our costumes all carefully packed into plastic dustbins by my mum and her assistant, June Rutland, and take our place on whichever of the several stages in the studio we were to be performing. Across the studio at BBC TV Centre, playing the song before us or waiting to perform after us in the show, might be David Bowie, the Bay City Rollers, Mud, Sweet, David Essex or any other pop star or band of the day. There was a community of artists who appeared regularly on the show – I remember kicking a football around the studio with members of Slade – as well as Pan's People, the girl dancers who were famous for their sexy but often cheesy routines. Each week they would do their bit, usually to a record that was going up the charts but where the artist was unavailable. We all got to know each other very well.

On one occasion I was driving home from *Top of the Pops* in my bright blue Rolls with my Womble head on the passenger seat. I came to some traffic lights and while the lights were red, put the head on, thinking it would surprise any driver who pulled up next to me – I just wasn't expecting the next car to pull up next to me to be a bloody police car! The constable in the passenger seat beckoned for me to lower the driver's window, which I did, while turning towards him with my Orinoco head pointing through the window.

'Alright, Mr Batt. You've had your little joke, now take the Womble head off and drive home carefully and we'll say no more about it,' he said.

Which I very obediently did.

THE CLOSEST THING TO CRAZY

ABBA and I continued to run into each other, our early career trajectories nicely coinciding. Notably, as well as shows like the BBC's Saturday night *Seaside Special*, we were often booked on the same German TV shows. After one such show we sat together in the hospitality tent, having dinner and drinking schnapps. We didn't want the evening to end and so we went to the local disco club just as the guy was locking up for the night. Seeing that it was ABBA – and possibly with a back-hander involved – he opened up especially for us, so we had our own five-person nightclub. The girls wanted to dance and the guys were deep in conversation so I chivalrously partnered the ladies on the floor. The DJ obviously thought it might be diplomatic to play ABBA's own music and soon I was spinning around the floor to 'Dancing Queen' with the two actual dancing queens. Just a fun night at the time, but later appreciated as the very special moment it was.

The Writing on the Wombles' Wall

At the end of 1974 something happened that convinced me I must stop doing the Wombles. Stop recording, stop building up the commercial success and pushing the 'band' to new heights. As it turned out, I was to carry on throughout most of the next year, but this incident was what really led to my decision to start winding things down.

Wombles Limited had, in their early contract with me, the right to put on a Womble stage show. How I ever allowed that to happen I do not know – one learns by experience, and things are different these days. They decided to mount a Womble stage show during Christmas of the first year of our success, perhaps thinking that the chart success would be short-lived and this would be their only chance to cash in. I had the right to supervise the music of the shows and so, rather than relinquish all control, I opted to cooperate with the producer, a young Bill Kenwright, who at the time was hustling and jostling to make his mark.

The very existence of a Wombles' stage musical was a threat to the credibility of the Wombles band. Don't laugh. I mean the *believability* factor. Most people in Britain thought of the Wombles as a pop group. Some kids even thought they were real, so how could they be on stage in Shaftesbury Avenue in the West End of London when they were at the same time on *Top of the Pops* or wherever else we 'real' Wombles were? Worse still, Bill Kenwright had put together a proposal for Wombles Limited that really appealed to their short-term 'cash-in' mentality. There would be *nine* shows, all over the UK, simultaneously! Nine casts were rehearsed in one rehearsal room in London, by one director. They would then be deployed to whichever unsuspecting cities and towns were chosen – Glasgow, Liverpool, Belfast and so on. All the shows were billed as starring 'The Wombles'.

It was a recipe for disaster. Everything about these shows, including the costumes, was cheap and nasty. In fact, they stank of everything we Wombles, as the pop group, tried hard to avoid. We couldn't stop Wombles' branding appearing on overpriced bubble bath bottles, but we could make sure that our records were good, strong pop songs – adventurous, well performed and expertly recorded. We were proud of the immaculate quality of our costumes, all handmade by my mother and her assistant, June, brushed and laundered for each appearance (US tour aside!), and we *never* fielded two groups simultaneously, or even two identical individual characters. Costumed Wombles had strict instructions never to be seen in public with their 'heads' off. They were stars, like members of any other group. Or so the public and I thought.

We were about to be disillusioned.

By now I was so tired of arguing with Wombles Limited. I'd reluctantly agreed to them opening garden centres with their inferior costumes; I'd succumbed to Max Robertson's supervision of my lyrics; I'd generally toed the line and watched them milk the situation for everything it was worth, while I just got on and provided an endless stream of hits without which no self-respecting bubble bath company would have given them the time of day. I personally often appeared *with* a Womble, but as myself, in civvies – chatting on the sofa with Sally James or other TV hosts, further identifying myself with the Wombles. A mistake, in hindsight of course. Meanwhile, Wombles Limited were cheapening the brand with every move. The public thought anything to do with the Wombles emanated from me, not Elisabeth Beresford's company. In fact, fifty years on, I still believe they think this is the case.

And then, just as 'Wombling Merry Christmas' was leaping up the UK charts – a certainty to be number one for Christmas, outselling our nearest rivals, Mud, by two to one, the story broke on the front page of a national tabloid. A picture of a girl, backstage in Liverpool, getting into a Womble costume, and a story about how nine groups of Wombles were appearing all over the country. And Great Uncle Bulgaria wasn't even a bloke! It was as if Father Christmas wasn't real and that there were lots of pretend ones. It was also as if Mike Batt was a greedy bastard who wanted to rip off the British public by fielding nine pop groups into nine cities to make nine times as much money. That would have been bad enough, but the shows were dreadful. I was told that in Belfast, outraged mothers stormed the stage in anger at the amateurish quality and demanded a refund. It was all over the papers.

That week, our record sales halved suddenly, Mud overtook us and made it to the prestigious number-one spot with 'Lonely This Christmas'. Bill Kenwright agreed to go face to face with me on *Nationwide*, the BBC's evening TV news magazine programme. Coincidentally he turned up wearing a black suit and I was wearing a white one. He had the wit and humility to point out that he was dressed as the bad guy and I was dressed as the good one but his humility didn't help much. We had our five-minute argument, in which I tried to explain to the public that the shows weren't the real Wombles, just as a store Santa Claus isn't the real Santa, but a fat lot of good it did.

Despite the disastrous stage show having robbed us of an almost certain number-one record, 1975 was another successful year for the Wombles. *Superwombling* was in my view the best album of the four studio albums, with 'White Tie and Tails', 'Superwomble' and other singles still all supported by multiple TV appearances including *Top of the Pops*, *Crackerjack!* and *Blue Peter*. Our chart placings tended to be a little lower, but frankly, I'd lost interest in taking the act into 1976.

I figured the Wombles had just about done their dash.

Planning My Escape

I was planning my escape. It had been great fun doing all my Womble activities and it appealed to my sense of the ridiculous as well as being very financially lucrative, but I had to move on. I could no longer continue in a situation where I was identified with the wider image of a character (or characters) over which I had no control.

THE CLOSEST THING TO CRAZY

Everything Wombles Limited did made me shudder because if they did something tacky, I was perceived to be the culprit.

I had entered the business with singer-songwriter aspirations. By now I was quite an accomplished singer, producer and arranger and I wanted to get back to making records of my own as an artist. I also wanted to write film scores. I had a word with Paul Russell and Dick Asher at CBS and we tweaked the Wombles' contract so that it would continue as a solo deal for me. It had always been that, but I happened to have been wearing a furry costume for the first four albums so there wasn't much to change. I continued to enjoy promoting the Wombles albums but would not make any more under the Wombles name. I began work on a serious solo album.

Meanwhile, during that second year of the Wombles' run of hits in 1975, I had a phone call from Tim Hart of Steeleye Span. Steeleye were at that time already highly rated as a folk-rock band. They were on Chris Wright's prestigious Chrysalis label, along with bands like Jethro Tull and Ten Years After. Tim wanted me to meet up for a drink with him and a couple of the other band members with a view to producing their next album. Apparently they liked the drum sounds on the Wombles' albums and had been impressed by the arrangements and production. I thought it had been quite perceptive of them to have seen the quality through the jollity – I suppose if they'd said I was crap, I wouldn't be saying how perceptive I thought they were!

Steeleye Span had had one big single hit, the beautiful, a cappella 'Gaudete' (1973), and had built up a big fan base by touring. Now they were looking to take one more step up the ladder. I met the whole group in a rehearsal studio – vocalist Maddy Prior, Bob Johnson and Tim Hart on guitars, Peter Knight on fiddle and mandolin, Rick

BUSY AND HOT

Kemp on bass guitar and Nigel Pegrum on drums. All the boys sang, too. There, during that first meeting, we thrashed out an arrangement for a traditional song that they had found, 'All Around My Hat'. They had already developed a lot of ideas for the arrangement and we stitched it together into a really tight and exciting piece, underpinned by a strong, up-tempo shuffle rhythm.

We made the album at Lansdowne Studios in Holland Park, AIR Studios in Oxford Circus and my other favourite studio, Wessex, in Highbury. I had gravitated towards Wessex Studios very early on in my recording career – in fact, it had been where Bob Reisdorff had chosen to record my first single, 'Mr Poem' – and I liked the Thompson family who owned it. Mr Thompson Snr (Ron) ran the business with his two sound engineer sons, Mike (who was a few years older than me) and Robin (who was just my age).

Mike, Robin and I made a lot of records together, including those medium-to-clunky Mike Batt Orchestra albums, and all the Wombles records were engineered by Robin, who was a lovely guy. We worked together from the ages of eighteen to about twenty-four and had a lot of fun. A few years later, Robin was to leave the company because of an ear problem. He went off with his young wife and daughter in a boat to realise a lifetime dream living overseas but got mixed up, allegedly, with a drug importation operation and was arrested for using his boat to smuggle cannabis into the UK. He served a term in prison and tragically died of a heart attack shortly after his release. I would guess he must have been no more than about thirty-five years old.

I loved working with Steeleye Span and developed a particularly strong friendship with Peter Knight. A strong character with a 'fuck-off' attitude and a raging sense of humour, he was one of those blokes who are annoyingly good at darts and snooker – probably from all those years in folk clubs. He rolled his own fags, sometimes as joints, sometimes not.

There were various undercurrents and rivalries within the band and it was my job as producer to ensure that none of this got in the way of the good atmosphere in the studio. The other thing you have to be, as producer of a band, is a pivot for everyone's ideas. Someone comes up with an idea, someone else says it's rubbish, you say, 'Let's just try it' or 'Let's not waste time on it'. You have to be the filter through which the band's ideas pass and add your own ideas in a way that doesn't unfairly dominate or distort the proceedings. It's a bit like being chairman of a meeting, although the role depends upon the band. With a different band, they might expect just to be told what to do. Working with artists who have plenty of ideas and bring a lot to the table is always more rewarding but often means you have strong characters around you because there is no art without ego, your own included; you have to be a bit of a diplomat.

'All Around My Hat' came out in the autumn of 1975 and went to number five in the singles chart. The album of the same name followed and was a huge success, reaching number seven. The *New Musical Express* ran a front-page headline – 'All Around Mike Batt' – to herald a fly-on-the-wall feature written by the respected rock journalist Charles Shaar Murray after a visit to AIR Studios when we had been working. The piece was very positive and I came out of it as the guy who, despite being a Womble, wasn't at all a bad producer.

The time at Langley Avenue falls naturally, in my memory, into two sections: Womble and post-Womble. There was a slightly iffy period towards the end of the two years of what the press dubbed

BUSY AND HOT

'Womble Mania' and me finding my feet as a solo artist. For reasons I can't fathom to this day, I released a succession of singles under my own name which were out-and-out pop records. In hindsight, I realise that the strongest pop influence on those singles was the band Sparks, who were so creative and mercurial. I was working with Steeleye Span, also on my more 'serious' album and promoting the Wombles. There would be three or four projects going on at the same time. I did have trouble saying no! At one stage I was promoting the single 'Superwomble' at the same time as I was working on 'All Around My Hat'.

In those days, to be on *Top of the Pops*, you had to mime. It was technically easier for the show (which went out live) if you did, and in any case, as we didn't have mouths, we Wombles had no other option! Nevertheless, to satisfy the Musicians' Union, you had to remake the entire record the night before your appearance. In other words you were not allowed to mime to the record itself, but you could mime to a specially made track for the show – made in one hasty, three-hour session.

I was in AIR Studios with Steeleye Span when the message came through that the Wombles were to make an appearance on *Top of the Pops* the following day, with no time to go and make a backing track. Being already busy with Steeleye Span, I asked them if they'd mind playing the TV remake of 'Superwomble' because the humourless bloke from the Musicians' Union was about to show up and 'witness' that it was indeed being remade. They sportingly agreed to do it. I taught them the track and we played it while the infamous and aforementioned Don Smith – 'Doctor Death' – from the Musicians' Union watched from the control room.

After the session, Don asked for everybody's name.

THE CLOSEST THING TO CRAZY

'Why do you want them?' I asked.

'Because the people who play the track have to be the same people who are on the show tomorrow,' said Don.

This was a new one on me but that's what had to happen. Don left the studio and I sheepishly asked the guys if they'd wear the costumes the next day and perform 'Superwomble' on the show. They thought it was a fantastic idea. Of course the whole thing would have to be a total secret – it wouldn't have been cool for a serious band like Steeleye Span to be caught being the Wombles. And so we arranged for them to meet with me the following day at the Kensington Hilton Hotel, where we would get into the costumes and be taken by blacked-out limo to the BBC TV Centre in Wood Lane, five minutes away. Somehow we managed to get them in, do the show and then get out again without anyone realising who was inside the Womble costumes!

CHAPTER SEVEN

Let's Get Serious Again

When I finally cut myself off from the Wombles in 1976, I still had a big hill to climb to try to get the UK media to take me seriously as a singer-songwriter. My string of chart-targeted 'poppy' singles didn't help. One such single – 'Summertime City' – became a big hit that year, reaching number four under the artist name 'Mike Batt (with the New Edition)'. It all came about by accident, really. Michael Hurll, a senior BBC TV producer, was making a series of Saturday Night variety shows from a circus tent that was travelling around various seaside resorts such as Bournemouth, Blackpool and Margate. He had asked me to write him a theme song. The idea was that the dance group from the show – the New Edition – would sing the song. But when it came to the session, I couldn't find anyone in the dance troupe able to perform a strong-enough lead vocal, so I sang it myself. There was no other option, as it had to be delivered the next day. CBS put it out as a solo record by me, and Michael Hurll I invited me to go onto the show and sing it on two occasions.

By this time, Dick Asher had been promoted to run CBS International from New York, replacing Walter Yetnikoff, who had stepped further up the corporate ladder to become president and CEO, worldwide. Asher had been replaced as UK managing director by Maurice Oberstein, a flawed and rather odd man who nevertheless had his good side and someone with whom I got on very well.

I said, 'Obie, I don't really think I should do this show, do you? It'll hardly help my image.'

'All publicity is good publicity,' he said. 'You should do the show.'

So I did the show, but it was a huge mistake as far as my credibility at the time was concerned. The record went to number four in the UK for two weeks and I looked like a complete schmuck in front of millions of people, stamping my feet and singing with, firstly, the New Edition on *Seaside Special* and then with Pan's People on *Top of the Pops* dancing around me. I wore flared trousers and Union Jack platform boots and had my big, ginger Afro.

Not a pretty sight. It was quite fun to be a 'human' pop star for a while, though.

The burden of becoming known as a singer-songwriter of any substance was becoming too much; the goal of transforming myself into a 'cool' or at least respected artist was looking less and less likely after allowing myself to be diverted by events rather than picking my own path and saying no to those who offered me things that didn't fit with that plan. The idea of being booked to do a session for the BBC's cooler show, *The Old Grey Whistle Test*, when my more 'serious' album came out would have been laughable. When CBS wanted me to re-sign with an extension to my solo deal a year or so later, I asked them to delete 'Summertime City' and never to re-release it. That's why it was never on the radio or included on compilations. I buried it. However, as time has moved on, I have become much more relaxed about 'Summertime City'. You can stream it now. I think it's a great little pop record and the footage of me and Pan's People performing it on *Top of the Pops* is hilarious and kitsch – I even quite like the Afro and flares!

To develop my career as a solo artist, I thought I needed to do live gigs with a backing band. I duly hired an existing group, who were from Manchester, put them in black leather top hats and called them the Mad Hatters. Stupid name, another bad decision. We put them up in a rented house and paid them wages, and Wendy became their manager, deciding that if they did gigs of their own, it would pay for their upkeep. It didn't, although it gave her something to do. She spent a *lot* of time with them. But essentially, it just burdened us with the responsibility of getting gigs for what was, in effect, a pretty average covers band – we never did play live together.

The Ivor Novello Awards

I have always enjoyed serving on industry boards. Initially, it was writer-representative boards such as the Songwriters' Guild (later, BASCA) and the Performing Rights Society (PRS) as a director then more latterly as deputy chairman of the British Phonographic Industry (BPI). Even in my twenties I enjoyed the debate and the issues, the contact with my peers in the industry, often lobbying government for change in copyright laws. It also entailed travelling quite a lot – on one occasion to communist-era Prague, and another to Copenhagen, representing the PRS at international conferences.

From early on I was anxious that the Ivor Novello Awards should be given a facelift. They really were a well-meaning but dusty, rather amateurish affair. The ceremony event was not befitting of the status of the awards, which are considered the British 'Songwriting Oscars'.

THE CLOSEST THING TO CRAZY

First, we changed the name of the Songwriters' Guild to the British Academy of Songwriters, Composers and Authors (BASCA), partly so that the award would have the status of being 'Academy' awards. We abolished the awful label 'runners-up' and started a system of nominations instead. Would you rather be a 'runner-up' or an 'academy nominated songwriter'? Then I moved the awards from Covent Garden's perfectly nice but unspectacular Connaught Rooms to the mighty Grosvenor House, where glistening chandeliers hung above the massive ballroom and coloured spotlights could sweep the grand event from the balcony.

It was while working on the design and upgrading of the Ivor Novello Awards in 1975 that I discovered the hidden art of using stills projectors to create animation. 'Hidden' because until then a stack of 12 Kodak carousel projectors might have been used to enhance product launches and indeed the company I used were in the business of doing just that. When I realised the visual fun that could be had from aiming multiple projectors at just one screen (instead of at many) to create a composite and moving image, a new world of potential kinetic projection art suddenly revealed itself; something which would fascinate me and which I would gradually develop for the rest of my career, for TV and stage production. It remained an original and fascinating art form even when video had become commonplace.

Back in those early Ivor Novello Awards days when pop videos weren't readily available, we were able to create eye-popping presentations using multiple stills, sometimes of the writers who themselves were perhaps not stars. Stars or not, this ceremony was their big day in the sun. We topped up the glitz of the occasion by making sure a big star was on hand to present each award, even if the writer was Joanne Bloggs, of whom you've never heard.

I produced and directed these awards for the first five years and I'm pleased to say that the even more grandly titled Ivors Academy have kept the ceremony at Grosvenor House and still now run it almost exactly as it was done back then.

Schizophonia

My first solo album, *Schizophonia*, came out in July 1977. Musically and stylistically, it was a return to the natural, unconstrained style that seems to be my compositional signature when writing for an orchestra with a rock rhythm section. Lots of contrasting ideas, licks, riffs, pace. Songs would alternate with ambitious compositions. The first half – a mini concept album on one side – had an Arabic feel. I never called it classic rock or prog. In fact, I distanced myself from the label 'progressive classic rock' from that period – I liked to think I was doing something genuinely innovative and unique. And yet I was – and still am – an ex-Womble. I was that guy from *Seaside Special*. So how could I also be perceived as artistically relevant? I couldn't.

I doubt that I will ever be taken seriously by the British arts fraternity because I don't speak the right language. You have to swan about and talk earnestly about art and the inner meaning of things to be taken seriously. I'd rather let my music speak for me but that presupposes people are listening intently, which no artist should presume. It seems sometimes that I'm too classical for the rock people and too rock for the classical people and, in turns, too weird for the middle-of-the-road people and too middle-of-the-road for the weird people! It is rather frustrating but I can't blame the media or the audiences – I accept that's just how it is.

I'm always quick to blame myself and criticise my own work if that's how I feel, but I'm proud of my solo albums as a body of work. However, art is a very subjective thing and I had already been through a period of clowning about and convincing everyone what a lightweight character I was, so, to an extent it was my own fault. The mistake I made was to think that I could mess about on *Top of the Pops* to my heart's content but when I said, 'Okay, guys, from now on this is the real me,' people would somehow realise and start paying attention. In the UK, few did. What I was doing didn't always follow the fashion of the day and I didn't fit in with what the press were paying attention to.

I was very happy with *Schizophonia*. I had put together a great rhythm section of the young Chris Spedding on guitar, Ray Cooper on percussion, Clem Cattini on drums and Les Hurdle on bass. They were actually the same guys who had played on the Womble records – all very respected and highly regarded musicians. I'd written some good songs. 'Railway Hotel', a song about a down-at-heel love affair in a seedy hotel room, has endured as one of my most rated songs over the years, covered by many artists despite never having been a big hit. The dramatic opening track, 'The Ride to Agadir', was a big hit single in Germany and other overseas territories and became the battle anthem for a South African special forces unit. The Arabic material happened to attract the attention of Elmo Williams, producer of the movie *Caravans*, based on the James A. Michener novel. It led to me being commissioned to write the score for the 1978 film. But before that, another film was about to appear along the horizon . . .

Burning Like Fire

I met Martin Rosen, producer of *Watership Down*, in 1975 when he was introduced to me by CBS. He thought he wanted songs for his film, then changed his mind several times – both before he commissioned me and after I had delivered the first song. He wanted to make a film that wasn't like a Disney film – rather, something more adult, like the book – he was just unsure whether songs might detract from that ideal. Martin brought in a hugely respected animator and film director – John Hubley, who, ironically, had worked in the early Disney studio, survived McCarthy's 'Anti-American' communist witch-hunt of the 1950s and was still celebrated as a highly skilled animation director. One of his famous creations had been the short-sighted pensioner, Mr. Magoo. Hubley did a lot of the early preparation for the film's story direction and artistic look.

What I really wanted was to be entrusted with the symphonic underscore for the whole film. Martin knew this, but he saw me as just a songwriter and wanted a 'big name' orchestral composer. I felt there should be a 'Delius/Vaughan Williams' flavour to the music and recorded a fully symphonic demo at my own expense with the London Symphony Orchestra (LSO). However, he commissioned Malcolm Williamson, 'Master of the Queen's Music', to do the score. When Williamson, who lived in Australia, turned up with only a few bars of unorchestrated music, days before the session, Rosen turned to Angela Morley to save him. Martin and I were good friends by then and he knew I was desperate to do it so I was disappointed that he didn't turn to me.

Earlier on in the process, John Hubley had briefed me to write a song for the movie. He wanted a song about death – it was a hell of a subject. I went home and thought about it for several days before concluding that the 'what happens when we die?' question is probably one of the biggest things we ever ask ourselves. Once I had that, the song came quickly. The 'Bright Eyes' lyric and melody enabled me to write about the wonder of life before it ends as well as the unknown, beyond.

THE CLOSEST THING TO CRAZY

When I had finished writing the song, I made a demo using a small orchestra. John and Martin loved it and asked who I had in mind to sing it.

'Art Garfunkel,' I said, 'but I don't suppose we'll get him so here's a list of other singers who sound a bit like him – with me at the bottom of it.'

Martin thought we should try for Art Garfunkel. He was, after all, a CBS artist like myself and the soundtrack would be on our shared label. Goddard Lieberson was contacted. Having been responsible for the introduction of the LP record, Goddard really was the father of the modern CBS Records. He had signed Barbra Streisand, Simon & Garfunkel and many other luminaries and had been a long-serving president of CBS. Lieberson loved the song and he called Garfunkel. Art also loved the song – he even asked if he could co-produce it with me, but I explained I never co-produced with people. I felt it led to slower, less decisive production and that his status as the artist would afford him ample artistic control. He took the point and a date was set. I booked a rhythm section and a string section with a couple of woodwinds, including the now-famous oboe that introduces the song.

Art was supposed to be at my house at 1 p.m. the day before the session because, having roughly worked out the best musical key for him to sing it in over the phone, I couldn't write the arrangement until I knew for sure, and that could only be done in person. Of course, this was before computer software could alter the key at the touch of a button.

Art arrived twelve hours late, at 1 a.m., having gone to the Savoy hotel for an afternoon nap. He left my house at 3 a.m., after which I had to stay up all night writing the arrangement for strings, guitars and woodwinds for the session later that same day.

LET'S GET SERIOUS AGAIN

The session was a nightmare. The afternoon was set aside for the rhythm section, the orchestra being 'overdubbed' immediately afterwards during the evening. Chris Spedding played acoustic guitar and Roland Harker was superb on lute. There were no drums on the afternoon recording – I added them later.

Art sat in the control room while I supervised the band in the studio, running in and out of the control room to check things as I went (the way I always work). We recorded a really good backing track for 'Bright Eyes', which was perfect but for one note of Chris Spedding's guitar, which had buzzed or twanged in one place and would need replacing. However, knowing there was a large string section waiting outside and that we had run out of time with the rhythm section, I decided to move on and bring Chris back the following morning to replace the offending note of guitar.

But Art wasn't happy.

'I thought you were a perfectionist when I heard the demo,' he said.

'I am,' I replied, 'but if we carry on now, the rhythm section will go into overtime. I think the track is great and I know what to do to repair the guitar note later. The strings are waiting outside and getting impatient so we would be in danger of running into overtime with a sixty-piece orchestra, which would just be irresponsible.'

Art didn't like it.

And then Martin Rosen turned up accompanied, without prior warning, by Goddard Lieberson, who was expecting to co-produce the track. This despite my having picked the studio, chosen and booked the musicians, routined the song with the artist, stayed up all night arranging it and supervised the recording of the rhythm section. There was a chat between Artie and Goddard and I could feel vibes coming off both of them. Goddard was still a powerful man, both in business and in force of personality. A much-loved and respected, witty and intelligent icon within the industry, I liked him enormously. This made it worse, as if I was about to get a telling-off from my favourite teacher.

We started recording the strings. My engineer, Mike Thompson, would always 'get the sounds' while I conducted out in the studio. I would dart in and out to talk to him just as I had during the rhythm recording. By now, the control room was full. Artie was there with his girlfriend, actress and photographer Laurie Bird – who, three years later would tragically commit suicide in his apartment, aged only twenty-five – plus Goddard Lieberson, Martin Rosen and John Hubley. While listening to the strings, Mike would ONLY be listening to the strings, so this control room full of newcomers could only hear the long, soft notes that are the main part of the string arrangement; like a slow string chorale, heard without Mike monitoring the rhythm of the twinkling folksy acoustic guitars and lute that form the main accompaniment.

I went into the control room to see if Mike was ready to record. There was a dark mood.

'Is there a problem?' I said.

'Yes,' said Goddard. 'I don't like the arrangement.'

Those exact words.

'What do you think?' I asked John Hubley.

'The strings sound a bit, er . . . pretentious,' he said.

They'd obviously discussed it.

I'd had enough. Every part of me wanted to tell them to fuck off. This was supposed to be my big chance to do a major movie and I knew the song was a hit. Was it worth throwing it all away because these people – distinguished though they were – had got the wrong

LET'S GET SERIOUS AGAIN

end of the stick and were bullying me on behalf of the artist, who was a delightful and brilliant person, but who had been giving off unhappy vibes? Certainly, Goddard, as a record man, was sticking up for the 'bigger' artist.

'Okay, I'm going,' I said very calmly. 'I won't embarrass you financially – I'll pay for the session, but you can't have my song. Goodnight.'

With that, I walked out of the control room, through the studio full of orchestra, got into my peacock-blue Rolls and started to drive off.

As I negotiated the narrow road that led past the church and away from Wessex Studios, I saw Martin Rosen running to try to catch up with me.

'You can't walk out now, this is too important,' he said.

'I just have,' I replied. 'The song isn't going into the movie.'

I was not given to Elton-style tantrums. And this wasn't one. This was self-preservation, albeit of the career suicide kind.

'What do I have to do to get you to stay?' he said.

'Get rid of everyone, including yourself, leaving me and Artie,' I said.

'I can't get rid of Lieberson,' says Martin. 'He thinks he's co-producing!'

'Well, tell him he isn't. Assure me he isn't – undertake to put it in writing – and he can stay, provided he lets me get on with the job.'

Martin went back inside and negotiated. I stayed, everyone else left except Goddard, me, the engineer and Artie. But Goddard couldn't just be a bystander. I went out to conduct the strings again. In the chorus there's a familiar part where the strings do a 'fall' or 'slide' between the notes – a 'portamento'. Given the length of the notes, the slide can start at any one of several places – the beginning of the initial note, halfway through or perhaps right at the end of the note. I had notated exactly where I wanted it. Goddard decided that the speed or placement of the slide was wrong.

'Can you come out into the studio and explain to the orchestra what you mean?' I asked, patiently.

Goddard came out and started singing different portamento slides to the band. We had already performed it perfectly about six times before all this. None of them could understand what he meant. I tried explaining it to them, trying different things. Then, looking at the studio clock, I realised it was five minutes to midnight and knowing that it was Sunday the next day, if we didn't record the strings in the next five minutes then we would go into overtime for going past three hours and then double overtime for it being after midnight, possibly even triple overtime considering that at midnight it would be Sunday. When I told him this, he said it didn't matter.

I said to Goddard, 'I've got an idea, try this. You go back into the control room and listen to this for an idea.'

He went.

As he was going, I said to the band quietly, 'Just play it as originally written.'

So they did.

'Finally!' shouts Goddard from the control room. 'You finally got it right!'

Of course they had played it like that an hour earlier, but they all went home richer because of the triple overtime. We, of course, had to stay and put vocals on. It was midnight. I hadn't slept the night before because I'd been waiting for the singer to turn up and then arranging the music.

LET'S GET SERIOUS AGAIN

And the fun had barely started.

Art goes into the vocal booth. He sings it. He sings it well – of course he does – but not quite with the right anticipation on the word 'Eyes'. In other words, he is singing 'eyes' on the beat and I want it anticipated. It's very important – actually it's part of the written tune to do it this way. We spend about twenty minutes trying. He doesn't really want to take my direction.

Goddard says to me, incredulously, 'Do you know who you are talking to?'

'Yes,' I say, 'it's Art Garfunkel, the artist I chose to sing my song and who wouldn't be standing here if I hadn't chosen him. By the same token that I was trusted to choose him, I think I have the right to be trusted to show him how the song goes. However brilliant he is, he isn't getting the best out of the song.' Artie is in the vocal booth and not listening to this exchange.

We try for a while longer. Soon, Artie wants to pause and he lights up a spliff. He's sitting in the dark in the studio.

I go up to him: 'Look, Artie, we could get this done in a heartbeat if we were alone. You are uptight because of the upset before and because Goddard is there. Why don't you ask him to leave us on our own and we'll nail it together? It's four in the morning anyway, he must be tired – I sure as hell am.'

Artie's limo has been waiting outside since 3 p.m. the previous day.

'Okay,' says Art, 'I'll suggest that.'

He goes over and talks to Goddard, who gets the point and leaves cordially.

'Just sing it in my headphones and I'll double-track you,' says Art.

So, I go into the booth and sing the song, phrased as I would like it. He then puts on the headphones and, while listening to my

THE CLOSEST THING TO CRAZY

phrasing, doubles it, recording his voice on the track next to mine. Art is a genius at double-tracking, his ear is so finely acute and observant. We take out my voice and it's there: him singing it; his voice, my phrasing.

'Okay, now I've got it,' he says. 'Now let me sing it without you in the headphones.'

So he starts at the top of the song and sings it through in one take. Perfect phrasing, perfect tuning, great expression. A proper, original performance, full of sensibility, awareness and control. This is the take we will end up using, unedited. It's perfect. It's also five in the morning. Artie goes back to the Savoy to sleep. No point my going home – Chris Spedding has been booked for 10 a.m. to replace his guitar part.

Chris duly turns up at the appointed time, repairs his 'offending' note in ten minutes and leaves.

That was in 1976. The following year, John Hubley died on 21 February during open heart surgery. It was poignant to realise that he would have known about his condition when he commissioned the song. Goddard followed him on 29 May, dying of cancer at the age of sixty-six.

'Bright Eyes' only made it into the final movie after being in, then out, then in again, three times.

CHAPTER EIGHT

Films and Family

In 1977 the Wombles came back to haunt me again in the shape of the film, *Wombling Free*. Organised against my will by Wombles Limited, like the musical, shot at Pinewood Studios on a low budget and directed ineptly by Lionel Jeffries, it was a horror. I had the option to write the score or let them appoint someone else to do it. So of course I did it myself. All I can say is that it was good scoring practice.

The shooting and staging of the musical numbers were imitations of the visual performances I had put together for big variety shows and *Top of the Pops* ('White Tie and Tails' in particular, for which my mother had made immaculate white-tailed suits for us to wear for television appearances, using plastic buckets covered in white cloth for the top hats). The story of the movie was patronising, dreary and unfunny; the magic of the musical Wombles as entertainers had been poorly faked – an opportunity missed. The whole thing was cringeworthy. For years afterwards it would pop up on TV at Christmas time and embarrass the hell out of me.

THE CLOSEST THING TO CRAZY

Caravans

In 1978, I had a phone call from Paul Russell, who was still head of business affairs for CBS UK (now Sony). He told me that Elmo Williams, the producer of a new, big-budget film, *Caravans*, had contacted him, looking for a composer for the movie. They already had a shortlist of John Barry, Michel Legrand and Maurice Jarre, all of whom were famous names as film composers, but apparently somebody had had a copy of my *Schizophonia* album on the location (Iran, just before the revolution) and they had often played it to get 'in the mood' before filming. They'd never heard of me but wanted at least to check me out.

I went to Munich on a snowy night to meet Elmo and his daughter Stacy, who was helping him edit the movie. They picked me up from the airport and we drove through the icy weather to a small room within the Bavariafilms Studios compound, where they showed me some of the footage on an old Steenbeck 35mm reel-to-reel editing machine. It looked spectacular. Based on the novel by James A. Michener, the film starred Anthony Quinn and Jennifer O'Neill. The authenticity and graphic breadth was awe-inspiring and I suddenly *really* wanted to score this movie. At a typical German pork-knuckle and gingham tablecloths restaurant we talked and got to know each other. Elmo, who had won an Oscar as the editor of *High Noon* (1952) before becoming head of Fox Pictures in the UK, was the producer and had to answer to the investors, who were all Iranian. The principal two were called Mehdi Bushehri and Dr Zhadi.

It did seem odd that the most fascinating character in Michener's book – a Nazi doctor on the run and travelling with the caravan, who is essential to the integrity of the story – had been cut from the screenplay completely. Again, it wasn't clear whether this was because of pressure from the Iranians who were funding the film with pre-revolution money, rumoured to have come from the Shah himself, or by decree of some well-meaning fool who wanted to make the film less controversial. Ultimately, James A. Michener got very upset and sued. In fact, things like this gross disregard for the storyline contributed to the ultimate blandness (and subsequent failure at the box office) of the movie, but at the time it had the look of epic desert films like *Lawrence of Arabia* and I was desperate to score it.

After a few more meetings with Elmo, it became apparent that the 'money' wanted one of the three big names to score the film. I asked if he would try to convince the investors to try an experiment before making their decision. In 1978 a reasonable fee for scoring the movie might have been £8,000 to £10,000. I asked him to pay *£2,000*, which I would use to hire a studio and the London Philharmonic Orchestra so that I could score one reel of the movie to picture (with the film playing on a big screen behind the orchestra) and the investors could come to the session and watch me working with the orchestra and hear the music.

He convinced them and, two weeks later, after working around the clock, I had scored three scenes from the film, where music was important: The moment where we first see the Caravan move off into the desert ('Caravan on the Move'), the song ('Caravan Song') and the storm sequence where the Caravan has to make a river crossing during a blizzard ('Storm in the Desert').

Everyone turned up at CTS Studios in Wembley. To take some of the formality out of the occasion and to help the orchestra feel the vibe, the studio was decorated to look like a scene from the film with sand, palm trees and even a couple of stuffed camels.

THE CLOSEST THING TO CRAZY

We performed the music with the film running. Thankfully my calculations had worked and the many 'synchronisation points' landed in the right places. The Iranians all seemed to like the music. They invited me, Wendy and Elmo to a Middle Eastern restaurant in Regent Street, where belly dancers stepped off the stage onto our long table so that the Iranian guys could stuff money into their bras and waistbands. There was such loud drumming that I couldn't hear a word of the conversation.

As we left, Elmo said, 'Well, are you pleased?'

I said, 'I guess so, but what about, exactly?'

'Didn't you hear? They've offered you the job!' he said.

The film needed two distinct styles of music. One was a sweeping orchestral, filmic score with a melody that could be used in many situations. I wanted that melody to be both poignant and triumphant, capable of being sad and happy, depending on the tempo and orchestration. The second type was what they call 'source' music, because rather than just adding mood for the audience, it was also part of the action – a group of musicians in a market place, say – being heard within the scene by the characters. To add authenticity, I studied a lot of Iranian music (although the film was actually set between Afghanistan and Pakistan) and did a tour of restaurants of those ethnicities in order to recruit drummers and even just a small crowd of people to stand in one corner of the studio, to clap hands and shout. I augmented this ragtag band with the top musicians of the day, the London Philharmonic Orchestra, my old percussionist friend Ray Cooper and Chris Karan, drummer of the Dudley Moore trio, who also happens to be an expert in world percussion, including tabla. I also gathered some fantastic Western experts on instruments from the region – oud, santur and others.

FILMS AND FAMILY

The sessions were exhilarating, although sometimes frustrating. The assistant editor would ring me at midnight the night before a session with a list of cuts they had just made, rendering all my sync points inaccurate. I would have to recalculate and cut beats out of bars or add half-beats in (creating ridiculous time signatures in some cases) to accommodate these last-minute changes. Sometimes I would even be told about such cuts just as I was starting to conduct a cue. The film would stop, I'd halt the orchestra and pick up the phone that connected to the control room.

'Roy's just remembered that he cut out the close-up just before the rain comes down,' the editor would say.

I'd take it on the chin, give them a smile, look down at the score, think for a couple of moments and then say, 'Guys, cut the second half of bar 134 and the first beat of bar 135. Then play as written until bar 160 and make 161 a five-four bar with the following notes for the fifth beat on the five four: first violins a crotchet F sharp, second violins a quaver D followed by a quaver C sharp, violas the F sharp below middle C and basses and celli, your lowest F sharp and C sharp respectively. Everybody else make the same rhythmical cuts and additions but remain silent during the fifth beat of bar 161.'

Pencils would come out. We'd try it to see if everyone had heard and understood and the session would proceed. It was as complicated and chaotic as it sounds but it was exciting stuff all the same. Indeed, I'd say my time writing and recording film scores has been some of the most satisfying and rewarding of my life.

The film premiered in London and at Radio City Music Hall in New York, in November 1978, but flopped badly. However, the record did something different. 'Caravan Song', sung so beautifully by Barbara Dickson, started leaping up the UK singles charts.

THE CLOSEST THING TO CRAZY

The album began to sell. Not just in England but everywhere. There was even talk of a possible Oscar nomination for the music – although the chances of that were really low on a movie that was otherwise a failure and were reduced to zero when CBS failed to get the records out to the Academy voters in time!

Then, just as the Barbara Dickson record was at number forty-one and was expected by all to make giant steps into the top twenty, it stopped dead in its tracks. I couldn't understand it. Why? Everyone was playing it on the radio and raving about it. Years later, the then managing director David Betteridge admitted to me after a few drinks that CBS had deliberately 'killed off' the record because they had what they thought was an even stronger single waiting in the wings, 'January, February'. It was already January and they couldn't wait any longer! So they killed our record by letting it go out of stock and rush-released the other one. Despite its modest chart performance, 'Caravan Song' remains Barbara Dickson's most popular song with her fans to this day.

The *Caravans* album did, however, keep on selling. It didn't matter to people that they hadn't seen the movie, they just liked the album. At one point it was the second biggest-selling soundtrack ever in South Africa after *The Sound of Music*. People used it for all sorts of things. Katarina Witt, the East German skating champion, used the instrumental theme for her most famous dance routine and the song still gets a lot of attention on Classic Radio stations around the world.

Tarot Suite

By now I was beginning work on my second solo album. The success of *Schizophonia* – outside Britain, in particular – had spurred me on and I wanted to make a truly cohesive album that had a dramatic concept on which to hang the ideas. I had always been fascinated by the artwork and the tradition of tarot cards. I wasn't really that interested in the occult – I suppose I was curious like anyone else – but I got to know the various tarot packs and read a lot about them. I decided to write an album, *Tarot Suite*, which would, once again, combine my more experimental combination of rock and symphonic instruments.

Unlike *Schizophonia*, which was only half a concept album, the idea for *Tarot Suite* was conceived before I began making it. The other difference was that I brought in other lead singers to help with the vocals. I recruited Roger Chapman, previously the manic frontman of Family, to sing the song 'Imbecile', which needed a really tough, harsh voice, and 'Run Like the Wind', which finishes the album. Colin Blunstone sang 'Losing Your Way in the Rain' beautifully. I sang the vocal on 'Lady of the Dawn', which became a big hit in Holland, Germany and South Africa. In fact, all across Europe and Australia, my own albums would sell hundreds of thousands of copies, by far exceeding the Wombles' sales. But not in my own country.

I'd been listening to a lot of Bartók when I made the album. This, combined with my love for the heavy guitar riffs of Hendrix and Zeppelin, gave rise to a continuation of the styles I had first developed on *The Big Revolt*. It emulated and built on the success of *Schizophonia*. Looking back, I think it was the most cohesive of all my solo albums.

It was when I was in the studio recording a guitar solo with Rory Gallagher that I received a phone call from a friend congratulating me on the sales figures of 'Bright Eyes'. The record had been doing only a few hundred a day, not enough to get excited about – but my friend said it had done 60,000 over the last twenty-four hours. I suggested he must have got the noughts or the decimal point wrong.

'No,' he said, 'I was in Oberstein's office this morning and he told me.'

I rang Obie: 'Did "Bright Eyes" really sell 60,000 copies yesterday?'

'Yes,' he said, 'great, isn't it?'

A quarter of me wanted to point out to Obie that it would have been nice to have been told, but the other three-quarters just wanted to go over the road to the pub with Rory and celebrate with multiple pints of Guinness.

So that's what we did.

'Bright Eyes' went on to become CBS's first million-selling single in the UK. It also went to number one in ten countries.

How We Made 'Bright Eyes' into a Hit, Against All the Odds

Only weeks earlier, CBS had dropped 'Bright Eyes' from their promotional priority list because it was not getting any radio play. BBC Radio 1 said it was too slow for them – 'Fuck off round to Radio 2 with it,' said a Radio 1 producer. This was in the days when really only Radio 1 had any hit-making power – or so we all thought – and that bred an arrogance in some of their producers and DJs which was a characteristic of many influential industry decision-makers, particularly those who didn't get paid much but suddenly had a lot of power.

Neil Ferris, a young promotion man at CBS's music publishing company, April Music, was angry because CBS director Norman Stollman would not authorise a Ford Escort company car for him. Neil was going to walk out.

FILMS AND FAMILY

'Don't go yet,' I said. 'Stay and let's try to break "Bright Eyes" together. The record company have dropped it but I think we can break it. I'll try to twist some arms at TV and you see what you can do with Radio 2.'

So he agreed and we went off on our separate missions. I secured an interview spot for myself on Noel Edmonds' Saturday morning kids' show, *Swap Shop*, where I knew the producer, having composed the theme music. We showed a clip from *Watership Down* and ran a competition, with me giving away some soft toy rabbits from the merchandisers of the film. Meanwhile, Neil had cracked Radio 2 and they started playing it a bit. Two weeks later and it was selling 60,000 copies a day – unheard of. Something about that record just got to people and we couldn't sell enough of it.

Even Radio 1 started playing it at that point.

Living in a Material World

Materially, Wendy and I had everything anybody could want. We had a busy and active social life, we shared a huge sense of fun and made each other happy on many occasions. The undercurrent of friction that existed between us was an ongoing strand of our daily life, but it was put aside often enough to allow a full and generally happy existence. It seems that you often remember the good things that happen and forget the bad – I do, anyway. Even when all around you is going apparently well, you can have crises of many different kinds, including cash-flow problems. I have always taken risks in business and sometimes paid out to make something, film something or record something that I know in my heart will never really pay me back, but I am driven to do so by artistic reasons, probably combined with ego reasons. I make no apology to myself for this – ego is part of art, without which there would be no creation by humans. This has often led me into hot water financially but, ultimately, on average, it has enhanced my life, and I hope those around me might agree that, on balance, it has enhanced theirs too.

At home, I worked from a huge T-shaped room which doubled as a dining room, but was configured like an office with typical '70s deep shag-pile, chocolate-coloured carpet and a jukebox, the contents of which were changed each week so that it contained the latest top thirty, in the correct order. The dining table doubled as a billiard table and the other part of the room housed an upright piano – my 'workhorse' piano, as I called it. It was where I was most days, with a Mickey Mouse telephone at my side for business as I sat at the piano and worked on songs or scores. I spent many hours there, often staying up all night to finish scores for sessions the following day.

The 'front room' of the house contained another piano, which was my pride and joy. I had bought it in Harrods on a whim one afternoon. It was a full-length concert Steinway, painted in 1895 with romantic scenes of lovers and shepherds in gold and willow-green by an artist called Simonet as a special custom design for the Shah of Persia. It had been completely overhauled before I bought it and played surprisingly beautifully for its age, if a little heavy in sound.

We were best friends with singing star Linda Lewis and her husband Jim Cregan, a fine guitarist and songwriter who had played with Cat Stevens and Cockney Rebel and who, towards the end of our time at Langley Avenue, went off to join Rod Stewart, becoming his main sideman for many years and co-writing some of Rod's biggest hits. They lived a few miles away in Cobham and it was easy for us all to get together and have dinner, either at local restaurants or at each other's houses.

One night they and Rod invited us to a party at a house nearby that Rod had rented for a big family Christmas. I drove us all in the big blue Rolls with the accordion and two Womble suits in the boot. Wendy and I changed into our costumes and I strapped the accordion on, to the delight of Rod, who answered the door to our merry-making. We all went in, touring the house and singing carols before the costumes came off and we could enjoy the rest of the party dressed in civvies.

It was at this party that I had my first line of cocaine – or *didn't*, to put it more accurately. It was discreetly pointed out to me that there was something happening in the billiard room and I went in with Jim. Lines of coke were arranged on the raised wooden sides to the billiard table and I was handed a rolled-up fiver through which to snort. Not having ever done this (at the ripe old age of about twenty-eight), I'm afraid I breathed quickly out through the bank note instead of snorting in – with the effect that all the lines of coke were blown irretrievably across the green baize of the billiard table. I was terribly embarrassed.

On the subject of drugs, a few words to clarify. I was blessed by the fact that cannabis had always made me nauseous, or physically sick, so I survived the psychedelic years without getting hooked – in fact, avoiding the experience. I was never worldly enough, nor did I move in the circles that would lead me to hard drugs, and to this day I've never dropped acid (even though I'm curious about it) and thankfully never experienced heroin. I don't subscribe to the idea that Lewis Carroll was 'on something' (like opium). Creative people often have very wild imaginations, purely naturally. I myself do.

THE CLOSEST THING TO CRAZY

Whenever I mention other people's drug use, it's very often people who went through a stage and then got clean, and even if they didn't, I'm not being judgemental. I only mention it in cases where the people themselves have been publicly vocal on the subject. If, years ago, I was working with a particular band or in touch with a social scene and was offered a line of cocaine, I would sometimes indulge, but again, thankfully, it hardly ever happened. Not even with Hawkwind or other 'psychedelic' folks. If they were doing it, they weren't telling me about it. My biggest artificial thrill these days is a non-alcoholic pint of Guinness.

In 1979, when 'Bright Eyes' had been number one in the UK chart for some weeks, I was in bed with flu when I received a call from Art Garfunkel.

'I just rang to say thanks and to share my pleasure with you that our record has done so well,' he said.

It was genuine and thoughtful.

'Yes,' I said, 'well worth all the hassle and friction at the session, wasn't it?'

'What friction?' he said. 'I only remember it being a very pleasant and thoroughly enjoyable experience.'

As I have said before, we remember the good things – or the things we want to remember. I didn't remind him of any of the details; what remained were the happy memories and a fondness between us that would see us work together again several times after that. I have been blessed to have had the opportunity to collaborate with him.

The Kursaal Flyers

During the latter part of the '70s I would often be asked to produce artists. One of these acts was the Kursaal Flyers, an up-and-coming pub rock band who emerged into the limelight courtesy of the record we made together, disappearing shortly thereafter when the guillotine of punk came down and consigned many existing acts to 'old fartdom'.

If the Kursaals had broken only a year later, with the same music, they would have been dubbed 'new wave' and would probably have lasted longer as a band. But we had a lot of fun making their album – *The Golden Mile* – from which we took the single 'Little Does She Know' into the charts, with the band appearing a couple of times on *Top of the Pops*.

They were a great live act, all presenting themselves as different characters. Their singer Paul Shuttleworth dressed and acted like a kind of spiv car salesman, while other band members wore different costumes (pedal steel guitarist Vic Collins wore a loud Hawaiian shirt and Lei flower garland). Will Birch, the drummer, was a driving force of the band and co-wrote a lot of the material with Shuttleworth and their guitarist, Graeme Douglas. They and their label CBS – who had asked me to get involved as their producer – were worried that their records to date (on Jonathan King's UK Records label) didn't carry the magic of their live set. I thought making them colourful in sound was the way to do it. A small, funky brass section here, some fruit machine jackpot sound effects there.

When it came to 'Little Does She Know', we were in Lansdowne Studios and I asked the band what they thought I should write as an arrangement. They went into a huddle and came back with a sketch of a kitchen sink. So that's what I wrote. The most OTT arrangement, modelled on a Phil Spector rhythm style, but augmented by a massive orchestra complete with cannons going off during the fade-out and even Handel's 'Hallelujah Chorus' creeping in. Combined with Will Birch's witty, tongue-in-cheek lyrics – 'Little Does She

THE CLOSEST THING TO CRAZY

Know that I know that she knows that I know she's cheating on me' – it was a heady mix of entertainment and irreverence, taking the single to number fourteen in the UK charts in November 1976.

Lilac Wine

Rather remarkably for the '70s, I had a phone in my car, with a proper big, black Bakelite handset. I was driving through Wandsworth towards the end of November 1977 when Derek Green, managing director of A&M Records in the UK and with whom I had a good relationship, called me. Elkie Brooks had a song, 'Lilac Wine', written by James Shelton and previously recorded by Nina Simone, that came over well as a live song but nobody had confidence that it could chart as a recording. It needed something special, he said, and he wanted it within the week.

So I booked an orchestra for the Monday – three days away – and set to, writing a big orchestral arrangement of it to emphasise the beautiful mysterious verses and a build to a big climax. I worked all weekend deep into the night, chain-smoking and drinking coffee, but by 6 a.m. on the Monday morning, I had to admit I would not finish it, with a two-hour drive to the studio still to navigate. So I rang someone to drive me in my car to the studio while I sat in the back with the score on a drawing board and a piano accordion to help me place the notes. We arrived at about 9 a.m. with an hour to spare before the orchestra were due. I carried on arranging at a small upright piano facing the wall. At about 10.15 a.m. I thought, *Funny, no orchestra yet* – but when I looked round they were all sitting there, having crept in quietly so as not to disturb me as I finished the arrangement.

Elkie wanted a really natural live performance atmosphere so instead of putting down a backing track and having her come in later and record the voice, we built her a vocal booth from acoustic screens right next to the podium from where I conducted the orchestra and could make eye contact with her. It's the way the previous generation had recorded when they didn't have multitrack, but it was exhilarating to conduct. We ended up using the first take. The record achieved number sixteen position in the UK singles chart in February 1978.

The Winds of Change

I had a business advisor called Michael Sinclair with whom I could discuss financial matters. After a while, I was able to confide in him on other, more personal matters, although it was not my general habit to do so. He knew that I was finding it hard to keep things going with Wendy; I was minded to leave, but I was, as is usually the case, torn because I couldn't bear to leave the girls. One day, as we were driving to a meeting, I clearly remember being on the Kingston Bypass on the way to London. I said to him, 'What if I leave – but take everybody with me? Maybe I just have a wanderlust that can be satisfied by all of us going on a journey together. At least, even if I'm wrong, it will keep the family together for a bit longer. We could drive to India in two Winnebagos, one for a home and one for an office.'

Michael thought I was crazy. I was.

I said earlier that even though 'Caravan Song' was written about a girl who wanted to get away from her life in America and go off on an adventure, the lyrics:

I wish I had the wisdom
To find some simple words to make you see
That the things that mean a lot to you
Don't always seem to mean a lot to me

were subconsciously addressed to Wendy just as much as they applied to the character in the movie. The chorus ends with the line, 'I don't know where I'm going, but I'm going'. Similarly, 'Run Like the Wind' on *Tarot Suite*, sung by Roger Chapman, included the lines:

One day soon I'm gonna run like the wind
One day soon.
Gonna break away from everything
One day soon.

It doesn't take a qualified psychiatrist to work it out.

The eventual boat trip was magical but also an insane career move. I left the UK just as I was getting a name for myself as a film composer and just as my solo albums were beginning to become noticed and were charting internationally. Although I did work, write and record throughout the expedition, with hindsight, it was not the best time to take a sabbatical. When I returned two and a half years later, my contemporaries and competitors had been beavering away and were now consolidating their careers on the next level. Meanwhile, I was off the list of rising film composers and I had a lot of catching up to do in my solo career.

On the positive side, it was a magical trip – rather like a caricature of real life, going from extreme to extreme. The ups were very up, but the downs were very down. My relationship with Wendy got worse but we shared some great highs. The boat, like our relationship, would go through violent storms and beautiful sunsets before its journey finally came to an end.

I was thirty years old.

PART TWO

CHAPTER NINE

Making Waves

If you want to drive to India with your wife, two kids, a piano and a secretary, don't choose a Winnebago: they aren't big enough. A band tour bus would have been the more obvious choice. However, towards the end of 1979, on the way back from the Winnebago sales lot, I stopped off at a newsagent's and picked up a copy of *Yachting Monthly*, wondering how much 'a boat' would cost. Obviously, that's a rather broad question, but in the magazine I saw a picture of a big boat for sale that caught my eye. I contacted the brokers and a few days later, details of a beautiful old girl called M.Y. (Motor Yacht) *Braemar* arrived in the post. She had been built in 1931, so in 1979 she was getting on for fifty years old and made of Lomar iron, which was apparently A Good Thing as it rusts more slowly than steel. Designed and built by a senior naval officer for his own leisure use, she had been used as a hospital ship during the war. She was beautiful, with a funnel and everything. Lots of mahogany everywhere, but all painted over.

I discovered that she had once been owned by Mr Fox, who had made his fortune with Fox's Glacier Mints. She was now owned

THE CLOSEST THING TO CRAZY

by John Jermyn, the Marquess of Bristol – reprobate socialite son of the then Lord Bristol. I fell in love with *Braemar*, just from the picture on the front of the brochure.

At the time I was in the middle of discussions about the extension of my artist contract with CBS Records. The conversation with CBS became driven by my wish to acquire the ship (*Braemar* really was a little ship, being 40 metres long and 200 tons). Paul Russell had been posted to Australia for his first managing director job within CBS and his successor as head of business affairs was Tim Bowen, who would subsequently rise through the ranks of the industry to become president of Sony BMG Worldwide among other things. However, when he and I met, he was in charge of getting me to extend my contract. Around then I was selling hundreds of thousands of albums as an artist in Europe, Australia and South Africa, so it was a serious discussion. I planned to take *Braemar* away for at least a year or two so the idea was to sign a three-album deal where the record company were locked in – that is to say they were committed to three albums from the start, with no opt-out possibility. I needed that commitment because I wanted to know I had a reasonable lump sum – and three definite albums to make – while I was away at sea. They agreed.

The money was good, too: £100,000 per album in 1980 was very chunky. I was fresh from the 'Bright Eyes' hit and there was a positive feeling to the negotiations. Tim was a bit worried that the life on the ocean waves might distract me from my songwriting and recording, whereas I expected that it would stimulate it. But, in order to afford *Braemar* and to run her for the time we would be away – she needed seven crew members, full-time – I needed to do deals for two *more* albums. I figured that if the other two albums were created by me but did not carry my name or voice as the artist, I might be able to sell the idea to a different record company without breaching my artist exclusivity with CBS.

I had lunch with my friend Chris Wright, the owner of Chrysalis. It had been he who had hired me to produce Steeleye Span, at the band's request, so we had experienced success together. We agreed that I could create a two-album project for Chrysalis based on the idea of a guy who falls asleep in front of his TV, floats into the TV set and goes off into a fantasy world. The project was to be called 'Rapid Eye Movements' and the fictitious band name would be Autopilot. We did the whole deal on a handshake right there in the restaurant. I now had a five-album commitment from two different record companies over two years.

I had never intended that this should be a 'grand' trip. It was just an adventure. However, they are grand things, yachts, and buying a 40-metre ocean-going beauty isn't something you can do without a little grandeur creeping in. I was never a sailor like my brothers, but if you buy a big bastard of a boat like *Braemar*, you have to run it properly. In this case that meant hiring a captain, a chief engineer, an assistant engineer/deckhand, another deckhand, a cook and a stewardess. If you fire any of them halfway round the world, you are contractually bound to fly them back to the place where you hired them, and when you hire a replacement, you have to fly them out to wherever you are in the world. Then you need power for generators, fuel (we burned a ton of diesel a day while at sea), food, harbour charges, ship's agent fees and the list goes on. The phrase 'carbon footprint' had not yet been coined. Most owners offset these charges by chartering their vessel much of the year, but *Braemar* was to be our family home, so this was a one-way, money losing machine. Rather like the big, red post boxes I used to put my sixpence pocket money into every week when I was five years old before I realised they weren't for savings.

I knew we would probably come back stony broke, but the idea of the trip and the work I could do along the way was inspirational and exciting. It might have started out as an emotional escape, as well as a change from the routine of my studio work and the static quality of my onshore life, but it had now taken on a whole new dimension. A voyage, an adventure, it was something that I felt would benefit my family at a time when we all needed it, as well as inspiring me creatively.

I sea-trialled the ship one afternoon in 1979, meeting the owner, John Jermyn, aboard her, where she was moored stern-to in the marina at Monte Carlo. The 200-ton ship managed the sea trial alright, but my marine surveyor, Bill Rich, pointed out that an awful lot of work needed to be done to her before she would ever be ready for a trans-continental voyage; the hull had weaknesses and the engines needed almost completely rebuilding.

Once the transaction to buy the vessel was complete, I hired a skipper, Larry Barnett, his brother John as engineer and two deckhands to deliver the ship from Monte Carlo to Cowes, Isle of Wight, where I had arranged for her to be dry-docked for all this work. I flew out to Monte Carlo again to join them for the trip back. Despite warnings of high winds in the Gulf of Lyons, we set off to cross the infamous gulf, notorious for the Mistral winds which are funnelled into it, claiming several ships a year.

After a long period sharing the skipper's night watch duty, I went below. It was a howling gale. I decided to remove all my soaking wet weather gear and get into bed. No sooner had I stripped completely

MAKING WAVES

naked than we took a huge knock from a wave on the starboard side and *Braemar* rolled violently over to port. I was launched through the air, through a wooden temporary bulkhead dividing my cabin from the next one and landed on our sleeping engineer, John, who woke with a start to find me, the owner, naked on top of him. Explaining how I got there, while in a howling gale and total darkness, was not the most urgent thing on either of our minds, but it became a story that was repeated with much mirth.

The refit in a Cowes shipyard was done with loving care but each job we did opened a whole new can of worms. I would spend days at a time down at the yard, sleeping at night in a room at the local pub. I supervised some of the work and helped with the descaling of the hull – a noisy, messy job – but I also painted some Japanese-style glass paintings for the walls and wardrobes of the main stateroom (our bedroom). We built a new, aluminium wheelhouse and fitted it out with the latest radio and navigational gear. In between days at the yard, I'd be back at home, writing material for the Hollies, having been approached by their label – Polydor. I was busy enough with boat matters, but the chance to work with this great group was too good to miss.

I wrote and produced three songs for the Hollies – 'If the Lights Go Out', 'Soldier's Song' and 'Can't Lie No More'. We recorded Allan Clarke's lead vocals and the other Hollies' brilliant harmonies at Lansdowne Studios. When we got to 'Soldier's Song', I knew I had the last verse of lyrics to write, but with time of the essence Allan started singing the first two verses as I sat in the control room producing, talking to him and simultaneously writing and finishing the third verse so that it was ready for him to sing just as he finished singing the second verse. Deadlines . . . the adrenaline of deadlines! It was the last job I did before leaving the UK on 4 April 1980.

THE CLOSEST THING TO CRAZY

I wasn't around to see *Braemar* moved up to Ipswich for further work. I had flown to Amsterdam Schiphol Airport, where I was met by the studio manager and driven to Wisseloord Studios at nearby Hilversum. There were just seven months to write and produce three albums before the planned arrival of *Braemar* at Scheveningen harbour with Wendy and the girls aboard, to pick me up and head south for the Canary Islands, ready for the Atlantic crossing.

We had contacted the studio to ask if there might be a house that I could rent nearby. They had drawn a blank, but came up with the idea of a 'luxury caravan' in the woodlands of their studio grounds, the rent for which they would pay instead of giving me a discounted studio rate. I had agreed, but when the studio manager drove me into the woods on the night he picked me up, the headlights of the vehicle rested on a small caravan no more than 15 feet in length.

'That's a luxury caravan?' I said.

'Well, it does say "de Luxe" on the side,' he replied.

I decided not to kick up a fuss. The 'Kip de Luxe' caravan was at the time probably the smallest, least luxurious caravan you could get. Kip means 'Chicken' in Dutch. No offence intended to chickens. The caravan would be my home for the next six months.

Three albums to create in seven months and I hadn't yet written a note. I hadn't even worked out the subject or theme for the solo album when I arrived.

While I was 'camping' at Wisseloord, the studio people also provided me with an old wooden edit suite building as an office. Essentially, it had a piano, so at least every morning I could walk the few yards from my tiny caravan home to my oddball 'office' shack and write all day. One day I befriended a small thrush that had fallen out of its nest. I took it into the office, where it lived with me until it was old enough and strong enough to fly away. I called it George and it used to perch on top of my score on the piano and shit all down it. You could hardly tell it not to. George was a nice distraction in what was generally quite a lonely existence.

I used to wander up to the canteen for lunch in the big, modern studio complex. During my stay there, the Police came and made their album *Zenyatta Mondatta*. Occasionally we would pop into each other's studio to see what was going on and all went together to a party in someone's house one night. Sting, Stewart, Andy and I sat in their car and had a couple of lines of their coke – I tried to snort rather than blow this time – before going into the house. It was amazing the way Sting just walked in, picked the most beautiful girl in the room and immediately disappeared upstairs. I was awestruck that anyone could have pulling power like that. Of course they were massive as a band, but he had that bit extra and he knew it. I think having 'it' is one thing, but *knowing* you've got it is what clinches the deal. I had often wondered whether you could convince yourself to know you've got it even if you haven't, but I suspect the subconscious is rather more powerful than that!

I decided that the solo album would be called *Waves*. It might seem odd to write all those sea-themed songs *before* going off on a voyage, but part of a songwriter's mindset is to be imaginative and I knew what the ocean was like. Lethal. But also beautiful and mysterious. I had especially experienced that feeling of awe when I had travelled to England from Monte Carlo via the Gulf of Lyons and the Bay of Biscay when we had brought *Braemar* back for her refit in Cowes.

I flew a UK rhythm section out to put down the basic tracks but overdubbed the Amsterdam Chamber Orchestra – session players

THE CLOSEST THING TO CRAZY

drawn from the mighty Amsterdam Concertgebouw Orchestra. The song that stood out as a single – and became a big hit in Europe – was 'The Winds of Change'. Once again, it epitomised my thoughts, with perhaps a little diplomatic, poetic licence in the final two lines:

> The winds of change are blowing hard in our direction
> We can't go back and we can't stand still.
> The winds of change may try to blow away my affection
> But they never will.

How I Broke into Colonel Gaddafi's Yacht

While I was living in Hilversum in 1980, it happened that the Eurovision Song Contest was being held in Holland that year and I thought it would be fun to drive down to the Hague to be there. At the same time, I could take advantage of the fact that a potential skipper for the *Braemar* trip was in Holland and the ship of which he was then captain was docked at the Van Lent shipyard on a stretch of canal on my route to the Eurovision venue. It was owned by the infamous Libyan dictator, Colonel Muammar Gaddafi, and it had fairly recently been used for a summit meeting of dangerous African leaders, including Idi Amin.

When I arrived for my appointment, the entire yard was seemingly deserted. I presumed there would at least be someone aboard, guarding the vessel, so I did what one does when approaching and shouted the name of the yacht up the gangway. No response. I stepped up the gangway and, from the top of it, again called the name. There was a noise of a generator coming from the open door to the engine room. Taking off my shoes, I followed the noise, expecting to find an engineer or someone. Nobody. I ventured along the side deck and called again. Nothing. I entered another door and went down below to find that I was in a magnificent stateroom with light beige suede wallpaper, luxurious fittings and what looked like an automatic weapon mounted on the bulkhead. To my horror I realised that I was in Gaddafi's personal quarters! I legged it back up to the main deck pretty sharpish.

Calling again, I made my way to the upper deck, where the French windows of the rear saloon were open. I entered, closing the doors behind me – I couldn't believe the yacht would be left like that. Suddenly it dawned on me that I had seemingly broken into Gaddafi's yacht and, if discovered by anyone other than the skipper, it might be an unfortunate encounter. I decided to get out sharpish. Except when I tried to open the French windows, they wouldn't budge. I tried for about five minutes. The headline 'Womble Singer Wasted by Gaddafi Bodyguards After Being Caught Breaking into Yacht' flitted across my mind. After much panic and confusion, I found myself venturing *deeper* into the yacht and it was only by a complete stroke of luck that I found a door leading to a service companionway ladder, which enabled me to escape. Climbing down to the main deck and breathing a deep sigh of relief, I noticed that the captain was arriving in a small car, and he greeted me from onshore.

'I see you found it, then!' he shouted.

We went to a restaurant for our interview and had something to eat. The captain was a really nice guy and clearly a first-class skipper. He told me he'd had enough of being with Gaddafi – it was all too tense. He would have been an ideal skipper for us but, ultimately, *Braemar*'s departure date and his availability didn't coincide so it was not to be. I drove onwards to the Hague and watched Johnny Logan win Eurovision for Ireland. Again.

THE CLOSEST THING TO CRAZY

Making the double album for Chrysalis was fun and weird at the same time. It was the beginning of the '80s and polyphonic synthesisers had only just been invented a couple of years before. Until then, synthesisers – like my trusty ARP Odyssey – could only play one note at a time, not chords. I found a young, very talented Dutch synth player called Peter Schöen.

It was in the days before programming, so I wrote the album score out for synths 1, 2, 3, 4, 5, etc., and Peter came in and played them by hand using his Prophet-5 synthesiser. For this album I wanted a lead vocalist who sounded a bit like me. I had made an album, just after I left Liberty/UA, with an artist called Vaughan Thomas. Vaughan never really had the killer instinct to make it in the business and by 1980 had a 'proper job' working in the offices of Hampshire County Council in Winchester. But he got time off and came out and did all the vocals in his very clean, pure, almost Beach-Boyish voice. He harmonised with himself beautifully, stacking up layer upon layer of harmony vocals.

One night Sting popped his head around the door as I was mixing it and perhaps identifying with the slightly higher-than-average register of Vaughan's voice and the unusualness of the synths, asked me to play a full twenty-minute side of the album through for him. Those were early days for the Police and he hadn't yet become the iconic heritage artist he is now. I had first met them a couple of years earlier when the rehearsal room in Leatherhead Surrey Sound Studios was used both by them and the Mad Hatters, my backing band. They subsequently recorded their first album, *Reggatta De Blanc* (1979), at that basic facility.

I found Sting to be genial and intelligent. During the recordings in Holland, we would sometimes order takeaway to share from the nearby Spandershoeve Indonesian restaurant. On one occasion, he and the band asked if they could come down to my makeshift office so that they could check the mixes of *Zenyatta Mondatta* on my more domestic Hi-Fi system rather than the sophisticated studio speakers.

Rapid Eye Movements was an adventurous double album and seemingly a favourite of people who collect all my old stuff. Sadly, it didn't get any marketing attention from Chrysalis when released in 1981 and, having sold poorly, the masters reverted to my company.

I spent seven months in my Kip de Luxe caravan and I finished the three albums in time to deliver them just before *Braemar* made her crossing of the North Sea from Ipswich to pick me up. John Barnett had joined as the permanent chief engineer, so my bursting naked through his cabin wall had obviously not dented his enthusiasm! Wendy and the girls had visited at reasonable intervals during my 'internment' in Holland, so it was not as if I hadn't seen them for months – but it was good to have the family hook up together again and there was much excitement as we left Scheveningen harbour and set a course due south, intending to pass the coasts of France and Spain and head straight for the Canary Islands, where we would rest up and refuel before beginning the Atlantic crossing, westwards towards Antigua.

Braemar looked fantastic after her makeover. The original woodwork had been protected since 1931 by seven different-coloured layers of paint which had been applied over the years (including green when she had acted as a hospital ship during the war). She had the genuine look of a real, period yacht. Her slow-turning twin 255-horsepower diesel engines had been rebuilt. Whenever we pulled into a port, among the admiring looks there were always some sailing types who looked down their noses at us for being a 'stinkpot' (engine-powered rather than a sailing vessel). These doubters soon changed their tune when they came aboard and saw

THE CLOSEST THING TO CRAZY

the level of seamanship that was necessary to guide the old girl in and out of harbour, never mind across great oceans. There was no gearbox. If you wanted to go from 'ahead' to 'astern', the skipper had to get on the blower to the engineer – stationed below in the engine room – to cut the engines and restart in reverse, using compressed air. This took ten to fifteen seconds, during which time the vessel was not powered and therefore could not be steered, making her vulnerable to any crosswinds or currents.

Our first days' travelling were not as we had jubilantly expected. We were only a few hours out when we developed an autopilot problem, so we headed for Cherbourg, where we were moored on a huge jetty behind a Cunard liner. Derek, our delivery skipper, left us at this point and was replaced by a Captain Birdseye lookalike called 'Happy' Henbest. Happy was an old sea dog, with a big, grey beard, who could park the ship on a sixpence. Aged about sixty, he really knew his stuff. The rest of the crew all looked up to him . . . when he was sober. Trouble was, he often wasn't sober and I frequently found myself standing outside the captain's cabin after he'd consumed a bottle of Scotch the night before, shouting, 'Wake up, Happy!', only to be met with a grunt and silence.

We were holed up in Cherbourg for about a week. The autopilot was fixed and during this time we made several excursions into the city, where I bought three powerful rifles. You didn't need a licence in France, I just went into a gun shop and bought them. We'd heard many stories of pirates, particularly on the Asian seas, who would take over a ship, kill everybody aboard and then use the ship for drug running before scuppering the vessel to destroy the evidence. I was trying to minimise the risk of it happening to us.

CHAPTER TEN

Atlantic Crossing and Caribbean Adventures

Our planned travel to Tenerife was confounded by a huge storm in nil-visibility fog in the Bay of Biscay on the first night, causing us to lose all our power and consequently our steering. We turned around and limped back north for the French port of Brest. At 5 a.m. we were boarded by two gendarmes and an official pilot, who told us that we must immediately cross the harbour under the pilot's command and berth ourselves alongside a huge Greek freight ship.

The port pilot had no idea about the subtleties of how to steer our old yacht and subsequently crashed us forcibly and dramatically into the side of a 400-foot Greek cargo ship laden with chickens and apples and bound for South Yemen. There was a massive bang, like an amplified car crash. We checked that everyone was alright and, apart from being shaken up, no one was hurt. The point of our bows had been crushed, but *Braemar*'s sturdy iron structure and design had saved her from further damage. However, there was a big hole in the side of the enormous Greek freighter.

The French pilot just looked at me and, with a Gallic shrug, apologised, walked off our boat and we never saw him again. An hour later, the gendarmes returned to pin a writ to our mast and to arrest me as the owner of the offending ship, taking me to a nearby magistrate. Pilots, however much they might be at fault, are not legally responsible, we later learned.

It had been an inauspicious beginning. We were stranded in Brest for several miserable weeks before paying a bond and being allowed to leave for the Canaries. On 24 November 1980 we finally set out, arriving in Santa Cruz in Tenerife on 8 December. I was shocked to learn of John Lennon's death the previous day, shot outside his Manhattan apartment, by a deranged fan. The demise of such a boyhood icon and influence was truly horrifying. I sometimes feel that Lennon could have contributed more to world peace by being less idealistic (sitting in a bag and telling everyone to love each other when you have plenty of money and live in a free country and 90 per cent of the people in the world don't isn't really very helpful), but he was a huge figure in my life – as he was for so many others. It was a hell of a shock.

Shortly afterwards we made for Southern Tenerife, where we berthed in Los Cristianos. It was to be our home during that Christmas as we prepared for the Atlantic crossing. The girls had a beach within walking distance and the shops were good.

Whether at sea or in port, Sam and Robin had lessons in the morning and free time in the afternoon. Wendy, as a trained teacher, did general subjects and I taught them music, French and art. We had taken with us all the books from their schools so that they could keep up with the same syllabus while we were away.

Just before Christmas it became obvious that Happy Henbest was not going to be able to take us across the Atlantic. There were too many incidents where the Scotch bottle had proved his undoing.

ATLANTIC CROSSING AND CARIBBEAN ADVENTURES

We appointed a new captain, via our agents in London. Basically a fishing skipper from Cornwall, he had had some yacht experience in the Middle East and was, at least at the beginning, dead keen. He put all the crew in white uniforms with badges of rank – I think mainly so that he could wear one himself. The ship did seem to be run tighter, but we also had ongoing problems with crew which never really stopped throughout the entire voyage. After Christmas my parents joined us for a short holiday and we spent a few pleasurable days cruising the coast of Tenerife, anchoring wherever we wanted to, water-skiing and relaxing. It was good to be able to share some of this extremely exciting adventure with them.

We were joined by our friends, Jim Cregan and Linda Lewis, for the Atlantic crossing. Making the trip in these circumstances was quite odd, although oddness has never been an unwelcome thing. I still had the fallings-out and fallings-back-in with Wendy, who had always had such an influence on the mood and the quality of life of those around her – positively or negatively. But Jim and Linda kept the atmosphere sociable and the kids were having fun. Robin was a cheeky little monkey who enjoyed winding people up, rushing around the boat letting off energy, very quick-witted. She loved to argue a point and would have made a good barrister. To this day she still talks like a very well-informed machine gun. Sam, the more arty one, was just as intelligent but more vulnerable and pensive. They both had piano lessons, but Sam was the more musical and was also learning the violin. She was a bookworm, reading all the time. They were great at making friends with local kids or children from other boats wherever we went, whether in the Caribbean or later, for example, a family of boat-dwellers in San Pedro, California, so their social life was not inhibited by the nomadic nautical experience.

THE CLOSEST THING TO CRAZY

These days, both of them are mothers with their own fast-growing teenage daughters. Robin with Piper and Lyra, and Sam with her daughter, Emily. All seem to be developing along musical lines – a source of great pride for their Grandpa Mike.

Our family accommodation was very plush, all newly exposed mahogany and oak. The master stateroom boasted a large four-poster double bed, which we had designed and which had been built at the yard in Cowes; the whole cabin was designed along a Chinese theme with my hand-painted glass murals attached to the wall-to-wall wardrobes and lit from behind at the point where they crossed the bedhead. The girls shared the aftermost cabin, right across the stern of the ship, which had two single bunks, one each side, and there was an additional, good-sized cosy double-bedded guest cabin that Jim and Linda slept in during the Atlantic trip. We had also installed completely new crew sleeping quarters for seven, and a spacious crew mess for dining and watching TV.

I started writing my next album – eventually to be titled *Six Days in Berlin* on this crossing, using the Knight upright piano that was bolted to the forward bulkhead of the music room, 'athwartships'. That is to say, you sat playing it, facing the way the boat was going. The seat was fastened to the piano so that it could still be played in rough weather.

Many moments of natural majesty occurred along the way. Once, a big whale surfaced only about 6 feet from the boat, just where I was standing on the lower side deck. I could almost have touched it. The whale was massive, about 15 metres – nearly half the length of our vessel. On another occasion we saw a beautiful big orca, which stayed and played with us for a while, ducking under the ship and appearing the other side. We often breakfasted on flying fish, which obligingly landed on the afterdeck at night, attracted by the lights.

ATLANTIC CROSSING AND CARIBBEAN ADVENTURES

When we arrived at Antigua, we slipped the local police a few bottles of alcohol and they stamped our passports as Linda Lewis sang them a couple of songs accompanied by her guitar. We anchored just off Galleon Beach at the mouth of English Harbour, which leads immediately to Nelson's Dockyard, a place so-named because it was a perfect natural harbour where Nelson had based the British fleet between 1784 and 1787.

Jim was devastated when he got a note from Rod Stewart's management recalling him to LA immediately for band rehearsals. Rod had given the band a special period of time off, and Jim had fitted the Atlantic trip into that time, but Rod had suddenly foreshortened the holiday and wanted Jim back straight away. So Jim and Linda left more or less as soon as we arrived in Antigua. But we remained in Nelson's Dockyard, on and off, for about three months. Each morning there would be schoolwork for the girls, then free time. I set to work seriously trying to get my next album written. It was an intense period.

While at sea I had been working on a symphonic, mostly instrumental album. On 19 January, I telexed Jorgen Larsen, the CBS Germany managing director, for help organising recording in Berlin. I was now under a feverish deadline.

Despite the pressures of work, there was always fun to be had. The last day of Antigua Race Week is Dockyard Day, like a big fete, and part of it is a competition for crews to make a raft out of anything they can find and then race it upstream to a designated point. We entered a team, which included most of our crew and the two girls. The raft came apart, of course, but they gamely kept on rowing while sinking, before ultimately swimming alongside as I filmed from the safety of *Braemar*'s upper deck.

THE CLOSEST THING TO CRAZY

In May 1981, we were visited in Antigua by a team of journalists from three different newspapers, and a very nice piece appeared in the *Sunday Express* magazine, among others. One of the press visitors was the beautiful but eventually tragically star-crossed Paula Yates. It was good to see her, as we already knew her a bit by then, and would meet again quite often thereafter. She joined us all for a pizza night out in the very makeshift pizza shack in Nelson's Dockyard, joined by Tim Rice, who had just arrived. He had come to stay aboard *Braemar* for a few days, which he jokingly declared was to escape the opening night of Andrew Lloyd Webber's *Cats* show. If it had been true, it would have been deeply insulting not only to Andrew but also to us. Of course it wasn't, it had been the only mutual diary gap we could find. He and I had tinkered around a bit when he had visited me only months earlier in my little caravan and workshop in Holland for the purpose of kick-starting his new idea of a musical called 'Chess!'. We tinkered with it a little more when he visited us in Antigua, but it was never going to work with me being away indefinitely. Ultimately, of course, he ran into Björn Ulvaeus and Benny Andersson and created one of my and Julianne's personal 'favourite ever' scores/libretti for a musical, so it was very fortunate for him (and us as theatre-goers) that he and I didn't end up writing it together. I have some very embarrassing footage of him belly-flopping and water-skiing which I shall have no hesitation in revealing if he ever denies any of this.

CHAPTER 11

'Shittin' in High Cotton'

Our first trip to Montserrat occurred shortly after Tim and the press folks had departed, when it had occurred to me to check out the island's AIR Studios as a potentially perfect place to post-produce my new solo album. Just years later to be tragically disabled by the eruption of its volcano, Montserrat was in those days a beautiful island and only a day's sailing from Antigua. It did, of course, lack a world-class symphony orchestra and an ace rhythm section, but the plan was to record the backing tracks for the album on a quick trip to Europe and then do the vocal overdubs and mixing at Air.

We anchored off Montserrat on a fine morning and I went up to the studio by moke, a small jeep-like vehicle that was the main form of transport on the island. It happened that the great George Martin was in residence. I had known George for years, albeit somewhat vaguely, mainly having run into him at his studio, Air London, on Oxford Street. After welcoming me, he showed me around the amazing complex where there was a good-sized studio space and state-of-the-art control room, plus a lovely swimming pool, great leisure facilities and a brilliant chef. It was designed for bands to hire by the month and to take their families, allowing them to combine holidays with work in a beautiful location.

I wasn't aware of the fact that Paul McCartney and Wings were the current clients until another moke drew up just as I was standing with George at the main door of the studio, looking out over the small lawn towards the bay. Out got Paul, and as he walked up the garden path towards us, he started singing, 'Big tits, wobbling like jelly' to the tune of 'Bright Eyes, burning like fire'. Laughing, he said, 'That's how we sing it in our house.' It was the first time I had met Paul and I was chuffed that he knew my song – it was a lovely icebreaker.

Paul was making a new album, which would eventually become *Tug of War* (1982), featuring duets with Stevie Wonder and others including early rock 'n' roll trailblazer Carl Perkins, writer of 'Blue Suede Shoes', who had been a strong influence on the early Beatles. In fact, Carl had arrived just the day before and, waking up in his bungalow on the beautiful island that first morning, had remarked in his southern drawl, 'I thawt ah'd dah'd and gawn to heaven' – and proceeded to write a song about the place, 'The Island of Montserrat'.

John Lennon had, of course, died only a couple of months earlier. Paul was thirty-nine years old when I met him and I was thirty-two. Lennon's death, which must have been a hell of a shock for him, seemed to be hidden somewhere inside him. He always puts on an outwardly unruffled face; we certainly didn't talk about John. I wouldn't have raised it, because it was such a huge subject, and there was no reason for Paul to do so, at least not to me, a new acquaintance at that time. Maybe he had chosen Montserrat as a recording location because of its relative safety and isolation. I don't

'SHITTIN' IN HIGH COTTON'

know. But it was weird to meet the only remaining half of Lennon–McCartney so soon after John had been so senselessly killed.

As we would be staying for a few days, we agreed to get together for dinner one night. Paul was fascinated by *Braemar* and the voyage, having seen her lying at anchor in the bay earlier that morning. I invited him to bring everyone aboard one evening. He said he'd like to bring Carl, Denny Laine, Linda and George.

'Of course,' I said, 'the more the merrier!'

Oh, and Stevie Wonder was due to arrive the following day.

On the night the McCartney contingent came aboard, our crew had organised a really fantastic spread for dinner and had it all ready to serve on the afterdeck. Funnily enough, I don't remember it being totally vegetarian. Certainly we were aware the others were vegetarian and made great efforts to provide a vegetarian-dominated meal, but there was also chicken, pork ribs and all sorts of carnivorous food.

Before dinner, I offered to show them around the ship, but Linda said, 'I think we'd rather just look around on our own if you don't mind.' Without waiting for an answer, off they went down the side deck and into the crew quarters. We thought this was extraordinary. I'm sure they just didn't realise. Even we, as the owners, never went into the crew quarters without at least knocking hard and shouting for permission to breach their privacy. One of our deck hands remembers running about in a panic below, trying to find a clean uniform shirt, and running into Paul and Linda, wandering through the crew's private accommodation. I headed them off as they reached the saloon, feeling that really it was my right and duty to accompany them on a tour of my own home.

Paul was quite relaxed about all this, perhaps even oblivious to it. I think he is so used to people being nice to him because he's

THE CLOSEST THING TO CRAZY

Paul McCartney that he assumes everything around him is cool. George Martin joined us and – I think having been a nautical type just after the war, long before becoming a record producer – he was full of inquisitive questions as we reached the wheelhouse. He wanted to know about the satellite navigation equipment, depth measurement equipment, autopilot and radar; he was interested in *Braemar*'s history, too.

Meanwhile, Carl and Denny were getting settled on the afterdeck and the drinks began to flow. Carl was still declaring himself to have landed in heaven and indeed the mood was very happy. Our crew, other than those serving drinks – a deckhand and the stewardess, resplendent in their new white uniforms with rank badges – kept discreetly out of the way.

As we sat down to dinner, I warned the party, 'I think I'm going to get drunk tonight . . . Just so you know.'

It was a great night. The food was beautiful, the conversation lively. At one point, Carl turned to Paul and said, 'Y'know what, Paul? Back home, this is what we call shittin' in HIGH COTTON!' His voice went up on 'high' and the vowel was delivered long and emphatically before coming down on 'Cotton'.

After dinner the evening developed into a jam session in the music room with Paul at the piano, Denny and Carl on guitars and me on accordion. We sang everything from 'Ilkley Moor Baht'At' to 'Let It Be' and Paul took his position as the leader of the sing-song, as you would expect him to. Then Paul said, 'Come on, Carl, play that song you wrote yesterday morning!', and so Carl picked up the guitar and sang 'On the Island of Montserrat, I never will forget . . .' twisting the pronunciation of 'forget' to 'forgat' to rhyme with Montserrat. He then demonstrated some truly fantastic guitar technique – something he had devised when, as a young guitarist, he couldn't afford

First day at school.

Family in Eastbourne (1954).

With brother John at Filey (circa 1950).

Cadet Company Sergeant Major (1967).

That Lady's Twins.

A session at Wessex Studios.

A session at CTS Studios.

Publicity shot (circa 1970).

Hapshash and the Coloured Coat (1969).

'Signing' with CBS Records (1973).

My mother at work (2000).

Glastonbury (2011).

Preparing for HM the Queen Mother's 100th Birthday march-past (2000).

Braemar off Montserrat (1981).

A gentleman is someone who has an accordion but doesn't play it.
I'm no gentleman (Atlantic crossing, 1980).

Julianne and me in character as numbers 36 and 17 in 'Zero Zero'.

We were married at Rippon Lea, Melbourne, on 2 January 1985.

Working on 'The Snark' with Sir John Gielgud ...

... and Stephane Grappelli.

Philip Quast and Mark McGann as the Bellman and the Baker, Prince Edward Theatre (1991).

John Partridge and Veronica Hart as the Butcher and the Beaver.

Ewshot Hall.

The Planets.

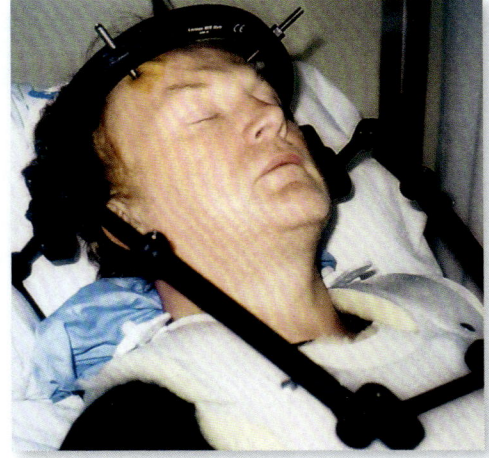

Broken C2 (2001).

Jeff Thacker, Katie, me, Paul Walters.

Michael Halsband shoots Katie album cover.

Billy Connolly, me and
Ozzy Osbourne.

Sir Paul McCartney presenting me
with LIPA Companionship.

Julian Lennon, me, Roger Daltrey and
Captain Sensible singing on the 'Snark' album.

Me and David Essex, nightclubbing.

Presenting Michael Jackson with
a BRIT award.

Rehearsing with Cliff Richard.

'SHITTIN' IN HIGH COTTON'

an echo unit to put his guitar through. He played a piece where he hammered the string a second time after each time he played it, giving the totally realistic sound of it going through a fast-repeat echo effect box. It was a masterful display. When he sang his songs 'Blue Suede Shoes' and 'Honey, Don't', it was *we* who thought we'd died and gone to heaven!

As the party reluctantly drew to a close and the guests climbed into the whaler to be driven ashore, Paul invited me to drop by the studio the following day. He and Stevie Wonder would be recording a new song, 'Ebony and Ivory'.

The next morning, Paul met me outside the studio in the sunshine, saying, 'You said you'd get drunk and you were true to your word!' We laughed, remembering Carl's wonderful turns of phrase the previous night. To this day, whenever I see Paul, he says, 'Mike, this is what I call shittin' in *HIGH COTTON.*'

'Come on, I'll take you into the studio. Stevie's putting a drum track down. I want to show you this fantastic new drum machine called a LinnDrum that he's brought with him.'

So I follow Paul into the studio and there's Stevie Wonder sitting at a drum kit to our left as we go in, surrounded by low screens to prevent the sound from whacking out all across the studio. He's in mid-flow, laying down the drums to 'Ebony and Ivory'. I felt a bit weird walking in right in the middle, but you could hardly say 'I don't think we should be doing this' to Paul. He was Paul McCartney after all. He went where he liked, did what he wanted. It reminded me of the joke 'Where does a gorilla with a machine gun sleep?', to which the answer is 'Anywhere it likes'.

'So you press this button here, you see,' says Paul, not keeping his voice down, 'and you get a bass drum, then you turn this knob and the snare drum starts up.'

THE CLOSEST THING TO CRAZY

All the time, I'm looking through the glass window into the control room where George Martin is trying to produce Stevie's drum track, surrounded by other people, including Linda. Stevie's bashing away, full volume, so Paul's having to talk quite loud to me.

After a while, Stevie stops playing – 'Hey, man, what's happ'nin'?' he says.

'Don't worry, Stevie, won't be a tick. Just looking at the LinnDrum thing with Mike – by the way, Mike Batt, Stevie Wonder, Stevie Wonder, Mike Batt,' says Paul.

Just then, we hear the upper-class voice of George Martin coming through a pair of talkback speakers in the studio: 'Chaps, would you mind doing that a bit later?'

So we move into the control room. Linda looks at me as if I'm some sort of axe murderer.

'You should never go into a studio when someone is laying down a track,' she says to me, not Paul.

Paul's standing right there but she's talking to me. I let it pass. I didn't reply, but neither did I apologise. Paul blanked it. He didn't come to my defence, so I blanked it too.

Once the drum take was finished, Stevie came into the control room and I was properly introduced. Paul, Linda and George thought the drumming track was great.

'No, I haven't tapped into the groove yet,' says Stevie. 'I need to try a few more times.'

So he goes back into the studio while Paul, myself and the others pop out to the pool area and leave him and George to it. An hour later, he's happy. And so is Paul – 'Brilliant, man, totally one hundred per cent better,' says Paul.

Which it was. Just shows, good is good but sometimes the guy playing it has to tell you when he's felt it could be even better. Sometimes it works the other way around and you have to discourage someone from playing his brains out when he already nailed it half an hour earlier. On this occasion, Stevie had been right to insist.

Linda had invited our girls to their house to play and so they went over for the day. That was nice of her. She developed photos while the kids played games and drew pictures. But our short Montserrat sojourn was coming to a close – the following morning, we were to set sail and leave the island behind.

It would be many more years before our paths would cross. I've always got on well with Paul. Not 'buddies' – I wouldn't presume such closeness – but friendly and always in good humour. We attended his wedding to Heather Mills in 2002, and we run into each other socially from time to time. More recently, I was honoured when he appointed me a Companion of his Liverpool Institute for Performing Arts (LIPA).

Six Days in Berlin

We motored back over the sea to Antigua the next day. Soon I would be leaving for Germany to work on the album which became *Six Days in Berlin*, so I continued preparing the music. I flew my copyist, Jack Wright, out to the boat from England. Jack was getting on a bit and had been a sax player in his younger days. Now he was in the late evening of his life and, following a recent heart attack, I thought it would do him good to come and do the job out on the boat rather than send the scores to England for him to work on. As my copyist, his job was to take my handwritten orchestral score and copy out the individual part for each musician. It was a skilled process, requiring precision and musicianship.

I flew to Berlin to record the tracks. CBS Germany had booked me a great rhythm section, including the legendary drummer

THE CLOSEST THING TO CRAZY

Curt Cress, and the studio was the Hansa Studio – most famously used by David Bowie, Iggy Pop and U2 – which looked right out onto the Berlin Wall, only a hundred yards or so away. A miserable view, but the starkness lent a certain edge, a bleak coldness, to the work we did. It was of course pre-Wall-coming-down days, and in stark contrast to the high life of West Berlin, which was landlocked by Communist territory.

The studio sounded great. A big, village-hall-sized room with a bare plank wooden floor and a Neve desk in the control room. The album suited the studio and I'm convinced it added an almost 'punk' energy and darkness to the production. I'd never embraced the punk thing even though, influenced by Chris Spedding, I often visited the boutique called SEX on London's King's Road run by Vivienne Westwood and then business partner Malcolm McLaren, where Vivienne herself would serve you. I wore some of the clothes – a canvas jacket that looked more like a straitjacket and narrow trousers – but the music didn't inspire me to imitate it. Where punk *did* move me to was an experimental and energetic area of my own. In other words, whereas before I had written using an orchestra and rhythm section to create my own (*absolutely not* classic rock) style, I was now feeling compelled to push that quirky style even further.

After I'd put down the rhythm section tracks, in came the Berlin Opera Orchestra to add the overdubs. They were a strange, old-fashioned bunch, meeting in corners and grumbling about things, and their sight reading wasn't great. There was a smattering of UK and US musicians among them who kept the sessions together, but from a conducting and general directing point of view, it wasn't like working with the LSO – it was bloody hard work! Nevertheless, we got through

'SHITTIN' IN HIGH COTTON'

it, and the darkness in their playing also comes through on the record. Berlin. Dark. Wall. Weird. Rain. Montserrat. Contrast. Sun. Sea.

I returned to Antigua for a few days, where life had been going on as usual at Nelson's Dockyard. We were soon en route to Montserrat again, this time to finish the production of *Six Days in Berlin* by adding my vocals and mixing the tracks.

The problem with my making albums while at sea and sending them back to England for the record companies to release was that I couldn't properly promote them. It was as if I was phoning them in. But I wasn't – I was working very hard and sending back what I thought was good work. I just wasn't appearing on TV or radio as I wasn't around to be interviewed. It was a folly. Even if I hadn't been going through the crisis of a musician trying to escape from the shadow of the Wombles and the contradiction of trying to escape from a marriage at the same time as trying *not* to escape from a marriage, I should at least have realised that you can't become a successful artist by absenting yourself from the countries where your popularity is starting to bloom. You can't become the next Ennio Morricone or Cat Stevens if you're moored in the Caribbean, giving your kids a French lesson. But you do become *something* else and I was becoming it – whatever it was.

Meanwhile, the album *Six Days in Berlin* bombed, relatively speaking. I lost some of the confidence of my audience. Nobody's fault but mine. I'm proud of the album though. I had ventured musically 'Where only the brave or the foolish would go'. (Not a line from *Six Days in Berlin* itself but from *The Hunting of the Snark*, a few years later.) As I write this, over forty years on, it seems more people are 'getting' *Six Days in Berlin* and it's pleasing to see that growing recognition.

CHAPTER 12

The Mighty Pacific

After a change of skipper and first mate, we spent some time in Caracas, then headed for the Panama Canal entering at the port of Cristobal. It's not cut like a straight, typical canal, but can best be described as a system of 'actual' quite narrow canals, big wide locks and lakes, the biggest of which is the massive Gatun Lake in the middle of the canal's geography. There are twelve locks, six to transit going west, and a parallel six locks going east, which are, of course, big enough to take ships much bigger than us. Nevertheless, when we went through the six west-heading locks, smaller boats lashed themselves to us because we were bigger and could keep them stable as we all went through.

Gatun Lake is 85 feet higher than sea level, so three locks take you up to it and three locks return you down to sea level as you head towards the Pacific. On 9 July 1981 we negotiated the Gatun Locks, the three stages up to Gatun Lake. There is a monument to the workers who died in the building of the canal, mostly from malaria. The girls and I had dinner on the foredeck in the last of the down-locks just as it got dark. We then went under the big bridge which carries a roadway from Alaska to Colombia and headed straight out into the Pacific, turning north without stopping.

The voyage continued in its caricature-of-real-life way. The ups seemed higher than normal life, the downs, lower. Now we travelled up past Guatemala with broken steering (having been hit by a floating object) and with only one stabiliser and the generator on the blink. We didn't put into Guatemala City – there was a war going on and our quest for adventure did not stretch as far as that. Being in the Pacific for the first time was noticeably different from the Atlantic. The Atlantic is shallower and consequently choppier than the rolling, beautiful Pacific. We limped up the Guatemalan coast, about 20 miles out from the shore, and eventually docked in Acapulco with an ever-growing list of repairs to attend to – a new generator, a water-maker (desalination device), repairs to the stabiliser fins, steering and autopilot attention. Nevertheless, our stay in Mexico was sweet, albeit frustratingly short.

When the ship was fixed and we were rested, we set out one evening towards LA, turning north as we left the harbour of Acapulco. The sun was beginning to set and we had dinner on the afterdeck. Just as we finished dinner, about a hundred dolphins broke the surface in an extended line each side of us, like a guard of honour escorting us onwards. There was a pink light in the evening sky, all around, not *just* in the west. The sea was powder blue. Sunlight danced on the small waves and the dolphins leapt and played. I had never seen so many dolphins all together; it was truly beautiful. We had become quite accustomed to four or five dolphins playing in our bow wave, but these guys were in what had to have been a deliberate formation each side of the stern. When people ask me about the boat trip, I always recall this as my favourite memory, contrasting with the ugly times we endured in storms and other conditions. The memory of that host of dolphins escorting us out of Acapulco harbour will stay with me forever.

Los Angeles

We reached Los Angeles and anchored off Long Beach, a couple of hundred metres from the Queen Mary, which was, and still is, a tourist attraction hotel, having been cemented into its berth. We would eventually stay in LA for three months.

It was convenient that we were in Los Angeles because we had quite a few friends there. Elmo Williams – the producer who only three years earlier in 1978 had hired me to write the score for *Caravans* – lived in Pacific Palisades with his wife Lorraine, a screenwriter. Jim and Linda, who had crossed the Atlantic with us, had a house just off Sunset Boulevard, which they had bought from Bruce Springsteen.

It was also convenient for me to meet up with the LA office of my publishers. Mike Stewart, the head of CBS Publishing, came aboard for lunch as we bobbed up and down at anchor. I served him the only fish I ever caught during the whole voyage – a mackerel which I caught with a rod and line over the side of the boat that very morning at Long Beach. It tasted awful!

One day, I had a call from Jim Cregan and Rod Stewart, saying that Rod had a new powerboat – a Riva 2000 – and asking if they could visit us. They were a little way up the coast at Marina del Rey. I invited them to pop over for lunch and about half an hour later they appeared along with keyboardist Kevin Savigar and tied up alongside us, out on our anchorage. Rod's boat was very impressive, built for speed and, of course, nothing like a yacht, but I am sure it must have been fun to own. He and the band were always great company. We'd dined at the Dome restaurant on Sunset a few times and there was always a high degree of mucking about and foolish behaviour. By contrast, we had a civilised, genteel and chatty lunch as we all sat on *Braemar*'s afterdeck, feeling relaxed and lucky.

When it was time to go, they set off back to Marina del Rey and we thought that was the end of the episode. However, about twenty minutes later, we had an SOS call from them, saying they were sinking. '"I Am Sailing" Singer Rod Stewart Drowns in Tragic Boating Accident' came to mind as a potential headline. There was nothing we could do so I suggested they should call the coastguard, who rescued the boat just as it was about to sink. Safely back in the marina, they rewarded their rescuers by sharing crates of booze that they had aboard as 'emergency supplies'. And so the day ended with Jim, Kevin, Rod and the coastguards all sitting on the dockside getting tanked together in the evening sun.

There were some fun times in LA. We followed the same daily school pattern with the kids: diary before breakfast, then lessons until lunch and free time in the afternoons. It concentrated the work and made the voyage enjoyable instead of denying them the opportunity to learn about and absorb something of the places they were visiting.

We also had a visit from Barbara Dickson and her manager, Bernard Theobald. They came to talk about the musical details of an album that CBS had asked me to produce for her. I was asked to write some new material for her and to arrange and produce other songs. The Queen Mary was a very convenient hotel, having been kept in the old style with all her original fittings, and the two

THE MIGHTY PACIFIC

of them stayed there. I flew back to Europe to make the album at Wisseloord Studios in Hilversum, where, only a year earlier, I had camped out for seven months writing *Waves* and *Rapid Eye Movements* in my 'luxury' caravan.

It was exciting to go back. I had written all the arrangements onboard *Braemar* after Barbara and Bernard had returned to England. The album that resulted from those sessions was called *All for a Song* (1982). I'm proud of that record, particularly 'Surrender to the Sun' (written especially for her) and 'Run Like the Wind', which I had recorded years earlier for my *Tarot Suite* album.

While in LA, we were deciding where to go next as we contemplated the Pacific crossing. We narrowed it down to Japan or Australia, but after hearing of massive, life-threatening storms and hurricanes in the sea around Japan, we decided to head for Australia via Hawaii and Fiji. This decision was made easier when I received a call from my old pal Paul Russell — by then managing director of CBS in Australia — who told me that the Australian Broadcasting Commission (ABC) had invited me to compose and perform a piece for the Sydney Symphony Orchestra at the Sydney Opera House to commemorate their fiftieth anniversary. I was thrilled to be awarded a commission like that and so we set off on the next leg of our trip with the idea that I would write the piece on the way.

We left LA, heading towards Hawaii as our first port of call, and after some days at sea, reached the port of Pearl Harbor. There, we berthed stern-to at the military harbour, where we spent several days resting up and restocking fuel and provisions.

The Pacific was a magnificent place to be. It was awe-inspiring to think that the nearest landfall was two weeks' journey away and that the ocean beneath us was 2 miles deep. I would sometimes,

THE CLOSEST THING TO CRAZY

very late at night, take a tray of Jasmine tea up onto the boat deck and sit there, meditating in my own way beneath the vast, infinite sky, completely aware of my own insignificance and totally at peace for those few precious moments. Free from the idea of a generator malfunctioning or a crew dispute or a creative challenge.

Communicating by radio was my job as the self-appointed radio officer of the ship. I would spend hours at the radio and telex machine at any time of day or night, dialling through different frequencies to find a way to bounce our signal off the ionosphere and back down to Portishead Radio – the main shipping signal station in the UK. As soon as I got a signal and a response, I would reaffirm my call sign as MSZJ (Mike Sierra Zulu Juliet) – the unique ID of our ship – and they would come on the line verbally, or more usually engage in a telex conversation with me:

'Hi MSZJ, is that U?'
'Yes, who's that tonight?'
'Alex on tonight, is that Mike?'
'Yes, how's it going, Alex?'
'Great, thanks. What have you got?'
'A couple of messages on telex – U ready?'
'Yep pls snd.'
'OK, here goes.'

I would then feed my first message, like a roll of caps from a toy pistol, into the gate of the telex machine and it would be on its way.

I would prepare my messages to CBS Records – or perhaps to my PA, Yvonne Warbey, back at our house in Langley Avenue – and whoever else I needed to contact. Sometimes it would be the ship's agent waiting for us in the next port, giving him a list of supplies we would need to collect on the quayside on our arrival. The messages, prepared earlier by typing punched holes into a rolled-up length of paper tape, would then be fed through the telex machine with a satisfying clatter after hours of trying to get a good enough signal. Messages back to us were received similarly. Of course, in the middle of the Pacific, the ships' agent in the next port was not our immediate concern, but there would be many messages of importance concerning work or to the family. One of these, which came shortly after we left Hawaii, was from Paul Russell to say that the ABC apologised that they could no longer secure the Sydney Opera House, but that they still had the Sydney Symphony Orchestra available and were asking if I could still write the piece but perform it instead in a TV studio. Of course, I was happy either way.

Indeed, the prospect of working in a TV studio gave rise to the idea that the timing was perhaps right for me to seize the moment and make the new piece *and* my next solo album one and the same. The TV transmission would be perfect publicity for the album. CBS and the ABC thought it was a great idea and I came up with a whole story about a futuristic world where love had long since been eradicated and our hero was a genetic throwback who falls in love with a girl and is sent to an emotional decontamination centre called Zero Zero. The magnificence and peace of the Pacific Ocean around me was clearly not the key inspiration for this futuristic and dystopian project.

These ideas were conveyed to the ABC and CBS by telex from midway between Hawaii and Fiji. It was all agreed. I began the composition, mapping out the duration and drawing in the number of sections so that I had a visual plan of the story. And when I

THE CLOSEST THING TO CRAZY

wasn't composing, I was sketching and designing the set, costumes and even some animated sequences for the show.

I sat at my piano in the music saloon and got on with writing the score, to be recorded on arrival. We were making our Pacific crossing over a period of seven weeks, plus a two-week stop-off in Fiji. That gave me what I most need when I write – a deadline. I also had the excitement of knowing my piece would soon be recorded by one of the world's great symphony orchestras.

I would *have* to get it finished in time!

Sometimes work was impossible because if the weather whipped up, the ship would roll from side to side, despite having had stabilisers fitted. You just couldn't sit at a piano writing music while the sea was rolling at you in massive waves that threatened to overwhelm the vessel. On one particularly memorable occasion a mountainous wave broke on the afterdeck. Something like that can sink you, but fortunately the power of the wave forced open the French windows that divided my music saloon from the deck and in an instant filled the saloon and made its way down into the family accommodation. One wave had flooded the entire section, leaving a good 3 feet of water sloshing around the family sleeping quarters. It took quite a bit of clearing up and was a shock to everyone, but it was thankfully the only time we took water aboard on that scale. This wasn't for the faint of heart. It wasn't all sunsets and dolphins.

We arrived at Fiji, where we spent two weeks. While the crew and family went sightseeing, I stayed on board most of the time working on the new piece, now titled *Zero Zero*.

Leaving Fiji on 11 December 1981, we arrived in Sydney on 19 December – past the Opera House and under the Harbour Bridge. It was very windy, squally and exciting. The lights were just

THE MIGHTY PACIFIC

coming on and it was far more thrilling than arriving on a beautiful clear sunny day. We docked in Darling Harbour. Nowadays it's a bustling tourist shopping attraction and quayside, but back then it was an old dog-end of the harbour, a derelict, crumbling quay. We stayed there for a few days then moved round to Rose Bay, where we were at anchor for most of our stay.

I guess it's fair to say that the personal highs and lows encountered on our voyage became even more exaggerated in Sydney. I'm abbreviating my account of it because there was such a lot of pain attached to the months we were there. The excitement of meeting everyone at CBS and ABC and the process of making *Zero Zero* are in themselves enough to fill a whole book, but the negative side of it – centred around an unholy battle with the unions – was initially triggered by something that came from a row between Wendy and myself and her insistent, unmovable demand that she and the kids should star alongside me in the *Zero Zero* TV Special.

Despite the probable extension of our marriage by two years, and a wonderful adventure for the girls, the boat trip had almost been an act of cowardice on my part. If I'd had the courage to face the pain – for everyone – before we'd gone away, it would have ended up as a cleaner divorce and of course the distress felt by everyone involved – particularly the girls – was now heightened. It was in stark contrast to what had been such a magical, shared adventure, with many exciting and happy moments for the whole family, but happy moments which preceded our inevitable break-up. Before we had set out, I knew I was just putting an Elastoplast over a deep wound, but I went ahead anyway, my idealism having got the better of me.

There's a phrase in one of the songs on my *Hunting of the Snark* album, written in 1983, about 'an optimist on the run'. I had unwittingly been

THE CLOSEST THING TO CRAZY

that optimist on the run when I had elected to take us all away on a boat. That was me! Shouldn't I have faced up to the fact that the game was up, the marriage unsustainable? I couldn't, and didn't.

Anyone reading about the subsequent sequence of events – that I arrived in Sydney with a wife and two kids and then sent the family home to England, got divorced and married a girl I'd met in Sydney – would put those facts together and presume the obvious. But it just wasn't what happened. Some people close to the epicentre of the marital earthquake will have seen me as having left the family home on arrival back in London, but in fact Wendy had 'left me' – certainly in terms of infidelity – secretly and on multiple occasions, with a succession of people – many years earlier, both before the boat was ever an idea and indeed during the voyage itself. So when, halfway through our time in Sydney, I began a serious affair with the beautiful secretary of Paul Russell at CBS, I felt fully justified, liberated and relieved after years of restraint and tolerance.

CHAPTER 13

Sydney

Her name was Julie Murphy. The minute I saw her on the day I walked into the offices of CBS in North Sydney, it was as if a bombshell had hit me. It wasn't a bomb that I ever expected to explode. To stretch the analogy, she wasn't even a 'bombshell' type: classy and beautiful, with short black hair and a cover-girl face. There had been many other pretty girls I'd seen or met in my life as a young married man and only ever felt that slight pang of temporary lust but done nothing about it. Not even a blink of a flirt. I would challenge most young men to deny that having happened to them. And so it was with Julie. A smile and hello, nothing more. I was married. Move on.

Or so I thought.

After a few weeks of many meetings with the ABC – who had by then agreed that I should direct and design the show in association with an experienced and brilliant co-director, John Eastway – I was in the middle of the sessions to pre-record the soundtrack with the Sydney Symphony Orchestra. It had been a long, productive day at the ABC Studios, but mid-afternoon, I was expecting some photocopied scores of my orchestrations to arrive from CBS. I finished conducting a particularly exciting sequence and as I turned around to find a towel to wipe my brow, silhouetted in the wide doorway, holding my scores and quietly waiting, I saw Julie Murphy. My heart leapt. I went over, took the music from her and told the orchestra it was time for a tea break.

I don't know where I got the courage from, but I asked, 'Could I have a word with you in the conductor's room?' I guess that's not a *very* brave thing to say, because I did need to talk to whoever was photocopying the music in case there were parts which might need further work. Anyway, when we were alone, the brave thing I *did* do was to ask her: 'I don't suppose you'd fancy a drink after the session, would you?'

It was a long, lingering drink. A bottle of chilled white wine in some cool north Sydney bar. The next night we would be having dinner together. The following day we would be lovers. It wasn't that difficult to keep it a secret – Wendy was often away from the boat at night with social engagements of her own. Julie would sometimes visit the EMI Studios in Castlereagh Street as I post-produced the soundtrack and we would slope off for a moment together. A really strong relationship grew from that. She had a flat in the Paddington area of Sydney, which she shared with a girlfriend. I would visit her there; I would meet her for lunch. We fell in love. It was the first time I'd felt that excitement since my teens. It wasn't just excitement, it was relief. As if I'd climbed up a steep, tall cliff and was now lying, exhausted and exhilarated, on the grass at the top.

Somebody at the studio must have mentioned to CBS that Julie had visited me at the studio outside of her working hours. By then Paul Russell had left for the UK to become CEO in London. And so the rumour started that Julie and I were having an affair. This surely can't have been unusual, but CBS refrained from extending her freelance contract, effectively letting her go under company rules for 'fraternising with an artist'. It was terribly unfair. She soon got another job, working for the famous Jamieson Street Nightclub in Sydney. And none of this, of course, stopped us from seeing each other.

The process of preparing the show went on. Life aboard ship, at anchor in Rose Bay, went on and 'normality' prevailed. Or at least as normal as life on a yacht with seven crew in Sydney Harbour, making a lavish TV special and having a secret affair can be.

As we moved into the stage of the *Zero Zero* production that involved dancers and actors, it became screamingly obvious that Wendy and the girls were not going to be allowed to be in the production. Very simply, Equity wouldn't have it. But that hadn't stopped Wendy from taking the girls to a rehearsal after which the cast kicked up about it and complained to the ABC. It was clear that both the production and our marriage were in simultaneous jeopardy – or indeed *beyond* jeopardy. Both were apparently over.

The unions cancelled the show and I asked Wendy to return to London with the girls. Time to call it a day. In any case, to avoid the oncoming hurricane season, *Braemar* would have to leave Sydney soon to get back through the Indian Ocean, up the Nile and into the Mediterranean. We'd put a lot of work into the show. Maybe I could talk the unions round? They weren't going to accept my family being in the show – but then again, neither was I! I had never wanted them in it. This wasn't a documentary. I resolved to stay in Australia until the 42-minute TV special could be made.

We sent the boat back to the Mediterranean with just the crew aboard. Then we moved briefly into a rented flat in Lane Cove, Sydney, before Wendy and the girls eventually got on a plane and left for London. I would join them once the show was made.

THE CLOSEST THING TO CRAZY

The Australian Equity guy told me in a personal meeting that he had deliberately waited until the eve of the studio date for the original *Zero Zero* studio production before telling its members not to take part – squandering an entire ABC production budget, with sets already constructed, costumes made and soundtrack recorded.

I trudged the streets of Sydney from the ABC offices to CBS Records and then to Actors' Equity, offering up various solutions. Eventually a deal was struck whereby my company would co-produce the show and I would have an option to buy out the ABC share of the Worldwide TV rights within a certain time, which I eventually did about two years later. Nevertheless, it cost the ABC the equivalent of three opera budgets to accommodate the new deal, subsequently denying Australian Equity members the opportunity of the employment those operas would have presented.

When the deal was done and the second studio production was set up, I needed to find a leading lady to play opposite me in the show. As the show's co-director, I had an office at Gore Hill Studios in North Sydney and asked the ABC to find me some people to audition for the role – the candidate had to be able to sing, dance, act and look great. The casting department put together a book of thirty-five photos. I flipped through the book of headshots and about halfway through, I saw a face I immediately liked.

'That one,' I said, turning the page, thinking the process would continue and I'd find a few more to meet. And I turned, turned, turned, page after page. I handed the book back. 'Is that everyone you think is suitable?' I said.

'More or less,' said the casting lady.

So the next day, Julianne White walked into my office. After an opening conversation, I said, 'Let's see you dance, if we may.'

'What, here in the office?' she said.

'No, in the studio,' I said.

I picked up a phone and asked if Wardrobe could bring over a leotard and dance shoes for her. We headed straight to a downstairs rehearsal space.

'Okay,' I said. 'Could you please dance?'

'Dance to what?' she said.

'Oh, just without music – you know, throw a few moves. Maybe some pirouettes or something.'

She thought I was nuts. But she danced. She ran around the studio, doing a jeté here, a pirouette there. She really *could* dance, and her acting CV was equally impressive. She was perfect.

And that's how I met Julianne and started working with her. I met her while I was still deeply and passionately involved with Julie Murphy and while Wendy and I were in the throes of separation. But there was no question of any romantic hook-up. Julianne was beautiful, but this was pure business – art, whatever we call it.

We filmed the show at Gore Hill just after the boat sailed and Wendy and the girls had flown back to London. I had us all in black-and-white chequerboard leotards and I played my role ('Number 17, but you can call me Ralph') using a blend of mime and acty-movement, while singing the songs. I was very proud of it as a piece of 'kinetic art', using hundreds of still photographs, all projected at one screen and controlled by a computer. For years I had developed and used the technique and would take it to its most advanced state years later in London in 1991 when I would present *The Hunting of the Snark* at the Prince Edward Theatre. We also had a brilliant Australian choreographer in Graeme Watson, who gave it a very quirky, idiosyncratic look.

THE CLOSEST THING TO CRAZY

So here I am in Sydney. The ship has sailed, the marriage is over – although there will be trouble ahead – and I've been floored by Julie, who had knocked me sideways the first time we'd met.

And then, during the post production, when I hadn't seen Julianne for weeks and had had no romantic contact with her, I picked up the phone. Would she like to have lunch? *Why on earth?!* I was happy with Julie and was not – until now – an unfaithful guy, but while editing the show I had become intoxicated by her. My heart was pounding. She said yes.

Lunch was on.

Bloody hell.

We were both smokers back then. After lunch, at Doyle's fish restaurant on the harbour in North Sydney, we stayed for coffee, smoking cigarette after cigarette. Neither of us wanted it to stop. I should have been back at the studio two hours earlier to supervise the animation, but nothing else mattered.

Julianne and I got together, of course. I broke the news to Julie – who seemed devastated but not overtly mad at me – I still remember our last few tender moments together. Even though it might seem sudden, as if my certainty was hasty or capricious, I really felt, deeply and instinctively, that I had found the person with whom I wanted to share the rest of my life. Not that Julianne really had. As it would happen, despite living together in Sydney for a couple of months, as soon as I returned to London to face the music with Wendy, I was to find out that I still had a lot of persuading to do to convince Julianne that we were a workable proposition – a long-distance relationship with a possible move to the UK all while parachuting into a shitstorm called my divorce.

PART THREE

CHAPTER 14

A Winter's Tale: The Heartache Hits

When I left Australia, it was a tough parting between me and Julianne. She had played no part at all in the break-up of my marriage, but we had lived together for a couple of months after Wendy and the girls had left and we were very close; we were a couple. Jules was cast in the well-known Aussie soap, *Young Doctors*. We lived together in a room at Kurraba Road, North Sydney, as house guests of two friends of ours, Paul Kenny and Karen de Heer.

Jules and I both knew we were in for a good kicking from life in the coming weeks and months. We were committed to each other, but we had also spoken of how difficult it was going to be to sustain a relationship at 12,000 miles distance *and* in the wake of what was bound to be a painful and acrimonious divorce. But we had no idea *quite* how bad it would be. Emotionally and physically, I was about to enter the nastiest and most heart-breaking period of my life and yet simultaneously a new and wonderful journey was beginning, giving each day a purpose which would sustain me for the rest of my days.

Our hosts, Paul and Karen, kindly allowed Julianne to stay on at Kurraba Road when I left. I travelled via Dick and Sheila Asher's lovely apartment in New York, where I stopped off for a few days before arriving back in England. Although I had made it clear to Wendy that it was all over, I somewhat ill-advisedly moved back into the family home and stayed in a guest bedroom. It seems mad now, and one could say I should have made a cleaner break of it, but at the time it was a hugely difficult logistical and emotional situation, despite, or perhaps even *because of* the kids, thankfully, being pleased to see me.

Suffice to say my stay was brief and I moved out to my sister Paula's house in Wentworth, where I stayed for several weeks with her husband and children. The pain and anguish of the divorce and Julianne still being in Australia created a bittersweet combination that was mentally exhausting, and I began to worry about my health. Julianne, by now, had started to realise that our arm's-length relationship was hard enough, but if the alternative was her jumping into the fire that was my life, that didn't make a lot of sense either. The idea had been that I would come back to London and sort out the divorce and that Julianne would follow me once things had calmed down. But they weren't calming down. In fact, they were getting uglier by the day.

Jules and I exchanged long phone calls and sad, anguished love letters. She was supportive and kind. Then one day a letter arrived, just as loving and concerned as the others, but mentioning that she was going off for a Sunday sailing trip with an actor from *Young Doctors*. Not with a group of people, just the two of them. It was to be the maiden voyage of this young actor's sailing boat. In those days I used to wear two watches, one showing Sydney time and the other showing London time. The night when I knew she was out with him – daytime of course in Australia – I got no sleep. It was indeed the beginning of a relationship between them.

A WINTER'S TALE: THE HEARTACHE HITS

Now I was in two hells.

As the week wore on and the phone calls between us became increasingly desperate, I was an emotional wreck. On the Thursday I made an impetuous decision, drove straight to Heathrow and got on the evening plane out to Sydney, arriving on Friday. I had to be back by the Tuesday morning, but at least I would have the weekend in Australia. So I used it. On the plane, I wrote a song called 'Please Don't Fall in Love'. It was one of the most poignant and sad songs I've ever written and it summed up my feelings exactly:

> I know that you're with him just now as I write
> I know you need someone to hold you at night,
> But I'm begging you, Baby,
> Please don't fall in love.
> I knew it might happen when I was away,
> But now that it's happened I just want to say
> That I'm begging you, Baby,
> Please don't fall in love.

Some months later, the song would go to number seven in the UK singles chart for Cliff Richard, but at that moment it was just a desperate message from me to her. I still had a key to the Kurraba Road apartment so I got there during the day on the Friday and waited until Julianne came home. What I would have done if she hadn't come home or if he'd been with her, I have no idea. She was suitably shocked to see me sitting at the piano when she arrived. We hugged for a minute and I sang her the song.

We went up the road to a restaurant and talked. I'd hired a car and suggested we go away for the weekend. We drove off and found a romantic little hotel in the countryside somewhere, nothing fancy, and we talked about trying really hard to keep it all going. We had a beautiful, peaceful weekend together and it was, in every way, as if we hadn't parted. On the Monday morning, I dropped her at the *Young Doctors* set and she walked away from me and, because they were working together, back to him.

I wasn't counting my chickens.

I got on the plane for London and during the flight I imagined them together all day. I was an idiot if I thought it could change her immediate life. By now she was becoming a star in Australia. She was surrounded by attractive male actors. She lived in beautiful, sunny Sydney. What kind of love would it take for her to give up her career, her family, her friends, the men who courted her and the sunshine to come to rainy England, where she was completely unknown, the innocent respondent in a divorce case and an object of bitter hatred?

The acrimonious divorce wore on. I stayed at my sister's house for some months. One day, my long-time friend Tim Rice came over to do some writing with me. We went down to the local pub for a quick pint of Guinness before starting to work and I told him the whole Julianne story. I also told him that David Essex had rung me the day before and asked if I could write him a Christmas hit. Tim thought we might be able to kill two birds with one stone: write a wintry song about a love that couldn't happen because of geographical or other reasons rather than the usual break-up. So we went back to the house and I sat at the piano.

'We need a great title,' I said. Or perhaps Tim said it. Somebody always says it. Most songwriters will tell you that a great title often sparks a song off. Tim started spouting ideas. I can't remember what they were, but about the twenty-ninth one was 'A Winter's Tale'.

A WINTER'S TALE: THE HEARTACHE HITS

'That's it!' I shouted, jumping up from the piano stool.

And it was.

We wrote some lyrics to the chorus: 'Winter's tale, it was only a winter's tale'. That's all we had. The tune I wrote was nothing like the one the song ended up with. Then we tried some verse lyrics and Tim came up with 'The snow has covered up your footsteps and I can follow you no more'. So we stumbled through a first-verse lyric together.

We ran out of time but Tim faxed me some more lyrics the next day. Although predictably brilliant, I didn't think they were quite right, given the intimacy of the story, so I asked if he'd mind if I had a go at finishing the chorus and adding a second verse. He didn't mind at all, provided that he got to approve them before they were published. It was my personal message to Julianne, written from the heart to the heart. I called Tim and he was delightfully relaxed about it. He knew it was such a personal thing for me. I had tried to emulate his theatrical style of lyric writing so that it appeared seamless when adding my own bits. For example, I had 'On a worldwide scale, It's just another winter's tale' but he suggested changing it to *'We're* just another winter's tale', which was of course a lot stronger and much more personal.

David Essex heard the song and loved it. I booked a rhythm section and strings for a day at AIR Studios in Oxford Circus. We cut the track there. Everybody knew we were making a smash hit. Of course, Julianne got the first copy off the press. My campaign to hypnotise her with personally tailored love songs was in full swing. The record reached number two in the UK charts just after Christmas – annoyingly kept off the number-one spot by Phil Collins' first solo hit, 'You Can't Hurry Love'.

THE CLOSEST THING TO CRAZY

Someone else who was impressed was Cliff Richard, who called and asked if I had any more songs like that. I did – 'Please Don't Fall in Love', which had been written a few months earlier about the same girl but hadn't been recorded yet. I played it to Cliff on the piano in my office in Soho rather than go through the rigmarole of doing a demo. He loved it and we recorded it, again at AIR Studios. As before, I sent Julianne the first copy of the record.

It was the second of what Julianne and I now call the three 'Heartache Hits'.

There was a time when *Young Doctors* finished its long run on TV and she nearly came over. Her flight was booked. But two days before she was due to get on the plane, the news came through that she had now been cast in a new TV soap, *Waterloo Station*. The trip to London was cancelled.

I was still living with my sister Paula and her family. Wentworth was beautiful, but you'd occasionally hear planes going over to land at Heathrow. I stood in the garden on the Sunday morning when Julianne had planned to arrive, but now wouldn't be. It was raining gently as I watched the planes come over. The lines 'I watched the planes come in on the early morning flights / But I could not stand to see them land without you' came into my mind. The fact that it was raining made me think of Buddy Holly's song 'Raining in My Heart'. I went inside the house and wrote 'I Feel Like Buddy Holly' in one sitting, taking no more than an hour.

A couple of days later I was with my friend Alvin Stardust and his then wife, the actress Liza Goddard. They were very kind to me during the horror of the divorce. We were having dinner by the fire in their house, with a nice bottle or two of red wine. I asked if he'd like to hear my new song – I wasn't plugging it to him, just playing it

A WINTER'S TALE: THE HEARTACHE HITS

as a friend. So I played them 'Buddy Holly' and Alvin was thrilled. He asked me if he could record it. Trouble was, Alvin was a great friend and had been very successful years earlier. However, at that time he was going through a really bad patch and hadn't had a hit for years. He was also saddled with the stupid name that his producer, Peter Shelley, had deliberately thought up to attract attention to the first hit, 'My Coo Ca Choo'. People had written him off; nobody expected that he would ever have another hit.

When you have a song like 'I Feel Like Buddy Holly', you ideally want a hot artist of the day to record it. But I've always hated the way people move in and out of fashion. So we recorded it, and it became massive. But first, we had to trick the press and radio producers, who didn't see Alvin as credible, into playing it. We issued it on a white label, with no name, and challenged them to guess who the artist was. That wasn't my idea – it came from Oliver Smallman, the radio promotion guy. Nobody guessed. By the time we told them who it was, they were already playing it and it was climbing the charts. The song reached number seven in the UK, becoming the third of the 'Heartache Hits'.

By now I was living in the office in Soho where I had played the song to Cliff. I had chanced upon an old friend, David Land (manager of Tim Rice and Andrew Lloyd Webber), who had offices above a tobacconist shop at 118 Wardour Street. There was also a flat that he owned, above the office, and he offered to let it to me. It had a bedroom, kitchen, shower and two reasonable-sized offices. At least temporarily, it was the perfect set-up for me, albeit very modestly appointed and old-fashioned. Suddenly I had somewhere to work and live. David was like a cartoon character. A small, round, jolly man, he had a wicked sense of humour and would greet me from his office every time I passed his open door on my way downstairs. He'd beckon me in and we'd trade filthy jokes. He laughed like the laughing policeman in the song. A real Soho character, he was rich but had the office of a small-time manager, with a couple of secretaries and an electric fire with wire-wound bars, only one of which was ever on, however cold it was.

By this time Julianne and I had more or less developed the reluctant understanding that our relationship was for 'practical romantic purposes' on hold. How could it not be? There was no certainty. We had to let it roll and see what happened. She was in a potentially long-running soap opera and I found myself single for the first time since I'd been eighteen.

I often stayed on David Essex's sofa during that time. He had a lovely flat just off Hyde Park Square. David was the best guy to have as your clubbing buddy. Well, sort of. He was like a magnet to women, so he was often back home with the best-looking girl in the club before I'd even said, 'Do you come here often?' or 'Isn't the music loud in here?' to her friend.

I had a very short but fabulous fling with a ballerina from the Royal Ballet. One day I rang her from Germany, where I was doing a TV show to promote *Zero Zero*, and she was with someone else, giggling and teasing me – probably, in hindsight, just one of the ballet guys – but it wound me up. So I wrote her a short but polite goodbye note followed by a sad but slightly self-pitying song called 'Ballerina, Prima Donna', which became a small hit for my friend, Steve Harley, going to number fifty-one in the UK chart in August 1983. Years later, we met again and I apologised for using her as song-fodder. She told me she'd been flattered that I cared. I don't think I've ever had a relationship where I *didn't* care. Sadly, caring makes you very vulnerable.

A WINTER'S TALE: THE HEARTACHE HITS

The innate magnetism between me and Julianne didn't go away and we kept in touch throughout this time. One day she rang to say that she'd received the news that her *Waterloo Station* TV show was cancelled after its low-rating, six-month trial and that this was in fact great news because it now meant she could come over and see me. Which she did. Just for four weeks – and with her friend, Sally Tayler, another actor in the TV show. We all stayed in my little one-bedroomed flat/office in Wardour Street, with Sally on a pull-out sofa bed in the office.

I had a month to convince Jules not to go back. I took it gradually, talking about all the good things we could do together, the fun we could have. We went for casual-but-smart lunches at Quo Vadis in Dean Street, a favourite watering hole for me, being so local. We did a lot of talking – we needed to know if we liked what we were rediscovering about each other and during those weeks we made a decision.

Jules and I have lived together ever since that visit, forty-two years ago, and we were married two years later, in 1985. Like one of Lewis Carroll's characters, I had sailed 12,000 miles of ocean to find something I wasn't even looking for or knew existed. But I had found my Snark; the true and enduring love of my life.

The *Zero Zero* TV special aired on Channel 4 in the first week of the TV station's existence in November 1982. I was quite upset when I realised that they had broadcast the sound of only one side of the stereo, leaving half the meticulously produced audio unheard. To make amends, they re-showed it again a week or so later. People still reacted well to it. But not well enough, and the album wasn't a hit. We couldn't get enough radio play on the single 'Love Makes You Crazy'. And that was that. End of project, after all those months staying in Australia to make sure it got made and to find the finance, as well as coming to an agreement with the union. This happens so often in our business. Ground-breaking doesn't always pay the bills. But you always have the work, you always have the art. *Zero Zero* now exists on YouTube and, years later, we re-released it on my Dramatico label, having acquired the rights from Sony.

I certainly can't imagine my life without *Zero Zero*.

One morning, over breakfast after I'd stayed over, David Essex said, 'I'm moving out, Mike. I don't suppose you might want to buy the place?' He'd only been there for just under two years. I bought it within the month. Julianne and I moved in and spent the next thirty-four years there as our London home. David was always very kind to us. It was early 1983 and I was producing an album for him called *Imperial Wizard* to follow up the success of the single, 'A Winter's Tale'. He looked at me one day and said, 'You look tired, Mike. Why don't you and Jules borrow my place in Spain and go for a holiday?'

I was indeed tired. We both were. The constant court appearances and vicious legal correspondence was wearing us both down, and it was to be at least a year before any divorce settlement was reached. So we hopped on a plane and spent a week in David's villa in southern Spain. And it was there that I wrote the first lines of my next piece, *The Hunting of the Snark* (1984), a concept musical album based on Lewis Carroll's nonsense poem of the same name.

> Out in the deserts of darkness and dreams,
> Out through the oceans of sadness we sailed,
> Venturing onwards through mystical scenes
> Blown on the whim of the wind that prevailed.
> We had no reason to doubt the truth,

A WINTER'S TALE: THE HEARTACHE HITS

> Driven by danger and discontent
> And the drums of youth.

These lyrics would sit undeveloped for many months until later that same year when I began expanding them into what was to become the first manifestation of the project – the original 'concept album' of the piece. I had first become properly acquainted with Lewis Carroll's epic poem during a visit to Foyles book shop in Charing Cross Road. I had been looking for a biography of Al Capone with the intention of writing a musical about him and I had literally tripped over a pile of hardback copies of a newly released book, *The Annotated Snark* by Martin Gardner. The book caught my imagination and set me off on the journey that I am still on, a mission to establish 'Snark' as a world-renowned musical production. It has become a lifetime's obsession. The fact that I had just returned from a journey at sea, not having known what, if anything, I was looking for, while having found something I didn't expect to find, was completely lost on me at the time. But looking back, there are so many things that my life – and that specific sea voyage in particular – has in common with the Carroll poem.

Those words I wrote at David's villa in the hills of Spain would become the first verse of 'Children of the Sky', the opening song of that lifelong project. Only later did I realise that they were unconsciously directed towards my two beloved daughters, Sammy and Robin, who had travelled those dark, stormy but often sunny seas with me. I love them – and their own beautiful children – very much indeed, but it's been a bumpy voyage. The damage will never really go away. Damage to them, damage to me, and to Julianne. It could have been so much more civilised.

THE CLOSEST THING TO CRAZY

Early on in my time with Julianne, in 1984, I was elected 'King Sod' – that year's head of the Society of Distinguished Songwriters. You have to organise the three 'songwriter' dinners and a Ladies' Night in December, which is a grand ball. I held mine at the ballroom at Claridge's, with music supplied by the Pasadena Roof Orchestra. The Queen Sod is the wife or girlfriend of the King and is expected to make a hilarious speech. So, out of the blue, Julianne had to conjure up a ten-minute standup routine. She killed it! The Marvelous Mrs Maisel would have been proud of her.

Meanwhile she was establishing a career here in the UK. Although she had some very impressive dance credits, having been a West-End singer-dancer in the UK at the tender age of twenty before ever returning to Australia and auditioning for me for *Zero Zero*, she had decided to remove all her dance experience from her resumé so that casting directors would take her more seriously as a straight actress, and she was soon performing featured guest roles in TV dramas such as *Minder*, *The Bill*, *Holby City* and *Brookside*. She found it easy to gather new friends with every job she did and already had many friends in London from her days in the West End before we'd known each other. Most of these people are still our friends to this day.

Several years later she was cast as Jackie, one of the two female stars of the heist movie *Sexy Beast* (2001) – with Ray Winstone, Ben Kingsley, Amanda Redman and Ian McShane. Directed by the Oscar-nominated Jonathan Glazer (it was his first feature film) it has become a huge cult movie over the years. The script by Louis Mellis and David Scinto is a masterpiece and much emulated.

In late 1983 I received a call from Anthony Camden, chairman and principal oboist of the London Symphony Orchestra, asking

A WINTER'S TALE: THE HEARTACHE HITS

me to guest-conduct them for a special one-off performance on 19 November. I had worked with the LSO several times in the studio but it was flattering to receive an invitation to conduct them on their home turf, the Barbican Hall. They wanted me to choose the repertoire and so I picked a mixed bag of my work, various songs and orchestral pieces. I invited Steve Harley and Linda Lewis to join me as singers and between us we shared the vocal duties. It was a great night and further established my relationship with that orchestra. This bond was soon to come in handy as my hunt for the Snark began.

CHAPTER FIFTEEN

The Hunting of the Snark – My Mad, Onward Journey

> They sought it with thimbles, they sought it with care;
> They pursued it with forks and hope;
> They threatened its life with a railway-share;
> They charmed it with smiles and soap.

Those were some of the nonsensical words that had caught my eye on that fateful visit to Foyles on the Charing Cross Road, London. Lewis Carroll had written his epic piece in 1876 as the follow-up to *Alice's Adventures in Wonderland* (1865). It's the story of ten characters, all known only by their job descriptions. I have already mentioned my self-identification with the two leading characters – the Bellman and the Baker – and they were joined on this voyage by the Butcher, the Bonnet-Maker, the Billiard Marker, the Beaver, the Broker, the Banker, the 'Boots' and the Barrister. They are sailing off in search of a mysterious beast – or conceptual idea – known only to them as the Snark. None of them knows very much about the Snark and whatever each character thinks he or she knows conflicts with the opinions of the others. For me it was the perfect vehicle for a musical interpretation. I would later take the liberty of adding an additional character, the Bishop – to represent the possibility that the Snark might, to that character, represent God. *The Hunting of the Snark* was to become the central and most personally cherished work of my life.

After many months of telling everyone that I was about to start this epic piece, I decided in 1984 that I should stop bragging and just get on with it. I met with the heads of several record companies. They all thought it was a mad idea – it was – but said they would love to hear it once I'd made the record. In other words, they weren't going to pay for it. As my own finances were severely depleted by the boat trip and the divorce, this wasn't quite what I wanted to hear.

With the memory of the London Symphony Orchestra concert still fresh, I thought I should talk to them about hosting another concert at the Barbican, this time to debut my – as yet unwritten – 'Snark' piece. I thought it would be a good opportunity to give myself a deadline to write it. The trouble was that the only date they could offer me for the concert was just three months away, and all I had was one verse of lyrics. The other challenge was that in those days a recorded album was forty minutes long to fill two sides of vinyl, and a concert was usually two halves, lasting about fifty minutes each. The LSO folks suggested we select a classical programme (Bizet: *Carmen Suite*, Brahms: *Hungarian Dances*, Dukas: *The Sorcerer's Apprentice*) for the first half and have the Snark after the interval.

Galvanised by the deadline, I began work in earnest. Most of it was written straight onto 24-stave score paper with a 2B pencil, in full orchestration, filling the pages from left to right across the manuscript paper. Even the lyrics were often created at the same time as the orchestration and written in as part of the collective composition. It's an exhilarating way to compose because the tune, lyrics and orchestration all appear bar by bar in full score as you progress.

So, starting with just that one verse of existing lyrics written on holiday, I began to develop the piece, coming up with the chorus for 'Children of the Sky'. I thought it was strong – catchy, positive yet melancholic all at the same time, perfectly reflecting the mood of the song cycle I wanted to write. Then I rang the actor Christopher Cazenove, who I knew socially, and asked him to narrate at the concert. Former Manfred Mann singer and blues legend Paul Jones agreed to be the Baker for this premiere performance. Other parts would be played by backing singers led by the former pop star, session singer Tony Rivers. Incidentally, my rule while writing the piece was that if the poem was spoken by the narrator, it would be pure Lewis Carroll. The songs would be by me, not using Carroll's words for the lyrics. I saw my lyrics as illustrative rather than a substitution. The only time I broke this rule was for the first line of 'The Bellman's Speech', where I pinched the line 'Friends, Romans, countrymen, lend me your ears' – but as Carroll had in turn nicked it from Shakespeare, I thought this was fair game.

It was a punishing deadline even by my standards, keeping me at the piano constantly throughout those three months, and against all odds, the music was ready just in time for the concert on 3 June 1984. We started formally, with the classical repertoire, and in the interval the orchestra all changed into blue-and-white stripy T-shirts and reappeared for the *Snark* premiere, jaunty and excited.

I was delighted by how well it was received. In the audience that night were Tim Rice, Benny Andersson and Björn Ulvaeus from ABBA, who had just finished writing and recording their musical,

THE CLOSEST THING TO CRAZY

Chess. That night they were inspired to adopt the same idea to organise their own concert tour of *Chess* with the LSO as a prelude to the fully staged musical. Also in the audience was the theatre producer Cameron Mackintosh, with whom I had developed a friendly lunch-pal relationship. He sent me a lovely gift of an early edition of *Alice's Adventures in Wonderland* and a note saying, 'This is a fan letter. It remains to be decided not WHETHER we do it but HOW we do it'. Sadly, he then got so deeply involved in both *The Phantom of the Opera* and *Les Misérables* that when the time came for 'Snark' to be mounted as a full musical in the West End a few years later, I would be forced to go ahead without what would have been his invaluable help.

Now it was time to record the album. It was up to me to finance it, even though I was not exactly flush. Art Garfunkel was my first port of call. He was a fairly good bet in light of our success with 'Bright Eyes' only a few years earlier. I was also, in 1984, recording a track with him for his 'Greatest Hits' album. On hearing the material, he agreed immediately. I now had the cornerstone of my star cast in place and was able to drop Artie's name when calling Sir John Gielgud's agent, who was happy when I mentioned a fee of £5,000 for a morning's work. It doesn't sound a lot these days but even for a big star, it was a decent amount then and it was worth it because it was the key to attracting the other big-name artists. I also asked the French jazz violinist Stéphane Grappelli to play some solos.

The main sessions for the album took place in one week at CTS Studios in Wembley. It took just two days to record the rhythm section, using a click to play against so that the 'holes' left between bits of rhythm section could be filled by the LSO, who would be recording on days three and four. Day five was the day I recorded Art Garfunkel's voice and Stéphane Grappelli's violin. Sir John Gielgud's narration happened the following week.

THE HUNTING OF THE SNARK – MY MAD, ONWARD JOURNEY

The session with Sir John was delightful – he was an incredibly gracious man. He turned up on time, wearing a blazer and cravat, and was generously happy to take direction from an upstart like me. He even called me 'dear boy'. Reciting poetry lines to music robs an actor of one of the devices often used to heighten the drama – the ability to change pace. He took to it after a few takes, realising how the narration all had to be spoken within the timing of the music and using dynamics and character to make it come alive. At lunch time we went to the CTS Studios canteen and queued up for pie and chips together. He had a relaxed, chatty manner but I was in respectful awe of him.

With seventy-five-year-old Stéphane, I was working with another hero. Like Gielgud, he had nothing to prove and was both relaxed and helpful. I've never known anyone get a better, more joyous and simply thrilling sound out of a fiddle. I wanted him to play his signature jazz licks over several tracks, but he said he liked the tune of the song 'Midnight Smoke' and wanted to play it as written. I agreed that he could record the tune 'straight' *after* he had done it in his inimitable jazz style! Once we'd finished, he and I went into the big studio and recorded an impromptu jam session just for the fun of it. His musicality shone from him.

I must find that recording!

I went back to the record companies and played them the self-funded, lavishly produced album, albeit still in its unfinished form. Where star cast members were yet to be recorded, they were temporarily represented by my own voice. This time, every record label in town wanted the album. I wasn't surprised; I thought it sounded stunning. The LSO were playing at their best, Garfunkel and Grappelli had added their classy magic and the safe, ancient voice of Sir John Gielgud narrating the Carroll poem between the songs gave the whole thing a certain gravitas. People talk dramatically about 'bidding wars' to help generate heat around records, but this really *was* one. I was only asking for about £150,000, but I got what I wanted and I chose Sony as the label. It turned out to be the biggest mistake of my life — well, one of them. I've made plenty!

On 2 January 1985, Julianne and I were married in the open air at Rippon Lea in Melbourne, which was *not* a mistake. Phew, something I did wasn't a mistake!

Peacocks strutted on the lawn and the sun shone while a celebrant carried out a non-religious ceremony. Jules wore a lovely cream lace and lemon dress made for her as a gift from our friends, royal wedding dress designers David and Elizabeth Emanuel. I wore a suit which I hand-painted for the occasion, but still resoundingly failed to upstage her! Sadly, my parents and family couldn't be there — it was a long way to go and they all had jobs. However, my mum did make a brilliant fancy dress bat costume, which she sent for someone to wear as a token family representative, but it was held up at Customs.

I knew most of Julianne's family by then. Her dad gave a great speech — and I responded in verse. Many of our Aussie friends attended the ceremony and subsequent dinner at the elegant old colonial mansion. It was a fantastic day. We'd agreed to do a live interview on Australian breakfast television the following morning, so at 6 a.m. I sang 'As Long As the Moon Can Shine' from *The Hunting of the Snark* on the piano in the hotel suite. A live, undoubtedly romantic, but rather inconvenient, breakfast TV moment!

Sony — in the form of Chairman Paul Russell and Head of A&R Muff Winwood — knew I still had to recruit the rest of my all-star cast for *The Hunting of the Snark* as well as needing to write two more songs. They let me go off and get on with it. With Garfunkel, Gielgud and

THE HUNTING OF THE SNARK – MY MAD, ONWARD JOURNEY

Grappelli on board, the others dropped into place quite easily, knowing that they were joining a prestigious cast. Next to confirm were Roger Daltrey as the Barrister and John Hurt as co-narrator. Then there was Cliff Richard as the Bellman and I even got George Harrison to play a guitar solo, after asking Ray Cooper to play him the backing track.

I was invited to George's home in Henley and we recorded the solo in his studio. It was a huge thrill, but I drank a bit too much beer. So much so that I was not inhibited from directing George as to each next suggested fret, even as he played. How he put up with me I'll never know, but his bottleneck solo was fantastic and it has his identity stamped all over it.

In the following months, while I was dealing with growing and unnecessary Snark-shaped tensions with Sony, Julianne and I got quite friendly with George and Olivia Harrison. George had been badly affected by losing his court case and having his song 'My Sweet Lord' declared to be an unwitting plagiarism of the Chiffons' 'She's So Fine'. He told me he needed something positive to pull him out of the depression of it all. One day he rang me and said he had loved doing the session on the 'Snark' album and suggested we do some work together on a Harrison solo album with me producing, both of us co-writing. Something he said in one of our initial phone conversations tickled me. When I said, 'So, George, when should I come over to yours again so we can write this masterpiece?', he replied in his lovely, slow, Beatle drawl, 'Well, actually something *crap* would do to start with!' Apart from being very funny, I thought that was really refreshing, and it's the perfect attitude to take when writer's block ever strikes – just write something crap, just to get going! You can always change it later or write something else.

THE CLOSEST THING TO CRAZY

On the day John Hurt turned up at Abbey Road Studios he was eating whelks out of a bag. I never could understand why anybody would want to eat a whelk. More relevantly, he had been to the pub on his way to the studio. I hadn't met him before but after a short while it was clear that it wasn't happening. He was missing cues, not understanding where the metre began and ended, getting cross with himself and sometimes with me. After a while, I said, 'Lovely, thanks, John – I think we have it.' He looked a bit surprised and said, 'Oh, if you're sure?' I assured him it was fine. But it wasn't – I just didn't want to waste any more studio time on it. I wasn't grumpy with him, just a bit sad. It was a huge blow. We'd lost John Hurt. Just because he'd been too pissed to work.

A few days passed and I called John's home number and got his wife, Donna, who at that stage I only knew as a voice on the telephone. I explained the situation – well, she sort of dragged it out of me really – and as I started to say, 'I didn't want to offend him and he seemed lovely but . . .'

She interrupted me: 'He was pissed?'

Sheepishly, I answered, 'Yes.'

'Damn! He really wanted to do this. Let me have a quiet word. Can you spare the time to redo it if I can persuade him?' she asked.

I assured her that we could.

A few days later, with the date rescheduled, John turned up at Abbey Road Studios as sober as a judge, and we had the most wonderful session in which he was witty, friendly and his work was magnificent. No one mentioned the war – Donna's word in his ear had obviously worked.

As time passed I got to know John much better. He became a very dear friend. When he was sober – or had only had a couple of

THE HUNTING OF THE SNARK – MY MAD, ONWARD JOURNEY

drinks – he was charming and compassionate, but after a few more he could reach the tipping point and become quite waspish. Never to me, as it happened, but I remember one evening just the two of us going from a pub in Victoria to the theatre next door and having to march him out of the stalls when he started calling out and heckling. Despite his demons, he was a lovely bloke.

I do miss him.

It still frustrates me that I ever let CBS have the 'Snark' album. They had just dropped me as an artist the year before and I knew their A&R director Muff Winwood didn't really see me as a credible artistic force. I first met Muff shortly after he had been appointed. I explained how I'd like to steer my artistic identity back towards the more serious direction of my younger days, to which he responded, 'Mike, to me you'll always be the bloke who sang "Summertime City" from *Seaside Special*!' Despite the fact that it had been a big hit, this was about the biggest put-down one could ever get, from someone who obviously thought of himself as more credible than me.

We all knew that the album needed two more songs and despite everything, Muff was pleased when I came up with 'The Snooker Song' for the Billiard Marker to sing and 'Dancing Towards Disaster'.

I recruited Captain Sensible to record 'The Snooker Song' and flew to LA to record Deniece Williams singing 'Dancing Towards Disaster' and other parts written for the Beaver. It was a funny session – Deniece couldn't sing the words 'I came as the Beaver on this escapade' for laughing. I hadn't really intended them to be funny, but the double meaning of the word 'Beaver' – more common in America – gave the text a much more obvious touch of humour. Eventually she pulled herself together and we recorded her part.

When I played the last two songs, edited into the final recording, to Muff and Paul, they were ecstatic. I was surprised therefore some months later to hear that they wanted to issue the album with just the songs, leaving out much of the narration and orchestral links. It was a complete volte-face on Muff's part and illustrated to me that he hadn't 'got' the point of the album at all. I thought it was a really bad idea and said so as diplomatically as I could.

Muff wasn't pleased – he wasn't used to letting artists make decisions that he didn't agree with. He went into a studio without telling me and edited the album the way he saw it. It sounded terrible. He had heard the original complete and said he loved it. Why the sudden change? This was the company that had had phenomenal success with Jeff Wayne's *The War of the Worlds* (1978), a dramatic concept with narration and instrumentals.

Paul Russell, who had always been a friend and advocate of mine, ran the company by relying on Winwood for every creative decision. He himself is not a musical guy and he decided to trust Muff's ears rather than mine. It was a stand-off that lasted for nearly a year and into 1986. Twelve months of sleepless nights, negotiation meetings and threats. Eventually I offered to give them their money back and take the album away to another company. They agreed, but seemingly in no hurry to release me into the arms of a competitor who might prove them wrong, they took nine months to negotiate the withdrawal.

Eventually I struck a deal with Starblend Records, a TV advertising specialist record company. The agreement was that they didn't need to pay me any money at all for the recording, but undertook to spend £100,000 on TV advertising. They released the album, paid for only £5,000 worth of TV advertisements and promptly

THE HUNTING OF THE SNARK – MY MAD, ONWARD JOURNEY

went into liquidation. The album therefore never had an effective UK release. All that work and painstaking effort had all come to nothing. I felt wretched.

Here, I should point out that my remarks about Paul Russell describe a brief episode in our relationship. As I write this, I look back on our many great times together, both personally and in business. We're still friends to this day. Our scrap over the 'Snark' was like two brothers fighting. One right one and one wrong one!

CHAPTER 16

The Phantom of the Opera

Although Cameron Mackintosh would not end up producing 'Snark', he did get me to collaborate on a small theatre production he staged at the Lyric Theatre, Hammersmith – a show called *Abbacadabra* (1983) based on the ABBA songs, long before *Mamma Mia!* The great lyricist Don Black and I wrote new lyrics to existing ABBA songs and I produced the records starring Elaine Paige, BA Robertson, Michael Praed, Finola Hughes and Anni-Frid (Frida) Lyngstad herself from the group. One day in 1984 while Cameron and I were having lunch in Covent Garden, I was fiddling with a rhyme I was writing for a private dinner that evening. I tried the verse out on him. He seemed to be very taken with it and must have made a mental note.

Soon afterwards I had a call from Cameron asking if I'd like to meet with him and Andrew Lloyd Webber at Andrew's flat in Green Street, Mayfair. I knew Andrew reasonably well. In the late '70s, before the boat trip, we had discussed potentially working together on what eventually turned out to be *Starlight Express*. They explained to me that they had been to see a musical production of

THE CLOSEST THING TO CRAZY

The Phantom of the Opera by Ken Hill. Cameron and Andrew planned to co-produce it with the idea that I could provide new lyrics. The music itself already existed in the form of arias from Grand Opera.

Andrew explained that he and Cameron wanted to bring Ken's musical into the West End and make it more appealing with new, relevant lyrics written by me. During the meeting, however, Cameron suggested to Andrew that he might contribute perhaps one fresh Lloyd Webber tune. Andrew thought for a moment, went over to a chest of drawers and pulled out a cassette. On it was a very rough recording of him playing something akin to what would eventually become the title song of *The Phantom of the Opera*, but without any lyrics and quite down-tempo. Of course I said I'd love to have a go at making it into a song. Andrew said he would record a clearer version of the tune on piano, with Sarah (Brightman, his second wife) providing a wordless guide vocal. The tape would be sent to my home later that day. The meeting ended cordially and, true to his word, a chauffeur-delivered cassette tape arrived later that afternoon.

I thought it would make a great title song, so I called it 'The Phantom of the Opera'. The lyrics came quickly, that very evening, but I thought what it *really* needed was a more up-tempo treatment, and the notes of what was effectively a downwards vocal portamento (slide) should be more defined quavers so as to fit my new lyric hook within a more vigorous rhythm – 'The Phan-tom-of-the-op-e-ra-is-here!' I had to pull the tune about a tiny bit to make it work – and just for the record, I'm not declaring a 'claimable' compositional function here – but it did change the musical personality of the song completely. It was what I would call 'producer input'.

I sent a rough piano and vocal version of the finished song to Andrew and Cameron. They loved it. The languid romantic ballad had somehow evolved into an up-tempo, potential hit song and not only that, it's 'hook' bore the words that were the title of the production.

Some time later, they asked me to arrange and produce a full track with Sarah Brightman and me singing – so I was, weirdly, the 'first Phantom' – but we all knew that my voice would be replaced once the proper duet partner had been found. The result was a powerful pop/rock/orchestral recording that just screamed 'hit'. Years earlier, I had done something similar with another of Tim and Andrew's songs, 'Oh What a Circus' from *Evita*, as a hit single for David Essex. For the 'Phantom' title song I had added a pulsing quaver rhythm using a Fairlight sequencer on the bass line and rock guitar licks to augment the feel, enhancing the ending by stepping the key up chromatically after each four bars as Sarah sang impassioned operatic-sounding motifs over the fade-out.

Perhaps emboldened by the idea that this sounded like a hit, Andrew was obviously thinking about the wider project. He invited me to lunch at the fashionable Langan's Brasserie near Green Park Tube station.

'Mike, I'm thinking of making "Phantom" my next musical. What do you think?' he said.

Ultimately, I don't think it mattered what I thought, but nonetheless he wanted to talk about it with me.

'But what about Ken Hill?' I asked, slightly taken aback.

'Oh, there's no copyright in a title,' said Andrew, which is true.

'I know that, but you've told him you're going to produce his version. You've given me his script to work on. He'll be devastated, won't he?'

THE CLOSEST THING TO CRAZY

'Not really,' said Andrew, believing it. 'Ours will be a completely different version.'

From that point on, it was Andrew's new project. And our record was no longer just a one-off potential hit to set up the Ken Hill 'Phantom', it would be used to launch Andrew Lloyd Webber's *Phantom of the Opera*.

My role changed several times. Firstly, I was kicked off the project as overall lyricist. On reflection, this might have stemmed from a misunderstanding over music publishing etiquette. To be fair, it was probably my fault for pointing out that, unless agreed otherwise, each writer initially controls the publishing of his half of a co-written song, and any changes to lyrics need to be agreed with the original lyricist. That's how it works in pop land and most of the world. But not always, of course, theatre, where things change around all the time. Some time passed and I heard nothing. However, Andrew worked further on the 'Phantom' show and presented the first act at his private Sydmonton Festival that year, with Colm Wilkinson in the title role. He had filmed the performance. I hadn't, of course, been invited.

Shortly after Sydmonton, Andrew rang as if nothing uncomfortable had ever happened and asked if I would like to discuss *producing* the *Phantom* album, despite my no longer being the lyricist of the show – apart from those indispensable lyrics which had given rise to 'The Phantom of the Opera' single. The 'genesis' of the song.

I needed time to think.

George and Olivia Harrison

A few days later, Jules and I went over to Friar Park, George and Olivia Harrison's house in Henley. George was his usual warm and

THE PHANTOM OF THE OPERA

welcoming self. He showed us around the studio, which had been newly decorated since I had last been there recording his 'Snark' solo. Jules and Olivia went for a long walk around the amazing gardens while George and I started chatting about songs and records. We discussed his apparent readiness to record an album, but he didn't want to stick his neck out until he had something really strong to offer. He was content to just enjoy 'buggering about' to start with. So we 'buggered about', me at the piano and George with a guitar given to him by Phil Everly, but after a few hours decided to stop for the night. We had come up with a body of a tune, a sort of Spanish bassline pop song, but nothing particularly exciting. There would be other days, we expected.

While we were all having dinner in the kitchen, Olivia mentioned she'd taken Jules around the fascinating underground caves in a boat and although it was now dark, George asked if I wanted to go. So we made our way through the garden, down the hole into the caves and slowly found our way through this fantastic underground labyrinth that ran beneath the house, out into the lake and back into the caves from the other side. Creepy but extremely pretty. Occasionally a bat would fly through – George thought that was a hilarious coincidence. Back safely in the house, we all watched a video of an Everly Brothers' documentary and then drove home, but not before George had generously gifted me a fantastic leather-bound copy of his limited edition book, *I, Me, Mine*.

And that's really how we wrote 'something crap', to use George's wise words. I guess we should have worked on it until it *wasn't* crap, but I was too embroiled in what was about to become a battle royale with CBS/Sony and, simultaneously, the strange dance with Andrew Lloyd Webber and Cameron Mackintosh over *The Phantom of the Opera*. Perhaps I should have delayed 'Snark' and concentrated on working with George. It would have been such fun and a great experience. He and Olivia came for dinner to discuss doing more music together, but fate would have it that, soon afterwards, George ran into Jeff Lynne. Jeff *did* invest time working with him – George's *Cloud Nine* album that they produced together was a global smash hit and out of that relationship came the Traveling Wilburys – Jeff, George, Roy Orbison, Bob Dylan and Tom Petty.

Somebody recently asked me if I might have ended up as a Wilbury if I'd persevered with George rather than 'The Snark' and other things. Frankly it has never once crossed my mind. Was it a sliding doors moment? Possibly. But firstly I don't have the same worldwide artist profile that Jeff had, and more importantly, I never say 'what if?' What if my car accident had been fatal? What if I'd done more film scores? What if I'd never had a hit? Hopefully it's not too soppy to reflect that each opportunity missed clears the way for another opportunity.

While still attached to the 'Phantom' project in the role of producer, I suggested to Andrew that he should hire Steve Harley as the potential 'real' Phantom to replace my temporary vocal. Andrew met him and agreed he'd be a great fit. Harley was, as most music fans know, sadly affected by polio as a kid and walked with a limp. He had developed a powerful upper body shape and was an intense and engaging actor – perfect casting for the Phantom.

Andrew signed him not just to sing the record that I was producing, but also to play the part on stage. Steve was ecstatic. The sessions with him and Sarah Brightman were interesting inasmuch as the two singers were completely different from each other as performers. Steve would enter the studio rather nervously, maybe covering it with a bit of friendly bravado, but with dark and serious intent, determined to do well. He would start off quite gingerly as he warmed up but when ready, his commitment was total. We would be working on phrasing, dynamics and emotional emphasis. He would pour his heart out and sing, even roar, with a passion and almost a fury, enabling him to inhabit the role of the character completely. I would have perhaps an hour with him at his dramatic peak and then it would be done. The magic would have been captured in that 'sweet time'. It was a bit like a director of photography for a movie using the 'golden hour' as the sun goes down and trying to shoot the scene just as the lighting was right.

Sarah, on the other hand, would have gone over the piece many times with Ian Adam, her singing teacher, before coming to the studio. She would not have allowed much more than an hour or so in her diary for the session. However, when she approached the mic and we ran the tape, she delivered a perfect performance from the start. *Technically* perfect, I mean. But if I asked her to try more or less passion in a certain place or a little less or more vibrato in certain places, it wasn't going to happen. She had rehearsed it the one way only. It wasn't unwillingness to work on the dramatic mood or the tension, it was just that she had worked out her part and that's what she delivered. A subsequent take of the vocal would yield exactly the same result. There was no point working further on it. She was delightful, and brilliant, just different. Harley would worry and push himself and allow me to cajole him into greatness – I would go on the journey with him. But Sarah walked in, sang it and went home.

'The Phantom of the Opera' record came out as a single in January 1986 and was a smash hit, reaching number seven in the UK.

THE CLOSEST THING TO CRAZY

The artist credit was 'Sarah Brightman and Steve Harley'. It set the scene for the launch of the show in a spectacular way.

It might take a whole book to describe adequately the ups and downs of my relationship with the Really Useful Group in the early days of 'Phantom'. As 1985 turned to 1986, Andrew and I continued to fall mildly out and mildly back in with each other. There was even a bit of tension with Cameron Mackintosh's office – I think, initially, over that issue with the music publishing rights. Being one of four kids in my family, I was used to banter and rough-and-tumbles with my brothers. It was all in good spirit and no damage was done. But, with hindsight, the business side of the Lloyd Webber/Mackintosh relationship couldn't be conducted in that way.

I found Andrew to be very sensitive to perceived 'sleights' that weren't sleights at all. He's also the most competitive person I've ever met. And who knows, maybe my own stubbornness got in the way? Maybe that was *me* being over-sensitive. It has meant that although I've produced, arranged for and co-written with him, we were never destined to be creative soulmates. I think what it boils down to is that if you work *with* Andrew, you have to work *for* Andrew, and that imbalance is what I find difficult in a creative collaboration. I don't find it difficult working for other people, though – film directors, for example – so there must be something different in his case. He and Tim Rice had initially been successful together as two young equals, striving for their first successes.

By chance, as I understood it, Andrew had run into Michael Crawford when he was picking Sarah Brightman up from a voice lesson and made the decision to cast him in the title role over Steve Harley. Both Steve and I were offered exit deals from the project. Steve was bought out of his contract with a cash sum, while I made certain undertakings regarding the contributions I had made. I signed over the music publishing rights to my part of 'The Phantom of the Opera' song and agreed that my royalties for that songwriting would be limited to records and non-theatrical use. Put another way, I would not be paid for their use in the 'Phantom' stage production, here or abroad. It wasn't a very smart deal. In fact, it was utter madness!

In my opinion, despite being an amazing actor and performer, Michael Crawford was never as strong a choice as Steve Harley. His polite and 'careful' delivery of the material on record and on stage was worlds apart from the passion and strength that Steve would have brought to the part. Steve's rendition of 'Music of the Night' – which I produced but can't imagine will ever be released – was delicate, hurt, impassioned and at the same time, full of love, drama and danger. I can't call his replacement a mistake, because look how successful the production has been through the years! But artistically, I thought it was a mistake.

In the years that have passed, I have always looked back with a surreal sort of pleasure on the times I spent working with Andrew. Despite everything, it was always exciting. Apart from surface tensions, we seemed genuinely to like each other, and since those days we have always maintained an overt friendly detente. Julianne and I subsequently joined him and Madeleine for dinner and attended their wedding and various other events and occasions. We've bumped into each other at the theatre or in restaurants and been sincerely cordial. I think there is a mutual respect between us and I look at his body of work with great admiration – he's a shrewd cookie. I genuinely never worry about not having been part of that spectacular ongoing *Phantom* success story. I see the knockabout moments as part of commercial and artistic life. From *Evita*'s 'Oh What a Circus' to 'Phantom', I'm glad to have contributed to his astonishing career. I know that his contribution to my own story and mine to his are just a balanced exchange of value between two artistic practitioners.

'Snark' at the Royal Albert Hall

While the 'Phantom' episode occupied my time, the CBS/Sony debacle and my re-acquisition of the 'Snark' album was dragging on and on. Yet somehow I was still in a high state of excitement about the record's potential. It was now 1987. I had organised a star-studded concert of *The Hunting of the Snark* at the Royal Albert Hall and it was too late to cancel it when all the record plans fizzled out – the concert would have to go ahead without the record being available. An unavoidable decision.

Billy Connolly played the Bellman, Roger Daltrey was the Barrister again and my friend Justin Hayward, Moody Blues frontman, was the Butcher, replacing Art Garfunkel (who was unavailable). Deniece Williams agreed to come over from America to play the Beaver and Julian Lennon and Captain Sensible both played their parts as the Baker and the Billiard Marker just as on the record. Ultravox's Midge Ure played the guitar solos instead of George Harrison. We filmed it with fourteen 35mm camera crews! Why pay less?! This was going to be one expensive evening to promote a record that was not even available in the shops following Starblend's insolvency. We did, however, raise £50,000 for the British Deaf Association. The not-for-profit show was promoted by the genial entrepreneur John Giddings, whose Solo promotions company also handled the Rolling Stones' tours and many other superstar acts.

THE PHANTOM OF THE OPERA

As for the hugely expensive TV recording, I licensed it to BBC TV for just £12,000 and they showed it at Easter in 1988, when there still was no record released. Despite the cost, I can't say I regret filming it. Not to have had a good video recording of it would have been a mistake for many reasons.

I have often made decisions to record or film things without knowing for sure that they will be commercially successful, but the thing I do know at the time of making these decisions is that I can't countenance the idea of the event happening and it not being captured for posterity. In other words, laying down wine that will hopefully be enjoyed years later. Call that self-indulgence or vanity if you like, but the way I see it is that it is more important for a piece to exist than for it to be immediately successful. It has often cost me dearly to carve that particular furrow, but it is not one that I regret as a lifetime habit. The TV recording, of course, also provided a good marketing resource for the ongoing story of the Snark.

As for the Royal Albert Hall concert itself, it was a triumph. The place was packed with punters, media, star faces and good friends. We even convinced a number of stars like ice-skating legends Jayne Torvill and Christopher Dean to be programme sellers. The mad, ambitious performance was received rapturously.

CHAPTER 17

I Watch You Sleeping

Being driven at speed in the back of an ambulance from the Wellington to the Portland Hospital in Westminster, Jules and I thought she was more likely to miscarry than to experience a viable birth. That evening, only seven months into her pregnancy, her waters had broken while we were at the Boat Show at Earl's Court. Devastated, and convinced it was a disaster, we headed for the Wellington to be told that the only chance the baby had was for us to be ambulanced to the Portland, where they had a Special Care Baby Unit. Against the odds, our son Luke was born at 4.39 a.m. on 17 January 1988 after a long and intense night, weighing just 3lb 2oz.

Luke was in an incubator in the Special Care Baby Unit for several weeks. It was often touch and go, but he pulled through and did not suffer any lasting injury or health issues, for which we are so thankful.

Around that time, Cameron Mackintosh's brother Robert asked me if I could write a song for a collection of Christmas songs being recorded by Cameron's cast members around the world for a Save the Children charity album. Focusing on the Nativity as an event involving a baby, I wrote a song with Luke in mind – 'I Watch You Sleeping'. I produced and conducted a record of it with Frances

THE CLOSEST THING TO CRAZY

Ruffelle (the original Éponine in *Les Misérables*) singing and the London Symphony Orchestra accompanying. It was an emotional time for all of us.

> I watch you sleeping
> Little angel face;
> And on behalf of the human race,
> Welcome to this crazy place.

The years between 1988 and 1991 were a financial balancing act. I was still trying to recover from the crippling financial blow of the debacle of the aborted 'Snark' record being unavailable, while paying the huge bill for the Royal Albert Hall production. On top of that, I was determined to find the funding to develop the 'Snark' piece into a full theatrical two-hour show and stage it in the West End. In the 'staying alive' department, I would take on work that was offered to me as an arranger/producer.

When Luke was just four months old, Julianne was cast as a semi-regular character – a smart young lawyer called Sarah Townes – in the long-running Channel 4 TV series *Brookside*. Despite the commute to Liverpool for filming, she accepted because it usually only entailed one night per week away from home, and even though her mother was staying with us for an extended visit, we hired a maternity nurse to stay over on those days and nights. Jules even managed to keep up the supply of breast milk by taking a breast pump with her so that she could express. She enjoyed the acting work, playing the role for eighteen months.

* * *

I WATCH YOU SLEEPING

I love making albums with just a solo voice and a symphony orchestra. It isn't done very much in pop music but it is artistically interesting because without guitars and drums, the orchestra provides all the moving parts and rhythm. Also, the soloist gets more space to be heard if there isn't a rhythm section banging away underneath. It became a kind of speciality of mine. In 1989, I made an album at Abbey Road Studios with Justin Hayward and the London Philharmonic called *Classic Blue*. He and I had often talked about doing something else together after the 'Snark' concert, and we landed on this idea of doing a set of well-known iconic rock songs in a purely symphonic way. The album, which was to become one of Justin's most popular solo albums, came out on Filmtrax records. It sold over 100,000 copies in the UK and has carried on selling steadily for years.

I was making a lot of albums at that time, including my own next solo album through a deal with RCA in Germany – *Songs of Love and War* – for which I was able to record my own versions of 'Caravan Song', 'Soldier's Song' and a new version of 'Railway Hotel'. The rest was brand new, original material. One particular new song, 'Sailing Ships From Heaven', I would one day re-record with Katie Melua as the lead track on her 2013 *Ketevan* album.

Another standout album in 1989 was one I did with Colm Wilkinson, the original Jean Valjean from *Les Misérables* and another extraordinarily impressive soloist who is among the most expressive and powerful singers with whom I have ever worked. We used Abbey Road Studio 1 with about a seventy-piece orchestra. The album *Colm Wilkinson: Stage Heroes* is one of my proudest moments as a producer and arranger. Soon after we had finished it, I was having a drink in our local pub – the Victoria in Bayswater – with John

Hurt, who was by then a good friend. I mentioned the album and he asked to hear something. The pub was only five doors from our London home so we went back to have a listen. John was so taken with it that by about the fourth track, he was in floods of tears. He was incredibly moved by it. And that's all down to Colm's vocal performances – they really were stunning.

Classical Gas, Gas, Gas

I had come to music partly through falling in love with Schubert's Symphony No. 9 as a young teenager and so, in addition to songwriting, I have a passion for composing and conducting – albeit self-taught. The first time I worked with the London Symphony Orchestra was when I hired them to play 'The Myths and Legends of King Merton Womble and His Journey to the Centre of the Earth' for the album *Superwombling* at Olympic Studios in Barnes, in about 1975. I got to know them well, as people. In fact, we got on like a house on fire. The first time they hired *me* was in 1984 for the concert at the Barbican.

I've always enjoyed what you might call 'straight' conducting. If I hadn't been a composer and songwriter, I might have had time to do more of it and make it my career, but my interests always pulled me away in eclectic directions and I would never be happy solely conducting other people's work. The closest I came to that was when Anthony Camden, principal oboist and chairman of the self-governing LSO, together with Clive Gillinson (later, Sir Clive), a cellist and board member, came to see me one evening at our Bayswater home and put to me what I thought was the most bizarre idea. They were waiting for news from the Arts Council about their grant for the coming year but were doubtful that the grant would be forthcoming for various reasons. The question they asked was both shocking and exciting: would I be prepared to become their chief conductor and music director if they didn't get their grant? They would 'go commercial' – still perform the classics, but lean towards (indeed, solicit) film scores and prestigious 'light' music (a description I always smile at when I hear it from classical folks).

I thought they were nuts! *Of course,* I agreed to be available to become the principal conductor of the LSO, should they ask me! I said, 'But I'm not familiar with a wide-enough range of the broad classical repertoire . . .' That didn't seem to worry them unduly. I was flabbergasted. They mentioned former principal conductor André Previn as having been learning repertoire as he went along, when he had joined them. But to me, Previn was in a different league. He was a brilliant classical and jazz pianist for a start. I wasn't. So what happened? Of course, they got their grant and Tony Camden called me apologetically for having 'wasted my time', but I said that I was flattered to have been asked. I continued to work with them quite often on sessions and of course we were to work together on *The Hunting of the Snark*, both on record and in concert.

What Does a Conductor Actually Do?

As the lights went down around me
And I opened up the score,
The room filled with the magical thrill
Of the Underground Overture.

People often ask me about 'proper' conducting. What does a conductor do? Just as I thought when I started out that there might just be some people who *can* write a hit song and others who will *never*

THE CLOSEST THING TO CRAZY

be able to, I thought much the same about conducting. I was, as I've said, keen to conduct from early on, but as with orchestration, I had no lessons from anyone. A book would tell you the patterns that your baton should make to conduct a four-four, a three-four, a six-eight, a nine-eight etc., but without experience there is a tendency to conduct like a robot. Down, across, back, up, repeat. And how do you signal the players in? In a recording session overdub, it's easy: we often have a click and maybe a verbal count-in. On the concert platform or when recording classically, you don't count Berlioz 'Symphonie Fantastique' in with 'a-one, two, a-one two, three, four!' It's a silent signal. One upbeat in or two? A full bar in or a single beat?

I learned my mistakes on the trot, flying by the seat of my pants. Conductors need to think, prepare, do mark-ups and reminders for themselves. I remember when I first conducted a *Carmen* piece with the LSO, one of the movements was in six-eight. I tried two fast preparation beats of the six-eight and the orchestra just fell to bits! Not laughing, just chaos. I felt like an idiot in front of eighty players. The tempo was too fast to beat 'in two'; it should be beaten 'in one'. Of *course* it should. Durrh!

I called a tea break to gather my thoughts. As he passed me on the way to his tea break, having hung back from the others, Kurt-Hans Goedicke, the timpanist, said, quietly and kindly, 'Mike, just give us a single upstroke, in one, of a full bar.'

When the band came back, I had composed myself. I stood ready and confident, made a swift but firm upbeat of one bar and when my baton came down, the LSO romped into the piece magnificently – all at the same time! I looked over at Kurt as if to say 'thanks, mate' and his eyes twinkled back at me in delight.

I WATCH YOU SLEEPING

If you've never played in an orchestra, you're not used to the signals, but one or two moments like that in my younger days put me on the right track. It does help if you have an inbuilt metronome. I don't know if mine grew from doing jingles that had to be 28.5 seconds long, or from working with film using precise timings, but I did discover that I have rock-steady timing. I can always tell when boiled eggs are ready, or what time it is without looking at my watch. It's like being the drummer or bass player of a band. Nobody wants a drummer or bassist who slows down or speeds up! But if you do, an orchestra will follow you and often of course the music requires it. The musicians follow every tempo shift and dynamic gesture, if they are good. Sir Adrian Boult wrote a wonderful book about conducting, *A Handbook on the Technique of Conducting*. Not much more than a pamphlet, it's fascinating. I learned half of what I know about conducting from just that one little book, and the other half from the musicians themselves during years of practical experience.

I've composed quite a lot of classical-style pieces, often in the form of symphonic suites related to media work I've done, such as my *Watership Down* suite and the *Dreamstone* overtures. I've had fun with many orchestras in the world including the Sydney Symphony, the Stuttgart Philharmonic and the State Orchestra of Victoria (Australia).

One of my proudest achievements, classically, is the recording I made of Holst's 'The Planets' suite with the Royal Philharmonic Orchestra at Watford Town Hall, which has one of the finest acoustics for orchestral recording in the UK. We recorded it using the Abbey Road Studios mobile recording unit. The record was produced by distinguished composer and critic Robert

Matthew-Walker and was the first 20-bit digital recording ever made of that piece.

I find it hard to explain adequately the bond you feel as conductor when you have a willing and friendly orchestra performing a concert or doing a day of recording sessions. It's the perfect combination of social and musical enjoyment.

Endorphins to the left of me, adrenaline to the right – stuck in the middle with you . . .

Another Emergency

Both of Julianne's and my children were born dangerously prematurely and both share dramatic stories that began weirdly at Earl's Court Exhibition Centre, a place we have only ever visited together twice! Luke had been 'born at the Boat Show' essentially and only just made it, being only thirty-one weeks and six days into gestation.

In 1990, with Julianne pregnant but not anywhere near due (about a month and a half away), we stood chatting to Christopher Dean and Jayne Torvill after their show in Earl's Court when Julianne suddenly started getting pains. Pains that she could read better than the first time she had given birth to a premature baby. I 'waddled' her as gently as possible to the car and drove straight to the Wellington Hospital, where she was under the care of Miss Mahnaz Keshavarzian (Ms Kesh), a delightful and caring Iranian specialist who had delivered Luke a couple of years earlier amid the drama of his emergency delivery. This new baby was already at thirty-four weeks, so our expectations were not so full of dread. There was, however, one *very* worrying factor: the baby had stopped moving. Was it still alive?

On examination, Ms Kesh said, 'This baby needs to come out NOW!' After asking how long it would take for a pain-reducing epidural injection and being told it would be forty-five minutes to take effect, she said, 'We don't have forty-five minutes!' and announced that she would perform an emergency caesarean section. She invited me to scrub up and join them so that at least one of us would be 'present', with Julianne herself out cold under a general anaesthetic.

And so, dressed in my green scrubs like a TV surgeon, I was privileged to witness the moving but challenging sight of this small and wonderful lady carving into my wife's abdomen like a Dickensian character carving into a giant Christmas pudding before our daughter, Hayley, was whisked out and moved to the paediatric team under the brilliant Dr Jake McKinnon before being taken off to the Special Care Baby Unit.

The amazing Ms Kesh never fails to send Luke and Hayley birthday messages every year, even to this day.

The Dreamstone

Around the time Hayley was born, I was commissioned to write the music for an animated TV series called *The Dreamstone*. Noting how good the animation was, I implored the producers to try to afford a budget that would enable me to write a symphonic soundtrack – I felt that such a soundtrack would reflect the quality of the animation work, giving it a Disney feel. The story was essentially that of the Dream Maker, a wizard who concocted and bottled dreams to be sent out across the land, populated by the Noops. The evil Zordrak (Lord of Nightmares) would try, using his idiotic army of Urpneys, to steal the magic Dreamstone, which was cut like a diamond and transmitted the good dreams throughout the land.

This premise – combined with hard and clever work from creator Mike Jupp and producer/writers Martin and Sue Gates – was an absolute gold-plated smash hit, beating the ratings of Steven Spielberg's animation show, an *Animaniacs* spin-off, on the opposite channel. It was so successful that, in all, fifty-two half-hour episodes were made. This was a fantastic opportunity to write some exciting symphonic pieces. As well as hundreds of episode cues, I composed five *Dreamstone* overtures, which were used throughout the series. Incidentally, one of the parts of my job that I enjoy the most is the orchestration. I have never once used an orchestrator or arranger to help with that side of what I do; I think of the orchestration as an integral part of the process and I personally believe if you have control over that process, you can create all sorts of little treasures that a separate orchestrator might never dare to explore.

'Better Than a Dream' was the main title song, which I sang myself, and the other favourite song was 'The War Song of the Urpneys', for which I recruited the unlikely trio of Billy Connolly, Ozzy Osbourne and heavyweight boxing champion Frank Bruno. It was such a laugh working with them. I recorded Frank and Billy in Abbey Road Studios in London but when I went out to LA to record Ozzy, Billy and his wife Pamela had just moved there and so I invited Ozzy and Sharon and Billy and Pamela to dinner at the Dome restaurant on Sunset Boulevard after Ozzy's vocal recording. It was one of the most hilarious dinners I've ever been present at.

The Good Ship Snark lay in the doldrums while I slowly realised that Cameron Mackintosh wasn't going to get round to producing it any time soon. I also knew he was strongly opposed to my directing it myself. A theatre producer and concert promoter called Stewart McPherson had approached me some time before the Royal Albert Hall concert saying that he thought he could put some funding together to contribute to the cost of the TV recording of the concert, and indeed his contacts provided finance to help the filming of that event. Now Stewart was keen on helping me move towards a full-length production.

At one stage Stewart set up a meeting with the Royal Shakespeare Company at Stratford, during which artistic director Terry Hands asked me about my vision for the show, knowing that I was keen on directing it myself. I told him that I'd always wanted to direct a piece where hidden musicians disguised as audience members would suddenly discard their overcoats and other disguises and join in. They were contemplating offering us a slot at Stratford, but those negotiations didn't lead anywhere.

Some years later I bumped into Terry Hands at a recording of ITV's *This is Your Life* for David Essex.

'You should have let us do *The Snark* at Stratford,' he said. 'I would have directed it in a very interesting way.'

'Tell me more,' I said.

'Well, for a start, I would have had musicians disguised as audience members, who would suddenly discard their overcoats and other disguises and join in.'

He said this with a straight face, clearly believing it to have been his own idea. I just nodded and smiled; I didn't feel the need to challenge him. It was a pleasant enough social situation, so why spoil it? But it did illustrate to me how one can adopt an idea and convince oneself that it is – or was – one's own.

It was in Australia that I first repeated the concert-length version of 'Snark' at the Melbourne Summer Music Festival with the State Orchestra of Victoria, where I had been appointed as artistic director/conductor in January 1990. The concert went well. Michael Parkinson provided superb narration and the Bellman was played by a robustly jolly Keith Michell.

My abiding mission, however, was to write it up as a full-length musical score and libretto for a two-hour theatrical production. That chance came when I received an invitation from two young amateur promoters who wanted me to come and do the show at the Hills Centre in North Sydney, followed by a week at the State Theatre in Sydney with the same orchestra and cast. I accepted on condition that it would be a costumed try-out of the full-length piece which I would complete especially for the occasion. And it was also essential to me that we would recruit well-known stars to play the parts – the ultimate public workshop.

We eventually returned to Australia in October 1990 as house guests of our good friends John and Sally Leaver and their two daughters, Kate and Sophie, who lived in a lovely house in Chinaman's Bay, North Sydney. The ink was 'still wet' on the orchestra parts, as we say in the business. I had recruited a stellar local cast. Daryl Somers, who had become a friend years earlier, was probably the most famous entertainer in Australia at the time, with his long-running *Hey Hey It's Saturday* show. He played the Billiard Marker. Philip Quast played the Bellman, A-list Aussie actor John Waters was Lewis Carroll, young heart-throb star Cameron Daddo played the Butcher, beautiful singing star Jackie Love repeated her role as the Beaver and the celebrated rock singer Doug Parkinson played the Barrister.

The show did very well, with a week out of town and then the week at the State Theatre. As a dry run for what could be, it had been an encouraging first outing of the full-length, two-hour musical, albeit in a concert format. It wasn't far off – indeed almost an exact blueprint – of what would become the fully staged show.

CHAPTER 18

The Mounting of the Snark

While we were in Sydney, our host and friend John Leaver said that he thought he could help us raise the money to stage the show in London. The London budget would be £2.2 million. He helped us, via his venture capital company, to draft a document that would be sent out to investors and, to start the ball rolling, put in an investment of his own.

Back in London, I went to see Gary Withers, owner of one of the biggest design and event companies, Imagination. I had first used his company when it was much smaller, back when I was setting up the Ivor Novello Awards in the mid-'70s. But Gary was frustrated because although he was now the market leader, his work was mainly for functions such as car launches and product presentations. He desperately wanted to be in theatre and he deserved to be. A charismatic, talented man, he ran his company in a stylish, business-like but mercurial fashion. He knew I had a vision for the design of the show and, as a consequence, I was adamant that I should direct it myself. This goes against the general traditions of advised practice in theatre but as this was going to be a revolutionary way of putting on a production, I felt it was essential that I was in direct charge of the lighting department and the design builders. Gary agreed that Imagination Limited would contribute some of the budget, albeit much of their contribution would be in services, and he gave us a big office from where I continued to fundraise.

I had devised a revolutionary and unique way to project pictures, scenery and lights using 200 Kodak carousel slide projectors. Constantly changing, often at a rate of ten slides per second, the animations of waves, birds, fish and clouds created a 'light box' in which the actors would perform. Although nobody at Imagination yet knew the particular cabalistic secrets about my light box, Gary assigned his technical audio-visual head Chris Slingsby and a brilliant young stage engineer/designer Will Bowen to help me to achieve mechanical, load-bearing and other physical and technical objectives. Slingsby had a thorough knowledge of how to get slides projected onto the right places from the right angles. The great thing was that Gary Withers, a fellow maverick, knew to trust me to deliver the artistic result I needed. His company would also get a very nice, well deserved, credit on the show billing.

The whole thing was one big juggling act. The money was being raised – and, finally, it *was* being raised – but we could not bring my stage design visions to fruition until we knew exactly which theatre we were going to be opening in. Given the number of projectors we would be using to create the desired visual effects, the exact angle and location of the projections would have to be calculated by Chris based on the layout of the actual, specific theatre.

I was driving down the M3 one day in April 1991 when Cameron Mackintosh rang me: did I think my show could be ready for September/October, because his Prince Edward Theatre had

THE MOUNTING OF THE SNARK

a John Caird show – *Children of Eden* – that was sadly closing unexpectedly early, leaving Cameron with an empty theatre. I told him I didn't have all my money yet and that it would be a tall order, but that the opportunity of such a great theatre *was* very tempting. I thought for a long time. In a West End full of long-standing hit shows, finding a good theatre is always one of the hardest things for any producer to do.

I took the plunge and told Cameron I could open on 31 October. He seemed delighted. His theatre now had a show and I had a deadline – and you know by now how much I love a deadline.

My days were split between drawing the artwork, talking to investors, deciding which flying bars would be allocated to which gauzes and screens and drawing out the required shapes for the scenery flats. I personally drew each slide in black and white and then, aided by a small team of assistants, coloured each one up, using lighting gels inside the slide mounts. We had Venetian blinds made of screen material so that the fifty-piece onstage orchestra could disappear and reappear suddenly. I had asked Will Bowen to achieve the impossible in engineering terms: to create a lateral bridge for the actors that would move not only up and down, but towards and away from the audience. He solved it ingeniously.

With regard to casting, we were gathering as we went. We still had Olivier Award-winner Philip Quast as the Bellman and David McCallum in place as Lewis Carroll. Mark McGann was to play the tormented, fearful Baker and I persuaded my friend Kenny Everett to be the Billiard Marker. Kenny and I had known each other for years. He had always been kind about my records, particularly the 'Snark' album. His work on TV and radio showed him to be a crazy, inspired performer but as he hadn't done a stage show before, he was uneasy. Once aboard, his own brand of nutsness added a lovely kick and indicated to the audience that this probably wasn't going to be your 'normal' musical.

Following formal auditions for the remaining parts, including the chorus, we worked for weeks in a rehearsal room near Waterloo. I had a hugely capable team around me. Jamie Hayes was my co-director and his experience in opera was particularly helpful. His brother was Martin Hayes, our production management guru, so there was a tight bond between the company and the management. Jamie was my secret weapon, really. I wasn't directing this show by myself – I had an experienced pro there all the time to catch me whenever I needed it. Which was often. Jae Alexander was invaluable as musical director and Jo-Anne Robinson (Gillian Lynne's right-hand woman on *Cats*) was choreographer.

We spent four weeks in the theatre doing technical rehearsals, which, as a director, is my favourite part. Finding the 'deads' (stopping points) for flown items, communicating with the flymen up in the flying gallery, working with the stage manager and the brilliant lighting designer, Andrew Bridge.

Those who say one person shouldn't write, design and direct are usually right, but in this case, I genuinely felt it was necessary in order to achieve the particular technical and artistic vision that I wanted to create. In those days, before bright LED screens and powerful projectors, light destroyed a projected image, so the lighting designer had to take direction from the designer. If I wanted Andrew to drop a blue light and replace it with a light mauve one, I only had to ask him rather than sidle up to a director and give him diplomatic notes to see if he agreed and try to fix it the next day. It happened instantly. This served us well in the technical runs. We

THE MOUNTING OF THE SNARK

pissed through them. Nothing went wrong, there were no moments of doubt.

The music was already written, orchestrated and tried, and had been triumphant in concert, so it wasn't as if that workload still rested on my shoulders, and the design was already done. So now I could concentrate on directing it. Not only to the standard I wanted, but also on time.

I had *one* job.

Finally, on Saturday, 5 October 1991, we opened for the first night of two weeks of previews. To be clear, these are commercial, paid performances that are open to the public but during which time the show may still need tweaks and adjustments. Critics sometimes sneak in for a peek without announcing themselves but that's not really supposed to happen.

At the end of our first preview performance, I was chatting with Nick Allott, managing director of Cameron Mackintosh Limited.

'You went up on time and nothing went wrong!' said Nick.

'I thought that was what you were *supposed* to do,' I replied.

'Yes, but we often have some sort of hitch that delays the preview dates.'

I guess at that level, with so much success under your belt, you can be a bit more forgiving of yourself for being late or having disasters, but this was a first time for me. I just thought it *had* to go right.

When I pressed Nick about what he felt might possibly be improved, he said he thought the second act could do with 'a bit more Snark-hunting'. I took his advice and over two late evenings during previews, I wrote a whole new song called 'Jungle Bridge' – aka 'Teddy and Me', in which we see the crew and characters fighting against the elements, singing a song questioning the wisdom of having come along on the expedition and wondering what the Snark is. By the second week of previews it had been choreographed, rehearsed, designed, lit and inserted, and it now endures as one of my favourite parts of the show. So, thanks, Nick!

On the first night the critics were delayed getting back from Paris. Cameron had taken them en bloc to see the opening night of the French production of *Les Mis* the evening before. There had been travel chaos on their return journey so they arrived just before curtain up and in a foul mood. We had no knowledge of this until afterwards. The cast excelled themselves, the kinetic visual aspects went perfectly and the orchestra played like angels. It really was an artistic triumph. We repaired to the after-show party at Imagination's headquarters just off Tottenham Court Road. There was an ebullient mood at the party and we all felt pretty great. Great, that is, until the first editions of the next day's newspapers began arriving at the party around midnight. First one review and then another tore us to pieces – tore *me* to pieces personally.

What we could understand least was that they had been wowed by the visual presentation, but they seemed to hate the score. Yet the score, which had been played successfully in concert and on record to great plaudits and audience feedback, was the one thing we were confident was already demonstrably loved by many before we opened.

Maureen Paton wrote in the *Daily Express* that there was 'not one memorable tune in it'. I appreciate that people can have opinions but that is just factually rubbish. I believe those few, but vital, critics had been overwhelmed by the visual elements (Sheridan Morley predicted the show would 'revolutionise theatre design for many years to come') to the extent that they had not really listened to the songs and tunes. The critics also seemed to hate *me*. It seemed the general implication was 'how dare this record producer upstart think he can write, direct and design a musical?'

We were shattered. To make matters worse, in the confusion, a gate-crasher had made off from the party in our limo and because we called the police, Jules and I had to go and make a statement at a police station, which kept us up until five in the morning, all the time fretting about the terrible reviews we had seen, more of which we picked up on the way home.

We went to bed very late in our London home and woke in the late morning the following day to the horrendous realisation that our lives would probably be changed forever by this blow. It was real. It hadn't been a nightmare. The show would have to close following such reviews. The company would go into liquidation – maybe we would have to go personally bankrupt. These weren't just bad reviews, they were personal attacks that spared no punches. Anyone who hadn't seen the show – which was of course most people in the country – would have thought I had just served up a piece of shit.

A friend, the renowned Royal Shakespeare actress Penny Downie, told us that during the interval on press night she had seen what she described as a 'coven of critics' conferring in the stalls aisle. I had noticed them too but had thought it must be a social moment. In the cold light of day it seemed that this was a half-time decision about a collective opinion. I don't think it helped that I didn't know any of the critics personally. Or that they had to run to catch the train that afternoon to get from Paris. Or that they were all bastards!

Our fundraising efforts had left us just £200,000 short of full capitalisation. This was to have been our advertising budget, post-opening. So, in addition to having the shattering blow of the critical hatred, we also had no way to advertise the very few nice things that were said, including Sheridan Morley's review in the *New York Herald Tribune*.

The following afternoon I addressed the cast and told them that shows, even *Les Mis*, had suffered this badly before, albeit not quite so personally. Cameron had advertised his way out of it and supported *Les Mis* until it had become a 'fixture' in the West End, and I resolved to do the same. I would raise the missing budget and build up a campaign of counter-measures – advertising and PR – and give oxygen to the opinions of those within the industry and public who *had* loved the show.

And there were *many* who loved it. I was snowed under with letters and faxes of appreciation expressed in strong and passionate terms. One very well-known 'big name' director told me that 'The Snark' had been 'One of the best three or four things I have ever seen on a stage'. And broadcast critics too were very enthusiastic. If everyone had hated it, I could have understood. But just the print critics? It didn't make sense.

I fought like a tiger trying to raise that extra funding. I had meetings with potential new investors; I had one investor on the hook who wanted to put £5 million in, but Gary Withers – probably rightly – suspected it was almost certainly a money-laundering situation. An existing investor – let's call him 'Terry' – who was helping raise the further funds brought a pretty female investor to see the show. She had pledged to provide £100K. He went with her in her Bentley, supposedly to her bank in Windsor to withdraw the money the next day (in cash? I never quite worked that one out), when the car was ambushed and he was taken prisoner at gunpoint. He

THE MOUNTING OF THE SNARK

had been the victim of a honey trap, set up by disgruntled business opponents who forced him to sign documents, beat him up and threatened to kill him and bury him in the garden. They kept him prisoner for several days.

We had expected him to return that same evening, but not until four days later did he contact us, telling this barely believable but true story. When Terry recovered from the shock, he visited the show again a week or so later. This time he was flanked by six former SAS bodyguards whom he had on retainer for at least the next six months.

They went everywhere with him.

The show survived only seven weeks at the Prince Edward. When 'The Snark' finally came off, I was still on the trail of new investment which might have saved it, but my hopes were dashed when Richard Mills, who managed the theatre, gave me contractual notice to quit because Tommy Steele wanted the theatre for *Singin' in the Rain*. With no theatre, I had nothing for any future investor to invest in and so I was forced to throw in the towel and put the company into liquidation. Richard said he had never in his long theatrical life ever seen a producer fight so hard to keep a show on.

There has been much argument about the merits of the piece since it closed. A Theatre Studies student, Andrew Loretto, even wrote his MA thesis on the subject, 'The Snark and the Critics'. It's a scholarly work and concludes that there was definitely something wonky going on within the critical community.

I'm going to afford myself a paragraph to tell you that the show we created was innovative, dazzling and thought-provoking. It broke boundaries on several levels and it inspired many future productions by others. Sure, it didn't have much of a 'story-plot' – but neither do *Cats* or *The Nutcracker* in my opinion. Lewis Carroll didn't write plots, but his pieces were still works of genius. His 'stories' were merely a series of fascinating encounters with strange characters. Even *Alice's Adventures in Wonderland* has no story to speak of; it's a series of vignettes or tableaux in which she meets the Caterpillar, then the Mad Hatter, then the Queen. You have to reach into the characters and enjoy his craftsmanship, his pure brilliance of presentation and the originality of his thought. So it was with us.

Even the introduction to this book will give you an idea of how I approached this piece; as a conflict between the philosophies and attitudes of the characters and surmising that we should all respect the views of others, as reflected in the closing song, 'Whatever You Believe'; all the while wrapped up in a jolly, silly, virtuosic piece of kinetic art – a curious confection if you choose to see it that way. If you listen to or watched the piece – (sadly, the full-length stage show was never filmed) – you would get that. For whatever reason, my vindictive critics were determined not to.

I'll admit that the injustice and aftershock of that experience have stayed with me for the rest of my life and I ask you to forgive me for the extensive account of my thoughts about it. But I do know that I created something magical and that I got it on in the West End and if I don't present it again before I leave the planet, somebody else will. One day.

CHAPTER 19

The Roaring '90s

Like the '80s, so full of simultaneous life-changing events, both positive and negative, the '90s, having started with a nasty Snark-shaped, existential bang, continued with the usual blend of projects, triumphs and disappointments. Where the '80s had begun with (and been continually dogged by) a divorce and a theatrical nightmare, the '90s present themselves in my memory as a decade of growth and recovery. Upwards . . . It was an upwards decade.

The period immediately after the 'Snark' show closed was not the most pleasant. The country was in the midst of a recession, the first Gulf War was raging and Jules and I were in serious financial trouble. We decided that she and the children should head for Australia, where she had a welcoming family set-up in Melbourne. I would be free to sort everything out in London and the kids would be spared the anguish of what would have been a tense situation. It was a good call – we could maybe all move and make a new start in Australia.

Although I wasn't convinced that Australia was the future for us and had no real intention ever of making a permanent home there, I kept an open mind. I was having to go through the ignominy of attending meetings with creditors and the dissolution of the Snark company. We had knock-on financial problems which went far deeper than the show closing and just one company swallowing all the debt. I did not go bankrupt, but it affected us personally due to all of the guarantees and obligations. I had no income to speak of and we were selling furniture to buy food. The dining table went. My favourite amplifier – a Mesa Boogie given to me by the Hollies as a thank you present for producing 'Soldier's Song' – went straight down to Denmark Street and achieved a fraction of its value. Whatever we could sell, we sold.

Normally, in such circumstances, we would have lost our beloved home in London, for which I was now unable to pay the mortgage. But the recession itself now helped us back up, to an extent. If Citibank had sued all their customers who were in financial trouble at that time they would have had almost no customers. Repossessing our house would have been pointless. Citibank would have owned a lot of houses and had no bank business. They accepted my offer of small capital payments in return for an interest freeze and that's how we managed to hang on to our home in Hyde Park Square.

Just as in the song 'Nobody Knows You When You're Down and Out', everybody ignores you when you've failed. Almost nobody rang me. I didn't secure any new work. Social invitations dried up. That first twelve months can only be described as my post-*Snark* exile. One person who came around – and I mean came around *every day* on his bike – on his way to *Les Misérables* rehearsals, was Philip Quast, who had so magnificently played the Bellman. Cameron had snapped him up to reprise his portrayal of Javert. Every day without fail he popped in to make sure I was alright. I had been diagnosed as severely clinically depressed and was under the care of a psychiatrist. The pills only lasted six months before I chucked them away. I wasn't suicidal but I was learning what the expression 'Black Dog' meant. Your veins are seemingly full of black treacle and you can't summon up the energy to do anything. Why bother? But at the same time I knew my depression was circumstantial and that when I achieved further success, it would go away.

That may sound shallow but it's the truth. It wasn't just about money, it was about reputation. It was the feeling that everybody who had not seen the show in those seven short weeks must have assumed that I had delivered the worst musical on earth. Some people were particularly unkind. The cartoonist in *The Stage* magazine dug deep on several occasions to hurt me as much as he could. Maureen Paton, who had taken so much pleasure in dumping on *The Snark* in her review, wrote a full-page article in the *Daily Express* saying how glad she was that I'd gone bust because it wasn't as bad as what she herself had to do, which was to sit through a performance of my show! From what dark reservoir of hatred and bile does a person have to draw in order to write such hurtful, crushing words?

Little things helped to keep my spirits up. The kids were still quite small and it was a pleasant and uplifting diversion to write to them and sometimes to draw them pictures. But I missed the family. I also had two good friends just down the road in Paddington, Lisa Katselas and Anday McCarron; she's a film producer of some note and he's a very talented singer-songwriter. They would often pop by with pizza. Little things.

I figured that if I could find something engaging enough to keep me interested, I'd have a reason to get out of bed every morning. Simultaneously, I began writing a musical called *Men Who March*

THE CLOSEST THING TO CRAZY

Away and a stupid, humorous book called *The Chronicles of Don't Be So Ridiculous Valley*, about an optimistic slug who has no hands but wants to play the piano and marry a fairy. These two projects, one quite a serious musical about a love story set against a background of the First World War and the Spanish Civil War (which contained a song called 'The Closest Thing to Crazy', at least ten years before it would become a massive hit with Katie Melua) and the funny slug book, occupied me and kept me going while no one rang me to offer me any work, despite all my previous success. I would have thought that my track record would have had people thinking, *Hang on, Mike Batt – he wrote 'Bright Eyes', scored this, did that etc. – he'd be great for our own project/record/film/show.* But not a work-shaped sausage was there to be had.

Until one day . . .

Green Shoots

Almost exactly a year after the closure of the 'Snark' show, I had a call from Maurice Cassidy, manager of the great stage star Colm Wilkinson. Maurice was ringing from his office in Ireland. He still managed Colm but he had a new client, a singer called Finbar Wright who had, until recently, been a Catholic priest and now had his own TV show. His lyric tenor voice was outstanding. Maurice had remembered how well Colm and I had worked together a few years earlier and wanted to know if I'd be interested in arranging and producing an album for Finbar, to be released by Sony, Ireland. The answer was that I would – and I did.

The material was a mixture of my own songs (including 'Whatever You Believe' from *The Hunting of the Snark*), famous standards like 'Catari' and more traditional material. We called the album *Whatever You Believe* and it shot straight to number one in Ireland. It's not a *huge* territory, but a number one still sold an impressive 30,000 copies. Finbar was suddenly a big star.

A second album, *A Tribute to John McCormack*, followed in pretty short order. It was recorded during a live-to-air TV concert on St Patrick's Day 1993, when I conducted the National Symphony Orchestra of Ireland. I also wrote a ten-minute overture called 'The Dublin Overture', which the orchestra played as part of the live transmission. The album went to number three.

I was back on the map.

Shortly after that, I had a call from Mel Bush, manager of David Essex, asking me to produce an album with my old pal. A straightforward TV-advertised covers album for Mercury Records. I have always got along so well with David, since our first meeting as label-mates at CBS in the '70s. We had a real friendship, which wasn't just musical. Of course, we trusted each other musically and had had significant success together, but I remember sitting in a café with him on the Edgware Road in London after a session years earlier and we were just having lunch, not saying much. He said to me, 'You know, Mike, I think it's a real marker of friendship when two people can sit together and not feel they have to make conversation.' He was right; so many people – even married couples – think they have to fill the blank spaces. Our friendship existed without constant verbal reaffirmation. The fact that we clicked in the studio was a joy, and this opportunity to work together was no exception.

David came and worked with me at our home near Hyde Park – the same home he had sold to me many years earlier – and we decided which songs we would record. Again, I set about arranging all the tracks, scoring for a full orchestra. We made the album at AIR Studios, where we recorded such tracks as 'Everlasting Love',

THE CLOSEST THING TO CRAZY

'Summer in the City' and 'Waterloo Sunset'. All the tracks were played as complete takes with the entire orchestra (i.e., not pre-recording the rhythm section). David came in over a period of a few days and we overdubbed his vocals – another process in which mutual trust between producer and artist is essential.

The album – *Cover Shot* (1993) – was a big success for Mercury Records and we were both very proud of it. Some years later (in 1997), we would follow it up with another album for Mercury, *A Night at the Movies*, again made at AIR Studios and Lyndhurst Hall. An equally fun experience, it would also chart high, selling well over 100,000 copies in the UK, doing everyone concerned a lot of good.

Meanwhile, by 1993 my one-year exile – when the phone never rang – was now suddenly and firmly in the past. But it had been a gruelling, often uncertain and lonely time.

The family returned from Australia. Luke and Hayley, having been booked temporarily into local Australian schools, returned with cute, but temporary, miniature Aussie accents. Life was starting to return to how it had been. I was still hurting from the injustice of 'Snark', but we moved on.

In 1993, less than two years after 'Snark', two seemingly similar projects appeared for me simultaneously. I said yes to both of them. They were, by complete coincidence, two unconnected, classically trained fourteen-year-old girls with very insistent, very wealthy parents. One was a singer called Sandra Schwarzhaupt and the other was the violinist Vanessa-Mae. Both were very talented. One of them would sink without much immediate trace, while the other was to have a spectacular international career.

Timing was important to both artists and their labels. I met with them both alongside their parents and was asked by their respective record companies to write and produce both artists. I would be paid a fee and a production royalty. This is the typical way producers are hired – you take an advance to help pay your bills and running costs and the advance is recouped from a future royalty, should the project be successful. The album I made with Sandra never really made much of an impression. We recorded at Abbey Road Studios. She was extremely good. Her voice was very young and sat right in that middle space between classical and pop. Her label, RCA in Germany, wanted to aim at a popular market but the stars weren't aligned for it to be successful, for whatever reason. You do your very best but you are still shaking the dice.

By the time I first met Vanessa-Mae and her mother, Pamela, I told them that our meeting was fortuitous because I had long been planning to write a violin concerto. Vanessa – a prodigy who had already recorded classical repertoire with the London Symphony Orchestra – immediately said to me that this wasn't what they wanted. She played me a Michael Jackson record.

'*This* is what I want to do!' she said.

I was incredulous: 'But you don't sing, you're a violinist!'

She was adamant. The direction they wanted from me was a pop direction, not classical. Which was frustrating because she was a true virtuoso. Not necessarily up there with your Nigel Kennedys and your Nicola Benedettis, but she played impressively, with all the right notes in the right order – most impressive when rapid, but in my personal view, somewhat less impressive on slow, expressive passages.

She was an acrobat rather than a ballerina.

Vanessa was nearly fifteen and, quite naturally, wanted to present herself in a cool way. It was a tough proposition, though.

THE CLOSEST THING TO CRAZY

I would have to design a 'sound' for her, create a style. I said I couldn't think of any repertoire that was both pop and virtuosic so I would have to arrange existing pieces or write new material. It was an exciting challenge to write new material and work to this brief, but I needed Vanessa to guide me as to what she liked. I played her some of the wackier oddball sections of my own solo album work. Pieces like 'Tarota' (from *Tarot Suite*) and other unusually-styled compositions from *Schizophonia* for the rhythm section and orchestra. She was excited that it seemed I could hopefully deliver something 'new-sounding', something more imaginative. I set to work, writing the album, rearranging a couple of existing pieces, including my own theme to the movie 'Caravans' and Mason Williams' 'Classical Gas', a guitar instrumental which had been a hit in the '60s, which I had always loved.

While composing, I programmed in some basics, like chords and drum and bass lines, while writing the pieces into my scoring software, constructing the violin parts so that Vanessa would have no doubt as to what to play. She had never recorded on multitrack in the way we usually worked. It was all very new to her but she picked it up quickly. I had bought her a white Zeta electric violin – the idea being that we would be able to match exactly the violin part using midi and mix it with various other sounds if we wanted to in order to get an enhanced, modern, futuristic effect.

At that age, Vanessa's playing sounded best on a real violin – the instrument she'd played all her life. She'd only had the white electric one for about three months. For that reason, we had three resources for each violin performance, firstly a midi-triggered note coming from my computer score which we called 'the shadow' (playing Vanessa's violin part) and Vanessa would play the part for real on both the electric violin and her own acoustic violin. We discovered that we could send the shadow to any effect we wanted (like a delay or a synth sound, for example) and when mixed with the 'real' violin sound, it could colour the actual violin sound. Sometimes, I chose to use what Vanessa had played using the electric violin, but often I used the natural acoustic instrument, usually mixed with the midi shadow.

Prior to the violin-playing section of this process, my engineer and I had spent some days programming the tracks by feeding my scores into the computer; I would pick a drum sound and then play the drum kit in, using a keyboard or have it coming off the score by midi. One of the most interesting tracks to do was 'Toccata and Fugue in D minor' (my arrangement of the J.S. Bach masterpiece). Because it has so many sections, there was scope to create passages with different drum patterns, sound effects, tempi, etc. In those days sound effects were best taken from CDs, and I had quite a few. To me the most effective was suddenly deciding to have a sound effect of a girl saying 'Fasten your seat belts' just before a change into an up-tempo section – that sort of thing. It gave a signal that we planned to be quite sonically irreverent towards the material, despite remaining, in notational musical terms, very respectful towards it. No one writes a better bass line than Bach. Maybe McCartney sometimes comes close! Anyway, whatever it was, it did the trick because EMI Classics loved it.

I think EMI Classics would have been happy if they had just recouped their £60K budget. I don't think *anyone* – including me – expected the album quite to go through the roof in the way it did. And why did it? I wasn't at the photo session for the album cover or the video shoot. I wasn't managing Vanessa; Mel Bush was.

Somehow, whoever did organise those sessions and directed the video, I doubt anyone thought those 'Lolita of the violin' pictures would emerge from the day's shoot.

There was media outrage. Vanessa appeared on Radio 4 *Woman's Hour* to discuss the morality of a fifteen-year-old girl promoting herself in that way. It even made the TV news and all of the papers. She gave interviews years later saying that all of this had been driven and shaped by her overbearing and ambitious mother, Pamela, whom she sacked as her personal manager a few years later.

None of the marketing or promotion was my idea. I think I helped her make a good record. I found her a white electric violin. I had created a sound for her, but my writing was not unlike the way I normally wrote. I think I wrote some good pieces; I produced them well, she played them well and I helped her to reach a standard and present it in the best way possible. Controversy alone could not have sold a poor or ordinary record, but without that controversy and with a less determined artist it would never have sold four million copies! Suddenly I was getting daily sales figures from EMI and their executives calling up to tell me that we'd suddenly 'cracked the Pacific Rim' or whatever it was that we'd cracked that day. Classical labels weren't used to selling these numbers – people were getting promotions and bonuses because of it.

I had written eight out of the eleven compositions – a serious step back into commercial credibility for me. Suddenly I had a big album, the lion's share of which I had created note by note from the ground up. And, as luck would have it, my publishing deal was up for renewal just as we hit the top of the arc of success. This meant I could now shop around the other publishing companies and score myself a nice big advance payment from the lucky bidder who would represent my songwriting catalogue for the next few years. It was incredible timing and, after 'Snark', was exactly the boost my career needed.

It reminded me of the day 'Bright Eyes' went to number one in 1979 and I was walking down Maddox Street, outside my London office. I ran into fellow hit songwriters Guy Fletcher and Doug Flett. 'Great news!' they said. 'Congratulations, Mike!' I said, 'Thanks, yes, and guess what else? My publishing deal RAN OUT YESTERDAY!' They knew what that meant. We did a little dance of joy on the pavement, which must have looked mad to everyone passing by. That's just what you want: to become free from your publisher just as you have a massive success. You're hot. Your gun is smoking. You walk into the saloon that day knowing that everybody knows.

* * *

In 1995, while the Vanessa-Mae album was being launched, I helped make another album of which I am enormously proud, and to which I still listen to loudly and regularly. Following the principle expressed earlier about a solo voice with symphony orchestra and no rhythm section, I worked with Gary Wilmot to create an album of theatre-song medleys with the London Symphony Orchestra at Abbey Road Studios. At the time, Gary was presenting a BBC TV show called *Showstoppers*. We linked up a medley of three songs from *The Wizard of Oz*, did the same with a pair of songs from *Carmen Jones*, *Gigi* and many other great shows. I knew Gary as a friend and admired his stage work enormously, but he shocked me in the studio by showing himself to be in possession of one of the finest voices I've ever worked with. His version of 'Luck be a Lady Tonight' is stunning – all the tracks are. It was issued as *Gary Wilmot – The Album* (1995) – a terrible title! – and later as *Gary Wilmot – ShowStopper*. Worth a loud listen one day when you get a moment and the neighbours are out!

XTC

In 1999 my old pal, sound engineer and producer Haydn Bendall, called me. A man of my own vintage, Haydn had been chief engineer at Abbey Road Studios for ten years earlier in his career and we have a long history of working together. He was there with XTC's Andy Partridge, producing the album that would become *Apple Venus Volume 1*. They were programming woodwind and other samples to create the orchestral sound Andy wanted, but had decided they needed a 'proper arranger' and a real orchestra for some of the tracks.

I was happy to help, but in those days I used to be embarrassed to charge friends for arrangements and so I told him I'd only do it if they'd accept my work as a gift. They protested in the way one might protest when a pal picks up the bill at a restaurant, although Andy did offer to buy us both dinner one evening as a thank you.

I was delighted to be doing the sessions, I always am. But working with brilliant people like Andy and Haydn, that's a real treat. 'Green Man' felt to me as if it needed a swirling, almost Indian-sounding string arrangement, and it suited my leanings towards Eastern music (along the lines of 'Caravans' and 'Schizophonia') even though the track simultaneously had a kind of pagan English folk feel. I just followed the mood of what I heard. That's the lovely thing about art: we all see or hear things differently.

With 'I Can't Own Her', Andy gave me a pretty free hand for the strings, albeit with lots of phone calls when I would play him bits on the piano. It came out sort of Beatley – it's a really gorgeous song.

THE ROARING '90S

A couple of weeks later, Andy and Haydn turned up at our Hyde Park home and we walked to a local restaurant, the Bombay Palace. It's a good restaurant, but to us it was just the local Indian.

'Oh, I see you chose somewhere nice and expensive as I'm the one paying!' remarked Andy as we approached.

Haydn and I exchanged knowing looks but said nothing. I'd read that Andy had a reputation for being a bit of a thrifty guy so I felt a bit guilty, but actually the restaurant wasn't particularly expensive. Suffice to say, we all had a great time. Andy's a lovely, kind and talented bloke.

Despite all our success together, I didn't make another album with Vanessa-Mae. Call it artistic differences to be polite, perhaps. Truth was, I couldn't get on with Pamela, her pushy mother. I suggested my best friend Andy Hill. An incredibly meticulous and inspired producer/writer, Andy wrote Celine Dion's 'Think Twice' and all the Bucks Fizz tracks with King Crimson co-founder Pete Sinfield. He's not an arranger but he's bloody good at producing and writing. Vanessa-Mae and her mum took my recommendation and got Andy to do the next record. And so it came to pass – Vanessa's second album produced with Andy sold a very respectable one million copies worldwide. They were happy, she kept on touring and Mel kept on managing her.

Throughout my friendship with David Essex, Mel had been his manager. Mel lived near my Bayswater home and we'd sometimes meet up for a spaghetti in the ASK Italian café in Kendall Street. One day, Mel arrived late and looking haggard. He ordered a big drink.

'What's wrong?' I said.

'I've been working with [Expletive Deleted] – his name for Vanessa's mother and [Expletive Deleted Junior] – his name for Vanessa!' he said.

THE CLOSEST THING TO CRAZY

'Why do you work with people you feel you need to call by those horrible names?' I said.

'Because we're making big money touring!' he admitted.

'I've got an idea!' I said. 'Let's form a label together, or at least a production company. And let's audition to find FOUR Vanessas! Two violinists, a viola and a cello. An all-girl electric string quartet. They can all have electric instruments. I'll produce, you manage. We'll collectively sign the act.'

We sat and fantasised for a moment. 'And *when* we launch them,' I went on, 'let's do it at the Royal Albert Hall! Let's start as we mean to go on, giving them the status that normally would take years to build up. It will be like launching Boyzone or the Spice Girls!'

The next day, Mel rang me: 'When do we start?'

I booked Baden-Powell House, a venue I'd used before, on the Cromwell Road and we put out a 'casting call' to musicians' bookers. Girls came trooping in, one every twenty minutes, all post-conservatoire classical standard. We auditioned all day. In that day we found a definite second violinist (Eos Counsell) and a couple of shortlisted viola players, but no absolute killer, genius first violin. Mel thought he knew someone who could be the cellist, who hadn't been able to be at the auditions.

There was a second meeting in a rehearsal studio with our shortlisted girls and this time, Mel had brought a beautiful Asian girl, Gay-Yee Westerhoff, as the potential cellist. She had worked with Vanessa and proved to be perfect. I had done a special string quartet arrangement of my piece 'Contradanza', from Vanessa's first album, with difficult-enough parts to test each player. By the end of the day we had chosen Eos Counsell for second violin, Bourby Webster as the viola player and Gay-Yee Westerhoff on cello, but we still needed our star first violinist.

THE ROARING '90S

After this, Mel had things to do and I was hired to score the music for the ITV series of *Watership Down*. We agreed that we would separately keep our eyes open, searching for the missing star, and keep each other in the loop. We kept the remaining 'band' girls on hold and got on with our other commitments.

A couple of months later, I had a call from Mel: 'I've found the ideal violinist,' he said. Her name was Haylie Ecker.

I was delighted. 'I'm just working on this *Watership Down* TV score and the album for Universal, but after that, say in about six weeks, I'll be free to carry on,' I told him.

However, the conversation quickly erupted into a raging row. Mel was telling me he wanted to go ahead NOW. I said it was impossible, reminding him that he couldn't proceed without me, not after the way the band had been auditioned and assembled – and it having been my idea in the first place! He slammed the phone down on me. I thought no more of it.

A lover's tiff.

Maybe six months later, Jorgen Larsen, the head of Universal Records International, invited me to his London office. He wanted me to meet his new president of Universal Classics, Costa Pilavachi, in case there was some project that we might find mutually interesting. We got chatting and Costa asked me what I was up to.

'Well, I'm working on putting together a new all-girl electric string quartet,' I said.

'That's interesting, we've just signed an act like that from Mel Bush,' said Costa.

It hit me like a sledge hammer.

'Oh, I expect you'll find that will be it,' I said calmly, but inside, all I was thinking was, *What a bastard! He's gone behind my back, developed the band and done the deal without me.* Somehow I managed to restrain myself from ringing him immediately and giving him both barrels. I guess, in hindsight, I should have done – it would have made my legal position clearer. Instead, I thought, *Let's just see what happens.*

After some weeks I finally received a call from Mel. He told me confidently that he had set up and signed the quartet, called it Bond and had made an album with the producer Magnus Fiennes. Again, this was my chance to fly into an outburst, but again, I didn't rise. He explained that the album was good but Magnus hadn't 'delivered a hit'. Mel proposed that I should remake one of the tracks, a tune called 'Victory'. I was gobsmacked. He'd signed the girls, given them a name, hired a producer, done a deal with Universal and not told me a thing. And then, just when he needed a hit, he had the bare-faced gall to phone and ask if I would do it.

I kept the call short and courteous: 'Oh, well send me the track and let me hear it,' I said.

Soon the track arrived. It was very ordinary, highly derivative Euro-middle-of-the-road, melodically predictable and unappealing. Why did I even give it a thought? Because I was curious, I guess. But inside I was still quietly fuming. Mel wanted me to 're-produce' it. Save his arse, effectively. Give him a track that might get radio attention.

Something in me made me want to work with this group, whose very existence had been my idea, so instead of telling him to fuck off, I said yes. I set about re-orchestrating the piece from scratch, completely re-writing the string arrangement and weaving new counterpoints in for the second violin and other players. We fixed a day for the girls to come over to the studio and spent a very pleasant day recording. Job done, I delivered the track.

THE ROARING '90S

Time passed and I received an invitation to Bond's launch concert at the Royal Albert Hall, hosted by Universal Records. A box, even. I thought it would be nice to take some folks from my office, so about six of us went along. We settled into the box and just as the lights were dimmed ready for the performance, I realised. The memory returned. We were in the *Royal Albert Hall*. This had been *my* plan! *My* vision! I could hear a voice in my head, in the local Italian restaurant a year or more earlier, *and WHEN we launch them, let's do it at the Royal Albert Hall! Let's start as we mean to go on* . . . For the first time, my blood ran cold. I felt as though I'd been fucked over, good and proper.

CHAPTER 20

Ewshot Hall

In the four short years since that year-long exile finished, we had not only managed to recover from financial meltdown, but through a succession of deals and hits had sorted out the financials of our Bayswater home with Citibank and added to our portfolio a beautiful eleven-bedroom Victorian country house in 20 acres of land on the Surrey-Hampshire borders. Having decided to 'choose our motorway' before shopping for the country house, we chose the M3 because I was born in Hampshire and it always feels like coming home to be driving south. I do believe there is a bit of the homing pigeon in all of us. Years earlier, Julianne had noticed that when we would take occasional weekend breaks in the country, I would apparently visibly relax when we crossed the Hampshire county border!

I had always said to Julianne that I fancied the idea of an old red-brick English house when we were older. Maybe I had grandiose ideas (grandiose, moi?) and saw myself as a Churchillian figure painting watercolours in the garden with a smock and a straw hat. I had meant when we were *much* older, as in our eighties and nineties, but the chance came earlier.

THE CLOSEST THING TO CRAZY

No sooner had the brochure for the property popped through our London letterbox, I knew I had found the perfect country home. The brochure had spoken to me but the house spoke even louder. You know that feeling when you walk into a house and it just speaks to you? It was that. As soon as I stepped over the threshold, I could see across the hallway through the open door of the dining room and out across about 50 miles of Hampshire countryside. It was everything I could do to stop myself from saying 'we'll take it' at that very moment.

The couple selling it were delightful – English, rather frail, but absolutely solid people. The place was in such disrepair and so big that they had retreated to the dining room and were living there to save on heating. It was sad to see the wheel of age turning. Once they had been the pillars of the local community, hosting the village gymkhana on the lower field and presenting the prizes. The local farmer later told me that Princess Anne had met Captain Mark Phillips at the Tweseldown Ball that had apparently always been held at the property. I wasn't at all sure that I believed it!

I made an offer for the full asking price. The next day I had a call from the estate agent. Their clients had decided to accept the offer. I was delighted.

We were to spend the next twenty years at Ewshot. After a year of rigorous renovations, adding bathrooms, a new roof, wiring the downstairs rooms for sound and converting the vegetable preparation rooms into a studio control room, we moved my two assistants into an office on the ground floor and life progressed. We kept the London place and became the best of friends with the M3. Our kids were still at school in London so at first we would spend the weekdays in London and weekends in Ewshot Hall.

EWSHOT HALL

The move to Ewshot occurred when I was scoring and recording the *Watership Down* album for the new TV adaptation. I was sitting at my piano in the drawing room one day, looking out across the breathtaking view. It seemed the perfect inspiration for a song for my *Watership Down* TV score. It is one of my lesser-known, but most cherished songs:

> Like the view from a hill, I can see you and me
> Like the view from a hill, it's so easy to see
> Here's where we belong, I feel it so strong
> And I see it so clear,
> As I always will;
> Like the view from a hill.
>
> Like a bird in the sky, I can see us below
> As it all passes by, I believe that I know
> This feeling of love, seen from above
> Goes on and on
> And it always will
> Like the view from a hill.

Not long after moving into Ewshot, I lost a bit of money on a TV-advertised Womble compilation, which left me with some cash-flow difficulties. People think that when you gain a degree of fame or success you must always be rich and secure. Some are. Characteristically, I sometimes sail a bit close to the wind financially and the new burden of acquiring and renovating Ewshot, combined with losing £700,000 on a Wombles TV campaign, was taking its toll. I decided I would create a new band. Just as I had conceived Bond,

THE CLOSEST THING TO CRAZY

I would conceive another act to allow me to compose and have fun in the area of pop/classical crossover.

I decided I would use Ewshot Hall as a base for a documentary about the creation of the band. Comprising four girls and four boys, the Planets would be the 'S Club 8' of classical music! I held extensive auditions, all of which were filmed. But how could I pay for the project without crippling myself financially? Get a major label involved.

With the Vanessa-Mae album and my own classical work, I was gaining a reputation as a go-to crossover composer and producer. While I try to resist identities that can be misconstrued or restrictive, sometimes it can have its benefits. EMI Classics were the perfect target as a partner for my ambitious project. I had lunch with the label's president, Richard Lyttleton, and told him about my plan. I hadn't quite got everybody auditioned yet, but when I had, and when we had the band ready to listen to, he would be the first to know.

With the eight chosen band members staying at the big house, we began shooting the documentary, filming rehearsals as we got ready to record the album. I was furiously writing arrangements. The whole point of having eight players was to enable them to play live without any sort of backing track or additional rhythm section. It would have been easier and cheaper to have had a smaller band, but I like the ethos of everything being live. So our percussionist had to be a brilliant classical percussionist but also very handy on drum kit.

Michael Kruk turned out to be just that. He ticked another unspoken box – he was like a younger, better-looking version of George Clooney! Beverley Jones, our bassist, had to brush up on bass guitar despite being a brilliant double bass player. All eight members were

EWSHOT HALL

virtuosi. They were post-conservatoire, classical players, all aged twenty-three or thereabouts, and they all looked fantastic. As with Bond, finding a first violinist was the biggest problem. Three auditionees decided it wasn't for them after we'd started filming – and in one case after shooting the album cover – but we parachuted Jonathan Hill in halfway through the process and he replaced all the other violinists' work on the tracks.

Julianne was, and has always been, brilliant with clothes and recruiting the right make-up artist and stylist or just taking bands and artists shopping. So, as always with our acts, and being an actress herself, she became involved as a kind of stagecraft/styling 'auntie'.

Once we felt the band were ready for presentation to labels, having filmed them at every stage, I kept my promise and invited EMI president Richard Lyttleton and his senior team (managing director Barry McCann and international marketing director Theo Lapp) to see the band perform in the big drawing room studio followed by dinner at the house with the band afterwards. The band played superbly for the three executives and then we all moved to the dining room where wine and conversation flowed, an atmosphere of celebration and positivity prevailed and, frankly, my new protégés charmed the pants off the EMI folks (not literally, I hasten to add!). The next morning, Richard and I agreed on a substantial deal to cover the cost of all the recording and pay the band for the contract period. This was the chance for EMI to have another Vanessa-Mae-style act on their label, and an exciting prospect for me.

Having eight people in a band is a bit like herding classical cats! Sometimes I felt like the teacher in the *Beano* comic with the Bash Street Kids, but we did have some good times together and made some musical sparks fly. It was an exhilarating time. We all lived together in the house and filming happened most days. Rehearsals, meal times, meetings at EMI Classics ... we captured everything that moved.

We had set a date for the launch – as is my habit – before even writing much of the material. A date for the album to be delivered. A date for live rehearsals to begin at the local Territorial Army drill hall, all ready for a concert on 13 September 2001 at the Royal Festival Hall. (*Not* the Royal Albert Hall – who on earth would choose to go *there?*) We also set a shoot date for the first video. This would occur before the concert so that by the time of the launch concert we could have the single and the video ready. I had chosen a spectacular monastery location up high in the rocks, thousands of feet above a winding river in the mountains of Segovia. I would be directing the video and a young producer called Alex was setting it all up for me, sourcing the location, the crane, the crew, the casting of extras, travel arrangements and costumes.

The shoot was to be across two days and two locations. The first day would be at the magical monastery and the second day at a beautiful Spanish village, where we would also sleep. This meant we had to commute from the village to the location, a matter of about an hour's drive through mountain roads.

We all flew out according to plan and were billeted in the rustic Spanish village, where we had a lovely evening dinner in the only restaurant there. There was an anticipatory, excited atmosphere. Everybody got to bed early because shooting needed to start as soon as the sun rose the next day. The substantial crew and crane company went out there at about 5 a.m., Julianne and the costume/make-up team left in another vehicle at 5.45 a.m., and at 6 a.m., another people carrier departed, carrying myself, Roger the cameraman and Salima the oboist, who was needed for the first shot. The band would follow an hour or so later. We were being driven by a young girl who had been hired as a runner. It was still pitch black at 6 a.m. All of us later said we felt she'd been driving too fast but we just hadn't liked to say anything.

I looked up from my seat in the rearmost section of the people carrier. I'd been fiddling with a cap they'd all given me the night before, with sticky gold letters attached, and was trying to make different words out of the letters. I looked up and, to my horror, in that slow-motion mode they say you go into in a critical emergency, I could see that our driver had tried to turn off to a right-hand fork, only to realise it wasn't the fork she wanted. She had swung the wheel to try to get back onto the left-hand bend of the mountain road but not quite made it. Here we were at 60 mph, heading either over the cliff or into a concrete block that we could see in the headlights. Either way, I expected to die. We hit the block violently and my neck was broken. The details of the moment have been described earlier, but suffice to say this was a dramatic and catastrophic turn of events that literally stopped us in our tracks. The shoot was cancelled and everybody had to go home. It was a horrible experience for us all. I was eventually moved to a hospital in Madrid.

After a week in Madrid, where a very fine neurosurgeon screwed the halo brace into my skull, I was taken by air ambulance back to the UK, landing at RAF Northolt. From there I was ambulanced to the Wellington Hospital and placed under the care of top neurosurgeon Mr Neil Dorward, who didn't look old enough to have A-levels. He looked after me very well and I was visited by quite a few concerned friends. Also concerned, not unnaturally, were EMI and the band members.

THE CLOSEST THING TO CRAZY

When it was safe to return home, we had a special hospital bed installed at Ewshot and at night I would sleep sitting up so as not to put too much pressure on my skull.

Mr Dorward had said, to reassure me, that as long as the brace was tight, albeit painful, I could walk around and do relatively normal things. The brace, which I would have to wear 24/7 for four months, prevented my neck from moving at all, so all movement had to come from the waist. I asked whether I could go to Spain, to which he said yes, perhaps thinking I meant a quiet holiday. But we still had a video to make. I had been able to persuade all the Spanish crew and villagers that we could shoot in two weeks' time – the exact same location, the same video we would have made. The band members recorded interviews for our documentary expressing their astonishment that this was still happening, and that I had announced to them that the original timetable would not be disrupted by the seemingly insurmountable circumstances.

I was in a lot of pain, but could still walk and talk. Roger the cameraman nobly said he thought he would be able to come too, despite his two punctured lungs. Salima, our oboist, gamely agreed to carry on, although she was still being treated for her injuries. And so, two weeks later, we were back in Segovia. Roger was walking with a stick and we had a qualified doctor and nurse with us at all times. There is some hilarious footage of me directing a moving shot on top of the mountain while gingerly running along a cliff edge, followed immediately by a Steadicam team, an assistant with a bottle of water, the doctor and the nurse. Somehow we got the video finished and delivered without changing our original release date.

When we began the rehearsals for the Festival Hall launch in the Territorial Army hall, I was of course still in the halo frame.

The band had to get used to performing what has to be loosely described as 'choreography', moving around the stage and into various playing formations to create a more entertaining experience than a static classical look. Initially there was an air of resistance until they became used to the idea of performing as a unit rather than sitting on chairs, orchestra-style. Once it was perfected, thanks to much stagecraft teaching from Julianne and expert friends of hers, we soon found ourselves rehearsing at the Royal Festival Hall on 11 September 2001, the day before the concert.

We were backstage when the first plane flew into the World Trade Center. And then another one. Glued to the TV in the green room, we didn't get much rehearsing done that day. Everyone stood around in disbelief, watching events develop in New York. Somehow, in our state of shock, we had to tear ourselves away so as to be able to walk through the set and do a soundcheck. In two days' time we would present the Planets to the world.

A One-Minute Silence

Apart from the horror of the situation and sympathy for those killed or otherwise involved, of course none of us knew whether the attack on the World Trade Center had been a one-off or the beginning of an entire plan involving attacks on other major cities – London, for example. There were obviously far more important reasons for being anxious, but that didn't stop us from having our smaller-scale, selfish concerns as to whether people would turn out for our concert in two days' time. But they did: the place was packed.

I made a short, welcoming speech, thanking people for coming out under the shocking circumstances. Saddled as I was with my halo brace contraption, I must have looked an odd sight. I also asked for a one-minute silence in remembrance of those who had perished in the terrorist attack in New York two days earlier. After that, I introduced the band, who came on and played a full-length set – virtuosic solos, pop-style production and all. It really was a stunning show. I was very proud of them. They looked – and sounded – amazing!

Jonathan Hill on violin and Ruth Miller on flute were striding about the stage, throwing shapes and trading intricate, daring licks, weaving counterpoints and harmonies in and around each other. Kruky (Michael Kruk) on drums and percussion underpinned a strong rhythm section comprising bassist Beverley Jones and our two classical guitarists, Ben Pugsley and Anne-Kathrin Schirmer. Salima Williams on oboe and Lac-Hong Phi, our phenomenal Vietnamese-Canadian cellist, made up the octet. The album was called *Classical Graffiti* and that night we launched it in style, without a single audio sample or playback aid.

Backstage afterwards, speeches were made, champagne flowed and there really was a feeling of elation, albeit tempered by the shadow of the previous days' events. I knew I hadn't let my EMI colleagues down and we had made the deadline despite Roger and Salima's injuries and my having sustained a potentially lethal broken neck. It was exhilarating!

There followed weekly marketing meetings at EMI Classics. Their offices were at 64 Baker Street, the former headquarters of Special Operations Executive in the Second World War, from where spies were sent out to be dropped behind enemy lines, often never to return. I felt their presence in every room and thought about the bravery of the men and women. What daring missions and secret deeds had been planned in those very spaces?

As we edged towards the album release date, the former espionage centre felt like a suitable location from which to cook up all sorts of stunts to try to compete with our rivals for media attention. We invited astronomer Sir Patrick Moore for dinner with the band at the Savoy and he cheerfully accepted. Afterwards, the Planets played a set in the Savoy restaurant, duly documented and photographed with Sir Patrick. We had them busking the queue at the London Planetarium on Marylebone Road and when I managed to get them hired as the support band for Deep Purple on a UK and European tour coinciding with the album release, EMI became very excited. Label MD Barry McCann and I planned a TV advertising campaign that would hopefully get us into the classical and even the mainstream charts.

A short time before the album release, I attended an appointment with Mr Dorward for him finally to remove the halo brace after all those months. It was a process that was both scary and liberating. My neck might have been healed, but I was still suffering from frequent involuntary flashbacks and a mental anguish about riding in cars that would take years to disappear.

Silence is Platinum

One aspect of the album's promotion that was particularly fun was the John Cage Affair. This started accidentally but once momentum started to build, it gave us massive exposure and we milked it for all it was worth, creating ripples of publicity that went right around the world.

It came about because, weeks earlier, Classic FM had said they loved the album. We had of course said we reciprocally loved their radio station and would like to advertise on it. They said they were

THE CLOSEST THING TO CRAZY

keen to pick the album as their album of the week, but there was one problem: the electric guitar. Many of the tracks featured Ben playing electric parts, with the other guitarist Anna sticking to her classical instrument. Classic FM's self-imposed programming rules forbade the existence of an electric guitar on their airwaves. They needed five tracks NOT to have electric guitar on them in order for it to qualify as album of the week, with one track played each morning.

As a result, I went back in the studio at Ewshot Hall with Ben and he replaced all of his raunchy guitar parts with a classical guitar. These tracks, which still sounded great, requiring no musical compromise, would be added to the running order *after* the other tracks, rather than replace the existing, electric tracks. But when I mastered the CD, to separate them completely from the album in its original intended form, I chose to insert one minute of silence after the original tracks and before the new acoustic versions. While mastering it, I said to the engineer, 'Why don't we give the silence a name? Let's call it "A One Minute Silence!"' This would stop people asking why the silence was there. Just in case there was any argument – or was it mischief on my part? *Possibly* . . .

I decided to credit the composers of the silence as Mike Batt/ Clint Cage, registering 'Clint Cage' as an official pseudonym with the Performing Rights Society (PRS). Each composer is officially allowed three PRS pseudonyms, I believe. EMI took it upon themselves to remove the first names, using just the last names, and that was how the label ended up with the composer titles 'Batt/ Cage'. This had the appearance to the uninitiated, of crediting, by implication, John Cage, who had famously 'written' a piece called '4'33"'. Hence my little joke. By claiming I had co-written the silence with myself under the pseudonym of Clint Cage, I was protecting myself from the comically unthinkable – a copyright claim from John Cage's estate.

The album came out on 7 January 2002 and was a phenomenal success. We had sold 150,000 copies and begun an uninterrupted run of three months at number one in the classical charts, when, one afternoon, I was sitting in the back garden at Ewshot, having lunch with my mum. My assistant appeared with an email from the Mechanical Copyright Protection Society saying that they were upholding a claim from John Cage's publishers, Peters Edition, for royalties on 'A One Minute Silence'. Once I'd realised they were serious, I started laughing almost uncontrollably. I explained it to my eighty-year-old mother, who rather wittily enquired, 'Which minute of their four minutes thirty-three seconds of silence do they say you have stolen?'

We had so much fun with this. It started with my speaking to Nicholas Riddle, the aptly named managing director of Peters Edition, and establishing that his claim was, to say the least, optimistic. Without admitting it, he good-naturedly agreed with me that whatever came of his claim, it would be educational to the world at large that copyright existed and was a serious matter but he was adamant that the claim stood because I had used Cage's name. I explained that my registration had been in the name 'Clint' Cage and no relation to John Cage – a pseudonym for myself.

I challenged him to a duel! We would meet at Baden-Powell House in South Kensington and the Planets would 'play' our 'A One Minute Silence' and then a young man from the offices of Peters Edition would 'play' the John Cage '4'33" Silence' on a clarinet. We set a date and invited the press, expecting a small turnout for a minor diary story.

THE CLOSEST THING TO CRAZY

In fact, three television crews, including *London Tonight*, plus several national newspapers turned up. The Planets came on in all their finery and as I silently conducted a printed but complicated succession of 7/8, 4/4 and 12/8 bars, all adding up to exactly a minute, they swayed attractively from side to side and uttered no sound. Then the clarinettist from Peters Edition got up and held the clarinet silently to his lips for exactly four minutes and thirty-three seconds. There was applause. Then there were questions. Nicholas Riddle, the performers and I all did interviews. We made it onto the national TV news and all over the press and the story went global.

After a couple of weeks, the fuss had died down and so in my efforts to spin the story out into another round of PR-generating excitement, I called Nicholas again. Assuring him that his case had no merit, I nevertheless agreed with him that the story also had value to both parties and the world as an example of the existence and importance of copyright. It was just spin really. With neither party admitting anything, I offered him an undisclosed sum (actually £1,000 to the John Cage Trust charity) as settlement out of court provided he accepted it in a sealed envelope on the steps of the High Court in front of the world's media. He thought this was a splendid idea and we duly met at the appointed place.

We both gave interviews, surrounded by the Planets. The press were goading Nicholas to reveal the amount of the settlement – 'Is it a four-figure sum?' No response. 'Is it five figures?' No reply. 'Is it six figures?' He looked over at me and I winked affirmatively. He nodded visibly to the press. This impromptu, implied white lie seemed to work. Next day the headline read 'Batt Pays Over £100,000 to Buy Silence'.

EWSHOT HALL

Again, the story went global. I was doing interviews for US radio stations, Al Jazeera TV and European newspapers. DJs would ring me on the air and tell me they'd made their own dub dance version of my silence. We would solemnly listen while they played it, silently. I maintained that my own silence was superior to Cage's silence because I had said in one minute what it had taken him four minutes and thirty-three seconds to say. Not only that, but my silence was digital and his was merely analogue. There was even an Oxford Union debate about it. I've always loved a story, but this one was a doozy! And it was (mostly) true.

Rather like Vanessa-Mae with her headline-grabbing video, the record would not have sold well had it not been good, and so it was with the Planets. If we hadn't made a really good album, it wouldn't have sold, however much we'd hyped it. The fact that we pulled every stunt we could to attract attention just made the album's journey into the charts all the more joyful, and indeed increased the profile of the band enormously. One of my proudest moments among all this activity – including the Deep Purple tour and wonderful headline Far East tour – was overseeing the band's appearance at the end of that year on the Classical BRITs TV show at, of all places, the Royal Albert Hall – the very place where I had seen Mel Bush launch 'our' Bond a couple of years earlier!

A second Planets album was considered, but partly because eight people don't always agree, and partly because their success was expensive for EMI (TV advertising was *not* cheap!), there was insufficient collective will and so they disbanded. It was a pity because they were all such fantastic players and it had been a tremendous experience. But there was also another deciding factor at play, towards the end of the Planets' success. I had decided that if

THE CLOSEST THING TO CRAZY

ever I were to manage another act, it would be a solo artist. There are so many reasons why. Firstly, in an eight-piece, they split royalties and advances eight ways, so no one gets rich. Then they have partners who may want them at home or they may leave. Replacing and training them up is an exhausting process and renders previous photography obsolete. Eight people still need feeding, clothing, grooming, etc. So we agreed to part ways with a smile but I'm pleased to say that I am still in touch with many of them to this day.

CHAPTER 21

Small Girl, Brown Hair

A year or two earlier, I had been taken to lunch by a promotion person, so that I could meet radio producer Paul Walters. I knew Paul vaguely but had never really met him properly. Paul was Terry Wogan's Radio 2 producer and – that rare thing – a Mike Batt fan! False modesty aside, we crazy, mixed-up ex-Womble multi-taskers need all the adoration we can get. Paul knew his music – and better still, he knew *my* music. His knowledge of my catalogue was phenomenal. He seemed to know every B-side for which I'd ever done a brass arrangement and every hit or flop single I'd ever had as an artist. I knew the Wogan show sometimes played some of my more UK-obscure European hits like 'Lady of the Dawn' and 'Railway Hotel', and it felt good occasionally to hear them on the UK's biggest radio show.

Shortly after meeting Paul, who incidentally was one of the nicest music people I've ever met, Julianne and I were listening to Eva Cassidy's big hit 'Over the Rainbow' on the car radio and marvelling at how it could be broken by one show: Wogan. With *some* help from Michael Parkinson, but essentially by Paul Walters, who chose all the records for Terry. In a world where tempo and a strong beat were usually the first two priorities for radio producers terrified that their audience will switch over, slow, meaningful records were so hard to break.

It was Julianne who said to me, 'You know who the most powerful person in the music business is, don't you?' As Eva Cassidy's record was playing at the time, I kind of knew what the answer was. The thing about Paul Walters was that he had complete autonomy and did not have to answer to the BBC Radio 2 playlist committee. Incidentally, for those who don't know, the radio presenters on daytime radio have almost no say (and sometimes not much interest) in what records are played. There are notable exceptions. But generally, the producer (or playlist committee) picks what to play.

I knew I had a powerful ally in Paul, who would be key to my breaking an act on Wogan – I just didn't *have* that act. The Planets had been fun, and good for flexing my compositional and arranging muscles, but as a songwriter, I needed someone with a special voice. Someone younger than me who could sing and sell my songs, rather than wait for established artists to cover them. I needed to 'create' a solo artist in the same way that I had created the Planets (or the Wombles for that matter). Of course, with a solo artist you don't really 'create' them so much as find them, encourage them, work with them and, as with anything else, put every ounce of energy and resource behind them that you possibly can. *Commit* to them. But the first thing I needed to look for was the artist. Where could I find one to whom I could commit the next few years of my life?

I began by holding casual auditions at music academies like the Academy of Contemporary Music (ACM) in Guildford and BIMM Institute in Brighton – places where people went to learn to be pop

SMALL GIRL, BROWN HAIR

stars, songwriters and producers. I was looking for a *great* singer. Male or female, it didn't matter. Finally, I decided to try the BRIT School, the Croydon college that had been established by the British Phonographic Industry (BPI), the organisation that represents the interests of UK record companies. No artist had yet broken from the BRIT School, but it was a hive of youthful ambition and activity.

I rang them and they suggested I put a notice on their board and they set up an audition for me. The note actually said I was looking for a singer 'in the style of Eva Cassidy'. On the day of the auditions, I took with me my sound engineer, Steve Sale, and we sat at one end of the room. About thirty students came in, one at a time, to play and sing. Katie Melua was about number fifteen into the room. She sang a song called 'Faraway Voice', which she said was about Eva Cassidy. She presented very casually: no make-up, hair pinned back. I wrote on my notepad 'small girl, brown hair, sang own song'. I wasn't blown away, but I was intrigued.

The next day, I rang Arthur Boulton, the teacher at the BRIT School who had organised the auditions, and I asked if I could see Katie again, this time at my London home, and could she bring a parent or guardian? Katie and her mum came to my place the next afternoon. We chatted and played a few more songs, one or two of mine, one or two of hers. Katie and her mum told me their story. Katie had been brought up in war-torn Georgia, from where they had been able to escape in 1992, just after the dissolution of the Soviet Union, when she was eight, and her heart surgeon dad had been able to get a job in Northern Ireland, just off the Falls Road. From there, they had moved to Redhill in Surrey, where her dad was now re-training as a GP and Katie was a straight-A* student, who had won a place at the BRIT School.

THE CLOSEST THING TO CRAZY

We agreed to have a piano and vocal session in my studio at Ewshot Hall. I decided to be neutral about material and chose 'September Song' by Kurt Weill. Katie picked it up easily and I laid down a quick piano track. She went into the room in the house where we did vocals and started singing. I was in the control room with engineer Steve. After she ran through the song I suggested maybe she could embellish a certain part of it. I was kicking the tyres a bit to see how she thought musically, not just what her voice was like. We ran the track. When it got to the bit she needed to embellish, she came out with something I'd never heard before and I don't think she had either. But it was so 'right', so original. It wasn't 'twiddle #326 from the *X Factor* book of vocal embellishments'. I burst out laughing. Not laughs of derision, but of delight that someone so new and untutored could find something so natural and original. *Now* I was blown away. I really thought at that moment: This girl could be a star. Just from that one twiddle. I signed Katie to my newly formed production company, Dramatico.

I had in mind an album with a retro, jazzy-lounge style but also with blues roots, and had a song of my own in mind, similar to 'September Song': 'Call Off the Search'. Katie had ambitions as a writer so it would have been unfair to stomp on those ambitions and just present my own songs, but she knew that her own material might not fit the kind of album I was planning. Her songs – like a lot of my own catalogue material – had a kind of folky quality and so by the time we started working, a style was emerging which was a mixture of all of the above. The big selling point was of course her amazing voice. Something to do with her Georgian heritage, perhaps, but she had a depth of vocal intelligence and breath control that you can't teach. She didn't even think about breathing technique; it was just there. I've known her sing one line of a verse, not take a breath and drop straight into the next line; then, if it suited her, she'd defy science and just glide right into the third line without breathing, like a bird floating on a warm current of air.

We spent several months developing her own material alongside mine. She knew the assignment was originally meant to be to make an album of my own songs but I also realised that there now needed to be a compromise and that she was worth it as an artist. I knew there was a lot of pressure on BRIT School students to be writers and Katie was feeling that. Until shortly before we'd met, she'd been doing what her 'cool' BRIT School pals were doing – synth and loop-based pop songs. Often about strange subjects.

I often take the role of a 'song doctor' with the artists I work with, and being in my mid-fifties at the time, I felt old enough and experienced enough to play that kind of professorial role, which was kind of how our relationship was. I pointed out to her that of the first six songs she brought me, they included one murder and two suicides! I did like 'Faraway Voice' – the song she played me at the audition – and yet I felt it needed a middle eight. She promptly wrote one and brought it back to me: it was just right.

We cut about five or six tracks and shot some video footage for an introductory EPK (electronic press kit, really just a video about the artist). The first day, we had brought a camera in and, after the attention of stylist and the make-up and hair squad, Katie looked down the barrel of the camera and the camera nearly fainted. She was a totally photogenic natural. She literally shone when seen through a lens. Not all beautiful people do. There are times in life when you *know* you have a gold-plated, irrefutable success on the cards. You *know* you aren't kidding yourself or anyone else. You just *know*.

THE CLOSEST THING TO CRAZY

Armed with the EPK and a few songs, I started setting up meetings around the industry. Brian Yates, MD at Sony Special Projects, with whom I'd worked on stuff like Wombles revivals, had always grumbled to me that I never brought him any new projects. 'That's because you run the special catalogue marketing division, Brian!' was my answer. But I thought, *Why not? He's a friend.* So I asked him over to my London place, showed him the EPK and then, da-daah, introduced Katie, who had been secretly waiting in the next room. Her forte was playing live and she did, right there in the room. No nerves, just a cool performance with guitar. It was totally captivating. Brian loved her. He organised a meeting a few days later with his colleagues at Sony, including UK chairman Rob Stringer and my unspoken nemesis, head of A&R Muff Winwood. About eight of us in a small conference room. She played, she shone, they fell in love.

Around that time, I also made an appointment with Costa Pilavachi at Universal (the guy who had told me he'd signed the Bond string quartet a few years earlier). A very cultured, personable and smart man, he came down to Ewshot Hall for lunch and a performance from Katie. He wanted the UK classical company to buy in but he was too senior, as international president of Classics and Jazz, to sign an act. He needed the UK company to buy into it. Enter my old mate Bill Holland, the UK Classics MD, fondly known as 'Champagne Bill' because of his habit of lavishly entertaining classical artists. Bill was a lovely, modest, polite guy, but he just didn't see it. He liked Katie, he had always said he wanted an opportunity to work with me, but he didn't get the songs, so Universal passed.

This left me with my on-and-off, bittersweet life partners, Sony. I knew Muff was not a fan of mine but he was the tastemaker-in-chief at Sony and he thought Katie was great. Chairman Rob Stringer and I worked out a deal: £500,000 for an album and a good percentage. In 2002, that was serious commitment. The songs we had at that stage were 'Call Off the Search', 'The Closest Thing to Crazy', 'Tiger in the Night', 'Faraway Voice' and 'Blame It on the Moon'. As we moved closer towards contract signature, I sensed something. Either it was a passing remark or just a feeling, but it led me to ask Muff directly if he wanted Katie and me to record this actual selection of songs once we had signed the contract. Unable to escape from giving a straight answer, he said, 'Well, I love Katie. But not with these songs.'

Good job I asked! I wonder why you didn't say that before? I thought to myself, but didn't say. I also had an inkling that he might also try to remove me as producer once we had signed so I went back to Katie and told her this. She was very alarmed. Not just that I had had to wring it out of Muff to get a straight answer, but also because she was very attached to the songs by then – 'Blame It on the Moon' was her mum's favourite.

Turning down half a million quid wouldn't be an easy decision for anyone, but for Katie, it was huge. She asked me what alternatives we had.

'Well, we could record it here at Ewshot Hall. I could pay for it and release it on my label, Dramatico, which has never released a record before but there's always a first time!' I said optimistically.

Without hesitation, she said she would prefer to do it that way.

Goodbye, half a million pounds. Hello, integrity.

This is the closest thing to crazy I have ever been
Feeling twenty-two, acting seventeen;
This is the nearest thing to crazy I have ever known

THE CLOSEST THING TO CRAZY

I was never crazy on my own,
But now I know that there's a link between the two;
Being close to craziness and being close to you.

We made the album. It was a joy. The band would come down to the house and stay overnight, which gave us a couple of days' recording time. Then we'd break off and reconvene for another visit a few days later. It didn't take long to lay the tracks.

The band comprised my then favourite bass player Tim Harries, drummer Henry Spinetti, who had been with Procol Harum and regularly worked with Eric Clapton, guitarist Jim Cregan, my close friend who had joined us so many years earlier on *Braemar*'s Atlantic crossing, and my lifetime guitar-stalwart, Chris Spedding. I directed the sessions from the piano. We were all positioned around the house, with Henry on drums in the hallway, most of us others in the huge drawing room, screened off from each other, and Katie in what we politely called the 'vestibule' – the coat-hanging room next to the toilet. The control room was right down the other end of the house. We were connected by headphones and microphones; talking and discussing the parts, very laid-back, stretching out, but totally focused when we were actually recording. The musical intimacy felt so good. We would cut at least four or five tracks a day, often breaking for dinner if the session ran later. It was an idyllic way to record. Katie sang a guide vocal to each take from her 'vestibule' position and at least a couple of her supposed guide vocals were kept as final, they were that good. This is the way we would eventually record all but one of the six of the albums we would go on to make together.

I had lunch with Paul Walters as I had got to know him quite well by then. I had never ever 'plugged' him, but this time was different.

I gave him a CD of the album, saying, 'Let me know what you think of this.' I added, 'By the way, we are probably leaving out "The Closest Thing to Crazy" because it'll be too slow for you guys to play. Just so you know.'

By the time I got back to my office there was an email from Paul waiting for me, saying, 'If you drop "The Closest Thing to Crazy" from the album I'll never speak to you again!'

The song received its first play on Terry Wogan's Radio 2 breakfast show a week or so later, just before the 8 a.m. news. Paul knew how to put a record in front of his radio audience. I hadn't begged him, I hadn't even really asked him – he just played it. Every week, twice a week, always just before or just after the 8 or 9 a.m. news. Paul's mailbag was jumping with reactions, all positive. He told us that he had a rule of thumb: for every one email or letter he received, there were a thousand or so other listeners who felt the same but hadn't chosen to write to him. For this record, had thousands of actual emails and letters.

I had literally 'gone shopping' for an artist that Paul Walters would like and it had worked! The only thing was, I didn't even have a distributor. Here I was, with serious radio play of an unreleased song on one of the most listened-to shows in Europe and I urgently needed a distribution deal. So I rang Steve Mason, who owned Pinnacle, the biggest Indie distributor in the UK. I was in Rome in a hotel, with Julianne on our summer holiday. He, too, was away on his holidays. But standing on the balcony of our room at the Hilton in Rome, overlooking the city, I struck a deal with him and suddenly Dramatico wasn't just a production company supplying labels with product (like the Planets to EMI), but a proper indie label with a distributor.

THE CLOSEST THING TO CRAZY

I only had three people in the office, but now we were a label.

What Katie Did Next

I often wonder what it must be like to step straight out of school into massive stardom and a number-one record. No three years in a scruffy white van playing the toilets circuit. No wishing someone would finance you, no making stupid TikTok videos until one clicks. No yearning. Just picked out while you are halfway through your A-levels and then suddenly, bang, you're there. A big star. I have to admit, in the nicest possible way, I'm a little envious of Katie for that.

Of course this was all still to come. Her song, 'The Closest Thing to Crazy', was on the radio, but still no one really knew who she was at this point. On a trip to New York, I signed her to the veteran agent Barbara Skydel at William Morris. On our first meeting with Barbara, she was so taken with Katie's 'look' – leather jacket, black jeans and ringletted hair – that she insisted we would be mad not to capture that look while in New York. While we were in her office, she picked up the phone to the late Andy Warhol's favourite photographer, Michael Halsband. An hour later we were in Michael's studio, a couple of blocks away. He took some shots in the street of Katie leaning against a bagel stand and some of her in the studio sitting on the floor with her guitar and a black background. From this session came the shot we would choose for the first album cover.

So we had radio play. We had an album cover. We had an album. I had organised a video shoot and additional stills photography for the CD booklet by top photographer Simon Fowler, all to be shot on the same day in the same venue, an old East End pub. I was directing the video as Simon was lighting each next set-up for the stills – I had to keep 'borrowing' Katie for a take of the video and then lending her back to Simon for stills while my lighting cameraman lit the next video scene. The stills were great for the CD booklet but nothing surpassed Michael Halsband's iconic cover shot. The video and all the booklet stills came in at less than £5,000. In those days that was ridiculous. People usually spent £30,000 to £50,000 on a video and £10K on a photo session. This was the famous video that we used in the TV commercial, with Katie in a blue singlet, moving into a new flat and falling back on the bed. I realised halfway through the shoot that we needed a 'boyfriend' for her, so I asked the on-set hairstylist Nick Peters to be the boyfriend. And then we needed two 'removal men' for a shot, so my assistant Pete Rutland and another crew member stepped in to complete the impromptu casting.

As we worked towards release, and knowing this was a make-or-break situation – disaster if it failed, massive paydirt if it worked – I set up three sit-down lunches in a private banqueting room at the Langham Hilton in London. Situated just over the road from the BBC, it gave producers no excuse for not attending. One of the lunches was for about twenty carefully selected radio folk, the second one was for TV and the third for press. Between each lunch course Katie performed one song with only her acoustic guitar. Her natural, relaxed ability to play without tension or fear and her easy conversational manner endeared her to a lot of the right people.

All this was of course costing me. Adding up the rhythm section, the orchestra, flights, the video shoot, the trip to the States, stylists, make-up, hair, the lunches, CD stock and monthly retainers to promo teams (in this case radio and TV pluggers Amanda Beel and Stuart Emery and press representative Sue Harris), it was all mounting up.

THE CLOSEST THING TO CRAZY

I was aware of the general wisdom regarding TV advertising: you only advertise on TV if the viewing audience already knows what the product is. So, *Eric Clapton's Greatest Hits*, for example, would be viable because everybody knows who Eric Clapton is. A TV commercial is too expensive and yet too short to introduce a new artist. Not long since, I had lost £700,000 on a Wombles TV advertising campaign, so I knew exactly what the hurt felt like. Nevertheless, I had always had a theory that *surely*, if done right, one *could* break an artist by advertising on TV, and I had that feeling about Katie. We had a song which was already sneaking into people's hearts on radio. Specifically, the Wogan listeners' hearts. A family audience, young and old. The way to them, I felt, was TV advertising – and preferably prime time.

So, Michael Dunne, our video editor, and I went into the edit room at Ewshot Hall and cut together a thirty-second TV commercial, the exact length of the chorus. I decided to put £50,000 into TV advertising on the first week of release. I'll tell you now, because it's not always obvious to people who think pop artists are rolling in it all the time, but it was the last £50,000 I had. I didn't make that known, even to my staff at the time. But it built confidence via Pinnacle, our distributors, when 'selling in' the album to the shops.

Back then, a CD would have cost about £13 at retail and Dramatico would receive about £8 per CD from the retailer. That's how big the shops' margin was! So, give or take, we would have to ship 6,250 copies to make our money back on a £50,000 TV spend. *And*, HMV, Woolworths and the other retailers were more likely to order if they knew we were advertising on TV. Particularly if we 'tagged' them in our commercials. One week it would be Woolworths, the next week WH Smith, etc. I'm working from memory but I'm guessing we would have gone out with about 10,000 pre-sales. But this was on sale-or-return, so it could all come rolling back later if it didn't fly off the shelves. I was completely invested in Katie. My belief was total. I felt, as her manager and principal songwriter, that whatever it cost to break her would be worthwhile because of the door it would open to the hopefully enduring success of our partnership.

On 3 November 2003, we released the album. Still with only two assistants, a book keeper and a studio engineer in my office at home. This was Dramatico Records. A tiny label. On chart day – 9 December – we were thrilled to see the album enter at number forty in the UK chart. At a celebratory lunch that week with Chris Maskery, sales director of Pinnacle Distribution, I was alarmed when he said, 'Don't be shocked when it drops twenty places next week, Mike.'

Maskery knew his stuff. He was on my side, but he reminded me that towards Christmas, the big artists were all releasing their albums. He knew for certain that twenty acts bigger than us would release the next week and our chart position would drop accordingly. Sure enough, the next week, despite continued TV ads, our chart position was down to number fifty-seven. It was hurting. Paul Walters was still playing the song twice a week on Wogan, bless him, and we'd had our Sunday Radio 1 Chart show 'New Entry' play by now, but the Radio 2 playlist committee had not yet adopted the record for general playlist support. To them, you either had Wogan or the other shows – not both. On the third week we were down to number seventy-one. It was like climbing a glacier with a blizzard in your face.

Because most people who loved the track already had it on the album, the single only made it to number ten in the UK charts, which was very good but not enough to tip the scales. Our press guru Sue Harris used that to get a piece in a national newspaper about how Katie might make it to Christmas number one. Of course, there was no chance of that, but it was good PR. Yet still, nobody knew what Katie looked like or how well she performed live. I *had* to get her on TV — that would be the decider. It might reverse the depressing plummeting-downward trend of the chart positions. But it was so hard to get on TV, with all the big acts in competition for the few spots available.

We got her a small TV show, something minor and local in Chiswick, west London. After the show, I went back to our Hyde Park Square home and agonised. I would either have to stop chucking money at it — money I didn't have — and wait until after Christmas when the competition was much weaker, or find another £150,000 for the TV advertising budget and blast us through Christmas with a middling chart position, hoping for some Christmas sales.

I made the decision: I would go for broke. Why change the habits of a lifetime? I would literally put all I had on one side of the roulette table and blast us, as best I could, through Christmas and, hopefully, out the other side.

Literally ten minutes after I'd made that decision, the phone rang. It was Jeff Thacker, producer of the *Royal Variety Performance* TV show. Jeff was an old friend, and had seen Katie perform at one of the media lunches I'd held. Although impressed by her, he had turned her down for the 'Royal', as it's known in the business. I was completely aware of this and had respected his decision.

'Hi, Mike, I've just rung to apologise for the bad news about Katie and the *Royal Variety*,' he said.

'Jeff, don't even think about it. I know you've said no and I know why. She's unknown, it's all fine,' I said.

'No,' he laughed. 'I'm apologising because you need to buy two plane tickets to Edinburgh and get her a new frock! Someone's dropped out of the show and we'd like Katie to step in.'

'You bastard!' I said, feeling the inner surge of joy.

The factor that had tipped Jeff over towards Katie as his replacement act had been the piece in the paper that Sue had obtained, spuriously rating her single as a potential Christmas number one.

I almost felt that this was divine providence resulting from my having made the decision to keep spending. My reward. Katie's reward. But now we had a national TV programme on 24 November 2002. Our hovering, low chart position, if supported by TV advertising and the *Royal Variety Performance*, would surely kick us higher, to catch the Christmas market just in time. Thanks to the *Royal Variety* show, Wogan and my TV spending, we were back up at number 34 on 23 December. What's more, in a casual conversation with Lucian Grainge (now Sir Lucian) – then chairman of Universal UK – he reminded me that sales in general, and consequently every major record company's TV spend, dropped by 90 per cent in January because logically it's madness to spend big on TV when everybody's exhausted and broke after Christmas. Of course, I took this as a cue to keep spending at the same high level after Christmas just to get chart position.

The album – *Call Off the Search* – made it to number one on 25 January 2003.

Call Off the Search kept on selling; partly, because it was a bloody good album and people out there really do know if something's good. Partly also because I kept advertising it on TV to maintain the sales and chart position. Why did it matter to me to maintain chart position? Because you got store visibility if you were high in the chart and without that, your position in the chart would keep dropping. Even so, you had to *buy* your store visibility by tagging the retailers in TV commercials and buying display areas and shelf space. Supermarkets and record stores had their own charts, but you had to give them big discounts, pay them actual money *and* tag the TV commercials or you didn't get in their charts and stay on their shelves. Stores would say, 'We'll take ten thousand units (on sale-or-return) and put you at number seven in our in-store chart if you buy an end-of-aisle display unit for £8,000 for one week'. There was a negotiation like that with every store chain, every week. We sold 1.8 million albums (six times platinum) in about nine months in the UK alone, with six weeks at number one, and broke Katie in some important European territories. It was such a thrilling, exhilarating time!

Katie was the first BRIT School artist to break. She and I had to put up with some nasty jibes from the likes of BRIT School alumnus Amy Winehouse before she was famous: 'Katie Melua doesn't need to write her own shit songs, she's got a manager to write shit songs for her.' That might have been about the time I took a dislike to Amy Winehouse! Katie never emulated anybody – she didn't even think about it, she just sang, and her voice was what it was: sublime. It did irk her inwardly that she was seen by the outside world as being produced by a 'Svengali' writer-producer and that it was the combination of my relentless marketing, belief in her as a singer and the strength of my songs that had made her successful and continued to grow her career. But what she was mainly feeling was joy at her success and relief that she could make her family comfortable financially and enjoy all of the good things about success.

CHAPTER 22

The Difficult Second Album

That much-used phrase 'The Difficult Second Album' is such a reality that it has become something of a well-known cliché. After breaking an artist – which is absolutely the hardest thing to do – *maintaining* the success is the next hardest thing to do. I was thinking about the second album from the day we first hit number one with the first.

In the interim, and while we planned album two, there had been a period of touring. I was part of the band in those days. It was a fantastic group with Jim Cregan on guitar, Henry Spinetti on drums, Dominic Glover on trumpet and Lisa Featherstone on upright bass. It was great to be going out with the band while still doing my best managing Katie using my BlackBerry handset, multi-tasking during soundchecks. We also launched Katie in the US after striking a distribution deal with Universal in early 2004, but after trying as hard as we did throughout our time with her, and spending a lot of effort and money, we would, sadly, fail to break her there significantly.

I had been writing on tour in 2004 and Katie and I did a bit together when we got home. Often she would play me a song, not as a collaborator but to see what I thought as a producer. Often I'd make a suggestion to change this or that. Perhaps just 'Try a raised melody in the second line to give it shape', general critique. But to me those were always her songs, I just helped a bit. We rarely collaborated as two 50/50 songwriters and I think we understood each other pretty well.

When promoting the first album internationally, in 2005 we went to China, where Katie sang 'The Closest Thing to Crazy' and I sang 'Bright Eyes' on a big TV show with an audience of 100 million. The lovely thing for me was that I was able to take my mum with us. After all she'd done for me in my life, from costumes to general inspiration, it was a great chance to enjoy an exotic trip together. The day after the show, we were treated to a private bus tour of Beijing, including a walk along part of the Great Wall of China. The interpreter-guide, standing at the front of the coach with a microphone, was telling us all about what we were seeing as we travelled through Beijing: the Emperor's Palace, the different-coloured red and grey roofs and what their significance was. She then said, after a few other facts, 'There are nine million bicycles in Beijing.' I turned to Katie and said, 'There's a song title!' and, thinking I was kidding, Katie chuckled, 'Yeah, right.'

The minute I got home again, I went straight to my piano and started fiddling about with ideas. I didn't want a comical song. It was one of the least important facts in the world . . . unless you happen to be a bicycle statistician in China. If the song could make that point it would become a serious song. Maybe I could juxtapose it with the most important statement in the world. What would be important? 'I will love you till I die'? That was a pretty important thing to say to someone. So I started thinking of other trivia, facts or questions you might expect to find in a quiz and then comparing it to other important measures of the depth of the love between the singer and the one being addressed. I often think 'I love you' songs are more powerful than 'He loves her' songs. Being written in the first person makes it so much more direct and personal. While fiddling with the lyric I was trying little 'feel' rhythms and melodic ideas on the piano and soon I had the shape of it.

The now well-known first verse went:

There are nine million bicycles in Beijing
That's a fact;
It's a thing we can't deny
Like the fact that I will love you till I die.

I played it to Katie and she was quite taken with it but had no idea whether we could pull it off as a band. We rehearsed it at the piano to get the exact right key for her – a semitone above or below can make so much difference – and then I set to, writing an arrangement involving the intro tune that ended up being played on an ocarina.

The band came down and settled in for a couple of days and we recorded in the usual way: residentially with a nice dinner and red wine, everybody sleeping over. Such a great, friendly way to record. Those are actually the times I miss most about Ewshot Hall and also about the ten years I spent working with Katie. Those idyllic sessions that just consisted of a band playing a track, with a guide vocal going down live and nothing pre-programmed. No tension to speak of. I do believe it reflected in the music organically – I can certainly hear it, anyway.

Album two, *Piece by Piece*, came out on 26 September 2005 after a seriously careful 'sell-in' to retail and a solid TV campaign. I edited

THE CLOSEST THING TO CRAZY

a sixty-second commercial for the album and asked our agency to get me a price for a national spot right in the middle of ITV's much-loved soap *Coronation Street*. When I was in my teens we used to work out studio costs in pints of Guinness. The cheapest studio was £8 per hour and Guinness was 2/6d a pint (8 pints per pound). So an hour of studio time was 64 pints of Guinness, which was pretty eye-watering! Later in life, we started talking about TV advertising costs in terms of Range Rovers. A single, sixty-second national spot (just one spot, one time) cost as much as three high-spec Range Rovers!

BBC Radio 2 had A-listed the single 'Nine Million Bicycles'. Pinnacle distribution had worked their magic and the sixty-second *Coronation Street* ad went out the day before the record went on sale. On the first midweek album chart and all through the week, we were at number one in the UK chart. In the final chart at the week's end, we'd made it. Our second number one! *Piece by Piece* breaking so big was for me the reward for enduring the imaginary recurring slow-motion video in my head of three Range Rovers driving off Beachy Head and smashing onto the rocks below.

Germany had similar success to the UK. But whereas our German office had done pretty well with album one, it did *spectacularly* well with album two. We sold a million CDs in Germany alone. Katie was suddenly internationally massive. Number one in Poland, Denmark, Norway, Holland. Three million records just in Continental Europe. At that point, she was the biggest-selling UK female artist in the *world*, despite not having broken in America.

Dramatico was expanding. We had opened an office in Germany in 2005, but a little later we also opened a US office at 1775 Broadway, one block away from Universal, our US distributors, at number 1755. We found a modest-sized but smart office suite of about 1,500 square feet and after a process of interviewing, I appointed Josh Zieman as president of Dramatico Inc. I guess it demonstrates, with hindsight, just how committed we were to breaking Katie in the States.

A year or so later I would buy a three-bedroom apartment at 1 Central Park West, just on the corner of Columbus Circle, overlooking the entire acreage of Central Park. A peaceful haven in a busy city. The memory of our visits there are cherished in our family and being there in person did make running the US company a hell of a lot easier – we felt like New Yorkers. And while we were determined to break Katie there, sadly, as I've said, it just never happened.

As a record label the artist roster grew to include a wide variety of international acts, including Carla Bruni, Gurrumul, Caro Emerald and Sarah Blasko and baritone Robert Meadmore, among others. With Katie, Dramatico was not only her label but also her management, so a large amount of the company's resources and staff was dedicated to her career. We dealt with her extensive touring down to the very last detail. I art-directed all her Dramatico albums and directed most of the videos for her records. On a more private and personal level, often with the help of our wise and experienced PR, Sue Harris, we protected her from any potentially negative publicity and looked after her pastoral well-being.

By the third album, *Pictures* (2007), Katie was well and truly established as a massive international artist. Stylistically, I knew she was sensitive to being perceived as a middle-of-the-road act. I hate the term, which denotes generality and easy-listening, even blandness. But Beethoven could be described as easy-listening; Joni Mitchell and Paul Simon, too – I don't personally see the problem with music that's easy to listen to. However, I knew Katie wanted to be seen as 'poppier' in the badass, BRIT School sense.

Pictures was a very good album but a touch confused, not fully maintaining our trademark 'cool', jazz-based groove. The lead single was my own song, 'If You Were a Sailboat' – later covered by Prince – and it got plenty of attention. *Pictures* went straight in at number two in the UK charts on 13 October 2007 – a great position, but not number one. I had suggested during the making of this third album that on album four I would step back from writing and producing in order to give Katie more artistic freedom. Therefore, I was slightly professionally miffed with her for making the – frankly – foolish mistake of announcing that fact to Neil McCormick of the *Telegraph* in her first launch interview for *Pictures*. You don't announce, before you've even released your third album, that its producer, and your mentor and guide, will not be producing album four. So this became the focal point of the *Telegraph* article rather than how wonderful album three was. Was there something wrong with it, then? Something wrong with *me*?

One other significant 'wrong' thing that happened was that the advertising agency who bought our media for us had persuaded me that if I paid up front for the UK TV advertising, I would get a lot more value. Many more Range Rovers' worth of screen time but for Ford Fiesta money! I fell for it and before the record was even released, wrote them a cheque for the full £800,000 I had budgeted for the campaign. The thing about TV advertising is that if you are Sony or Universal, and a TV-advertised album isn't performing, you simply switch your bulk-spend to another artist or artists. In our case, with only one TV advertisable artist, we couldn't cancel or re-direct the TV spend if we didn't sell the records: it just went straight to our bottom line and couldn't be unspent.

THE DIFFICULT SECOND ALBUM

The album did do well, certainly over a couple of million copies. Just not quite as well as the others. But my advertising error damaged the trading position of the company and gave us a cash-flow problem for a while. Looking back, with 20:20 hindsight, this was the first crack that would lead eventually to Dramatico's decline.

Pictures would be the last of the three 'big' Katie albums.

Prince

During the sessions for *Pictures*, we had a call from Prince's tour manager, asking if Katie would like to perform a duet of 'Nine Million Bicycles' with him *that evening* at a big private function in London. We were in the middle of recording a track with the band, who would be staying overnight for more recording the following day, but decided this was an opportunity not to be missed. Having rather expensively given the band the afternoon and evening off, we duly appeared backstage a couple of hours later, Katie clutching her acoustic guitar and me in my management role. We were greeted cordially by Maya and Nandy, Prince's two fantastic backing dancer/singers, who I had recently met on a promo trip to Los Angeles and who told us that Prince often played 'Nine Million Bicycles' and 'The Closest Thing to Crazy' on stage.

As we were talking, Prince appeared and joined our group. A strikingly small man with an unsurprisingly charismatic presence. After chatting affably for a while, he casually announced that he'd changed his mind: Katie *wasn't* going to be invited to duet with him but we were welcome to stay and watch the show. He also asked if Katie would like to 'hang' with him after the show. She declined. To say we were crestfallen would be an understatement but I bit my tongue and we duly stayed and watched the incredible show, in

THE CLOSEST THING TO CRAZY

which he did an amazing version of 'Nine Million Bicycles' but with Maya and Nandy providing backup vocals.

I don't know what it was about my songs that so much attracted Prince. Obviously he had become a Katie Melua fan, so that must have led him to the material. But to be doing two of them on stage was a great surprise that gave me an enormous psychological boost. More heady still was the day, some time after the release of *Pictures*, when he called me up at home.

'Hey, man, I love your song "If You Were a Sailboat", but it's got girl-centric lyrics. Can I change a couple of words? Would that be cool?'

He was ultra laid-back but very polite and I was impressed by his courtesy – most artists would just change the words and not tell you. He wanted to change the line 'If you were a cowboy, I would trail you' to 'If you were a gypsy, I would trail you'. That was it.

Of course I agreed. I was delighted to have him perform my song.

About a week later, his office sent me an mp3 of the track. It sounded fantastic. He'd made the lyric changes and added a really cool beat to it. What I didn't notice in my excitement was that he'd snuck another word change in. Where I had written 'If you were a preacher, I'd begin to change my ways', he'd substituted 'If you were a witness, I'd begin to change my ways'. I'd forgotten he was a Jehovah's Witness. Not that it mattered, of course.

Sadly, Prince died before the song could ever be released. A great loss of an insanely talented musician. He was only fifty-seven. About a year later, I posted the song online, but I received a 'cease and desist' letter from the lawyers of the Prince estate so I promptly and obediently took it down. I have a feeling someone might have reposted it but, whatever the situation, I really hope one day his estate will release the song – it's a great version.

CHAPTER 23

The House and the Palace

Usually an artist would make an album every two years – touring the previous album for a year, then making the next one in the second year. Katie's fourth album took far too long to write and make, and that essential momentum was lost.

With me standing aside as writer-producer, I suggested to Katie that T Bone Burnett might be a good choice as producer and writing coordinator for album four. T Bone had just had an enormous success with the Robert Plant and Alison Krauss album *Raising Sand* (2007) and he had a cool profile that I thought might work for Katie. She loved the idea so I got in touch with T Bone and we went over to meet him in LA at the Beverly Wilshire hotel. T Bone had set up writing sessions for Katie with some of his writer friends. There were several more writing trips to LA and Katie wrote with various people T Bone teamed her up with, but none of the demos really cut it. There came a point when she and I realised two years had already passed, but we had no songs. T Bone was quite understanding about it and we agreed to part ways.

This left us at the beginning of 2010 with no new album and we needed one by the year end. I suggested to Katie that we try to organise writing sessions with some writers in the UK who were very strong potential partners. I asked Guy Chambers if he'd like to write a couple of songs with Katie. He agreed straight away and altogether they wrote five songs, all of which ended up on the fourth album. The best of these, commercially at least, was a three-way co-write with Lauren Christy called 'The Flood'. Two more songs came from a session with seasoned hit songwriter Rick Nowels. Suddenly it seemed we had a collection of songs but still no producer.

I was on my own in the kitchen at Ewshot Hall one weekend when I had an idea: what about William Orbit? Was he still producing? He was a cool cat. His success with Madonna had been immense and he had that experimental, edgy streak that I knew Katie would so much appreciate. I didn't know William personally but tracked down a number and gave him a call. He was delightful – he said he was flattered, but he just wasn't sure. He sounded reticent, even a bit nervous; he'd been away from the coal face for a while and wasn't sure he was ready to re-engage.

I said, 'Shall I send you the songs anyway?'

He agreed to listen, and only an hour or so after I sent the songs over he was back on the phone. He loved them, he loved Katie – he was just a bit unsure about his own readiness to go back into the studio. He also knew we were in a hurry. Even if we went like the clappers, there would still be a three-year gap between albums. Where would we get the musicians? What studios would we use? I said I would be happy to do all the heavy lifting preparing the sessions; I suggested we could use Katie's usual session band and that I could try to book a block of time at AIR Studio 1.

This was attractive to William because it took the pain out of the whole thing. We already had the songs, the studio and the musicians.

THE HOUSE AND THE PALACE

Of course, he needed to meet with Katie and see how they got along. But I knew – they were perfectly matched.

As the mixes started to come through, I was thrilled. Thrilled we had an album at all! The songs were a million miles away from albums one to three in style, but 'The Flood', a dramatic power ballad, sounded like a hit. Sadly, great though it was, 'The Flood' only made it to number thirty-five in the singles charts. *The House*, however, made it to number four in the album charts. Alas, it was not appealing to Katie's solid fanbase so it didn't stay long in the charts despite selling a few hundred thousand copies worldwide. Where previous albums had gone platinum or multiple platinum, this one only made gold in the UK. These days, with streaming, you'd kill to sell a few hundred thousand records, but that fourth album marked the mass exodus of Katie's fanbase, even though our TV advertising campaign was as ballsy as always.

Even though we would go on to make two more albums with me once again at the production helm, we never got Katie back to the sales of the first glorious three albums. Once you lose the trust of your fanbase it's hard to get them back. And three years – in our case – between albums had been too long a wait. Altogether, in the ten years of my professional relationship with Katie Melua, we spent over £10 million on TV advertising in the UK alone and we sold 11 million records worldwide. The only way to sell Katie's records in sufficient numbers was by TV advertising, and for those albums, *Secret Symphony* and *Ketevan*, we kept on doing it.

Touring – particularly a *big* tour taking in the whole of Europe – remained an artistic joy and by this time we were touring with two buses and three big trucks. I would watch the show from the sound desk position and when we got to the solo acoustic song that often comprised the last encore, I brimmed with pride on behalf of my uniquely talented and ultra-special artist holding 15,000 transfixed people in the palm of her hand. There are so few artists who can do what she did and command the silent attention of such a huge audience. During the last song I would make my way quietly through the crowd to the side area just in time to greet her as she made her way off stage. Those were magic moments.

Brian Fucking May

What perhaps hasn't come across strongly enough in my telling of the Katie Melua story is the immense amount of fun and creative satisfaction we all experienced. There were many exciting moments. A memorable concert in the Kremlin comes to mind. Katie's international reputation was legendary in Georgia, her homeland, and the Kremlin concert reflected that. Our hotel, the Kempinski, had a terrific view across the river towards the minarets of Red Square and we were picked up and bussed into the Kremlin, where there was a full-sized theatre stage.

During the trip, Katie's friend Georgia burst into the room saying, 'Guess who I've just seen in the hotel lift! Brian fucking May!' Katie, a life-long Queen fan, was very impressed and we wondered why they might be in town, because it wasn't for the Kremlin show. During that afternoon's rehearsals, we were all in the stalls of the theatre in the Kremlin, waiting for our moment. I stepped aside and called Brian's mobile and told him the story of him being spotted in the lift.

'Can you have a quick word with her?' I asked.

He agreed.

I went over to where Katie was sitting in the theatre stalls and said, 'Phone for you.'

THE HOUSE AND THE PALACE

She looked puzzled but took the phone from me: 'Hello, who is this?' she asked.

'It's Brian fucking May!' said Brian in a dry but delighted voice.

She burst out laughing. They chatted for a while and he thanked her for being so complimentary about them in the press.

Royal Moments

During those heady Dramatico times I coincidentally renewed my relationship with the Royal Family. Not that we were ever close!!! I had been commissioned in 1997 to write the official celebration of HM the Queen and Prince Philip's Golden Wedding Anniversary. It was for the massed bands of the Coldstream, Grenadier, Scots, Irish and Welsh Guards – 150 musicians in total, plus another 100 pipers. 'Royal Gold' was performed at the Royal Tournament with the Queen and the Duke of Edinburgh present.

I had been very proud to do it. Sadly, my retired lieutenant colonel dad died a week before the Royal Tournament and missed a great evening of hobnobbing with generals and brigadiers. It was clearly a good introduction to the Establishment and I must have got my name on somebody's list because after that I was asked to compose several royal pieces, most notably the theme for the Queen opening the Channel Tunnel with President Mitterrand of France. I had written a song called 'When Flags Fly Together' – the international optimism of which sadly seems somewhat out of kilter with today's frosty, dangerous world:

> So raise your flag next to mine
> Raise your eyes beyond your borderline;
> And we will stay strong forever
> As long as our flags fly together.

THE CLOSEST THING TO CRAZY

That was in 1994. Twenty-two years later, Britain would vote to exit the European Union.

In 2005, I answered a call from Buckingham Palace asking if Katie Melua would kindly perform for a Music Theme Day for children who had been involved in a youth scheme, culminating in a concert in the Palace ballroom. Of course we said yes. After the performance of 'The Closest Thing to Crazy', where I accompanied Katie on piano, the Queen's private secretary Sir Robin Janvrin took us up to meet Her Majesty and Prince Philip during a lunch reception in the Picture Gallery. It was the first time I'd seen the Queen since the Royal Tournament. Katie got on very well with her and Her Majesty told us how much she loved 'The Closest Thing to Crazy' from listening to Wogan every morning while she had breakfast.

The Master of the Household, then Air Vice Marshal David Walker (now Air Marshal Sir David Walker), included Katie and me in a rare sleepover dinner at Buckingham Palace at the invitation of the Queen in May 2007. It was a dinner for about thirty people with about a dozen of us staying over before leaving after breakfast the following day. This was accompanied by a request – or possibly a 'Royal Command' – for Katie to sing and for me to play 'The Closest Thing to Crazy' after dinner.

A couple of weeks before the event, I whispered in David Walker's ear that the piano in the music room at the Palace was not a fantastic instrument. It was more of a piece of decorative furniture with a family history but musically it played like an old, neglected pub piano. If they wanted a *really* nice-sounding performance, maybe I could get Yamaha to do us a good deal with a C3 parlour grand for the evening? This duly occurred, and three footmen struggled up in the lift with the piano just as we arrived in the middle of the day to help them set up.

We were shown to our rooms, but not before David had quietly said to me, 'Is there any protocol that would prevent Katie from having a smaller suite than yours?' He explained that the Ambassador's Suite was bigger and had a view out across the art gallery side of the palace, but the suite across the corridor was much more feminine and beautifully decked out with soft furnishings. Of course, I told him it was *fine* for me to have the bigger suite! We were assigned a valet each for the duration of our stay and invited to a special, more casual drinks gathering with Her Majesty just for the few of us who were staying and before pre-dinner drinks with the other guests. It all felt very special.

The Queen was relaxed and chatty. She was quick to note that she wasn't the musical one in the family, but her sister, Margaret, had been. I told her I'd met her sister only once, but as I had been wearing a Womble costume at the time, it hardly counted. Suddenly, she said, 'Actually, I've got a dog called Womble.' She waved almost dismissively over to Prince Philip, who had his back to us, talking to Katie and others a few feet away. 'It's *his* dog really,' she said, 'and his real name is Vulcan, but the children call him "Womble" because he looks like one!'

Over the next few years, I would often be asked to help with musical or entertainment matters at the Palace. I was once asked to record US Secretary of State Condoleezza Rice performing a Brahms quintet for piano and strings, accompanied by players from the London Symphony Orchestra including the foreign secretary David Miliband's wife Louise on violin. The Queen exited her quarters through the famous mirrored door into the White Drawing

Room, where a number of US generals and others were waiting with us in a greeting line. She was accompanied by just one dog – a Dorgi (a Corgi-Dachshund cross).

Condoleezza and the string quartet began to play to an audience of perhaps fifteen, including David Miliband, and we recorded the performance. The Queen had the centre, front-row seat. At first, the Dorgi sat under Her Majesty's seat. However, as soon as the performance started, the dog began to 'ooze' forward away from under the Queen's chair and started exploring, creeping on its stomach. Mildly annoyed, Her Majesty leant forward and quietly pulled it back, giving it a sharp slap on the rump by way of warning. It stayed in place for a short while longer, needing a few further gentle reprimands from the Queen. Ms Rice proved herself to be an extremely talented concert pianist. We printed off only four CD copies: one for the Queen, one for Condoleezza, one for the Royal Archive and another for me. The event was not to be released publicly, but I'm pleased to note that there is a short official video clip of a few minutes online.

At another dinner with the Queen, maybe a year later, Julianne and I were waiting in the music room with the other guests, including the opera singer Dame Kiri Te Kanawa and adventurer Bear Grylls. As Her Majesty emerged from the White Drawing Room I was surprised when she immediately made a beeline for me.

'Good evening, Mr Batt,' she said. Then, leaning in almost conspiratorially, 'There's a piano over there!'

I wasn't quite sure why she mentioned it. I couldn't imagine she was asking me to play. I thought she might be making a private joke about the fact that it wasn't a Yamaha replacement but the usual old clunky one that was always there.

THE HOUSE AND THE PALACE

'Yes, Ma'am, let's leave it there, shall we?' I said, hoping I'd correctly understood the joke.

The Queen smiled politely and moved on.

A little while later Bear Grylls said, 'You know you've just disobeyed your monarch, don't you? She was asking you to play!'

I was mortified. She must have thought me terribly rude. David Walker would have briefed her by suggesting she ask me to play it, knowing I wouldn't have had the cheek just to sit down and start tickling the ivories without invitation, but I wasn't in on it.

Anyway, after dinner and after we'd all been down to the art gallery to view the collection of pictures of Queen Victoria, the Queen was just leaving and so I approached and explained that I was embarrassed, having misunderstood her, and hoped my *faux-pas* would be forgiven.

'Oh, it's quite all right!' she said before departing for her quarters with her small entourage.

This confirmed it. She *had* meant me to play. And I had refused her.

CHAPTER 24

I Will Be There

For an artist so young, it was vitally important that we were always on hand – me, Julianne and Sue, our publicist – to provide the right level of pastoral care for Katie as she navigated her career and the potential emotional trappings and pitfalls. We would always act swiftly to protect her.

One such occasion, which we kept quiet about at the time, but about which Katie has spoken very openly to the press since, was her nervous breakdown in 2010. It's been speculated that it was overwork that led to it and, being a sensitive soul, I've often imagined outsiders or family, or even Katie herself perhaps attributing it to the demands made by me and Dramatico in working her too hard. Nothing could be further from the truth. Katie herself has said, 'There wasn't one thing, a clear black and white, but different things mounted up.' To have helped her through that experience and ensured that she could heal without the outside world – and the media – knowing about it was one of the achievements that Julianne, Sue and I look back on with the most relief.

THE CLOSEST THING TO CRAZY

It was a worrying time for us all, of course. We had been through so much together, both professionally and personally. We'd lived the moments with her. We'd had intimate, almost parental, discussions about everything from the pure technique of songwriting, on a professional basis, to the trials and joys of her day-to-day family matters, the bliss of acquiring British citizenship, nuances of music business politics, the sensitivities of her personal relationships and many other matters. The bond had been unbelievably strong.

In September 2012, Katie married James Toseland, a twice World Superbike champion she had met a year or two earlier as an audience member at one of her gigs. Dramatico staff organised the wedding, which was at the Royal Botanic Gardens in Kew. It was a beautiful day and Katie had asked us to put it all together. I wrote a song which I performed at the wedding.

James seemed a really good guy and, having retired from motorcycle racing because of a wrist injury, wanted to get into music. He formed a hard-rock band partly because he thought that was his audience, the bike community. Katie's brother, Zurab, joined him as a guitarist.

At the point they first met, we had been making the fifth album, *Secret Symphony*, which was full of songs done mainly with a symphonic line-up. We were very proud of it and it did quite well, selling a few hundred thousand copies – just not well enough to recover the losses of the financially disastrous fourth album.

When we began the sixth album – *Ketevan* – in 2013, Katie asked my son Luke, who had engineered some of our previous sessions, if he would co-produce with me and co-write with her. It was a perfect situation because Katie loved Luke's work as a solo artist and perhaps it diluted, in her mind, the notion that I was her sole mentor and producer. We made the album in the studio at Ewshot Hall and I think it's a fine album. Indeed, on it is one of the best songs I think I've ever written – 'I Will Be There' – which Buckingham Palace had commissioned for the Queen's Coronation Jubilee and with which I was able to honour my mother at the same time as the Queen. They were both the same age (eighty-six) and yet my mother, Elaine, was so sadly dying of peritoneal cancer. I hoped she would still be able to attend the concert at Buckingham Palace at which we would play it for her and the Queen, but tragically she died the week before the concert. You may remember that exactly the same thing happened to my dad a week before my first ever Royal performance. At the Buckingham Palace concert, we left my mum's seat empty. Katie sang the song with her incredible, instinctive technique. The last line is almost nature-defying in the way she controls her breath. At the time of writing, the video of the studio recording has clocked up 41 million YouTube views.

Oddly, while we were making that record, I had stepped into the control room to hear the playback when an urgent call came through from Denise, my secretary, saying that a letter had arrived with a Royal crest on it. She read out to me the notification from Buckingham Palace that the Queen had appointed me a Lieutenant of the Royal Victorian Order (LVO). I was quite emotional to hear it – I had some A-levels and a Cycling Proficiency badge but had never 'won' anything like this before! It was later explained to me by the Palace folks that the Royal Victorian Order was created by Queen Victoria so that the monarch could honour people without going through government. It was the personal gift of Her Majesty the Queen and usually only awarded to those who work at quite a senior level within the Royal Household. I felt then, and still feel to this day, specially honoured.

THE CLOSEST THING TO CRAZY

Ketevan came out in late 2013 and did sales which artists and record companies these days would love. But they were very low figures compared to the glory days of the first three albums. During my time managing Katie, I had learned many lessons about marketing and, incidentally, I also think I taught some lessons to a few folks in the industry about total commitment to an artist. But, knowing the decreasing sales pattern since album four, I made a big mistake: I should have ramped down the marketing expenditure as the music became less typically what Katie's audience was expecting. Or I should have tried harder to influence her not to veer too far from what her audience loved and expected. Change isn't *always* positive and sudden musical change can be as risky as hell, commercially. I'm a born risk-taker, but that fourth album hadn't been a clever move. If you spook your audience, you have a lot to lose. Whether Katie sees that as a lesson, I don't know, but she eventually got what she wanted − complete control over her creative life − because her six-album record and management contract with us was soon to expire.

Katie signed with BMG Records after a protracted and sometimes challenging negotiation in which BMG acquired the catalogue of six Katie albums from Dramatico. I don't even receive a producer royalty on any of the tracks we made together. She and I have occasionally met up and had coffee and chats and, in early 2022, Julianne and I had lunch with her in a pub in Kensington.

Katie was in fine shape, happy to have found a new man in her life after her divorce from James Toseland in 2020. Our lunch was just before she became pregnant with Sandro, her baby son. We talked about the things friends talk about, hardly touching on records and songs. She was about to give some lecture workshops on songwriting

I WILL BE THERE

at Cambridge University – she takes an academic approach to the study of poetry and lyric writing, something I find interesting. She so much wants to write and works extremely hard to improve at it – even more than singing, at which she is uncannily, naturally, one of the best in the world. I now watch Katie's career from afar and I look back with fondness on our years working together.

CHAPTER 25

The Shape of Things to Come

During the ten 'Katie years', other things were happening. Despite my disapproval of the 'too cool for school' attitude of the BRIT/BPI – which I still maintain – a few people there had noticed the rather audacious and somewhat spectacular rise of Dramatico, and in 2007 I was invited to join the BPI board, soon being voted deputy chairman. I had already served on many industry boards such as the Performing Rights Society (PRS) and the Ivors Academy when I was younger.

The issues back then were different, but just as important. I really enjoyed my seven years with BPI and made some great friends there. I hope my experience as a writer, artist, manager and label owner was able to help bring balance to discussions in an industry where different factions often have opposing but valid interests.

As well as the growing record company, I renewed my relationship with the Wombles. Despite my early paranoia about any potential negative effect on my musical credibility, I must admit I have always loved them and, besides, as the years have passed, other people's love and respect for the Wombles and their music appears only to have grown stronger.

While I owned the song performance and recording rights, the underlying character and TV production rights had changed hands several times over the years. I was anxious to avoid a repeat of the mistakes others had made in the '70s — the awful film, the poor-quality stage shows, all the terrible things that I had no control over, but which the public assumed I must have been involved in.

I knew the Canadian company who had most recently bought the rights had been involved in a Canadian stock market scandal and were in some sort of financial difficulty, so I wondered if an offer to buy the underlying rights from them might be timely. I made an offer and, after some wrangling, in 2011 paid quite a sizeable seven-figure sum for the rights I didn't already have. Marcus and Kate Robertson, the grown-up children of Elisabeth Beresford, also retained some control — mainly merchandise and book rights. I thought if they threw in what they controlled, we could co-own one company that would, for the first time, own 100 per cent of *everything* Womble-related under one roof. What Kate and Marcus contributed fell short in value of what I had paid for the TV production and underlying character rights, but I still gave them 50 per cent of the new company: Wombles Copyright Holdings Limited. I also somewhat rashly offered to pay them a big cash sum if I failed to produce a TV show within a certain time. There was absolutely no reason to do that — I'm sometimes not as clever as I look!

The Wombles at Glastonbury

The most memorable thing I did in 2011 was to accept an offer for the Wombles pop group — essentially myself and a selection of hired musicians — to appear on one of the bigger stages at Glastonbury. Surprisingly, we Wombles had never played a full, one-hour totally live

THE SHAPE OF THINGS TO COME

gig before. I say 'we' because I always remember I'm a Womble and the pop group appearing without me as Orinoco seemed unthinkable. But I had a hard-earned experience in a Womble costume and I knew how hot it would get, particularly in the sunny weather. Being driven through Manhattan on a flat-bed truck to promote ourselves in a humid August of 1974 had taught me that in the wrong circumstances, it might prove dangerous. So I picked two guitarists to 'relay' as Wellington, two bassists to relay as Cholet and Alderney, and two drummers to relay as Bungo. The plan was that, identically dressed, under cover of a front-of-stage stunt moment, I could get team 1 off stage and replace them with team 2 halfway through the act. We had some unashamed 'humans' – a keyboardist, a violinist and a sax/flute player (not costumed) – to augment the live act rather than a backing track. I had already demonstrated my preference not to use backing tracks with the Planets and for me this was still a matter of principle. The problem was there could only be one lead singer or the game would be up. That was Orinoco. That was *me*.

So, at the age of sixty-one, I gave myself the job of rehearsing and performing a live sixty-minute set in full Womble clobber, while my younger two sets of bandmates would get to take half the show off to keep cool and safe! Just a year before she died, my 85-year-old mother Elaine rose to the occasion and, with her faithful assistant, June Rutland, resumed her responsibilities as chief costume creator, including working out a clever way to cut out the inner part of the glove fingers for the guitarists so that their real fingers could contact the guitar strings while the audience-facing glove fingers would remain intact.

Rehearsals took place at Music Bank Studios, near Tower Bridge, and involved training the two teams up, both in and out of costume and concocting the distraction in the middle of the act (Superwomble appearing and cartwheeling across the stage) – to cover for them as they left the stage and returned, reborn! Never one to leave musicians idle, I had team 1 return to the stage after a long rest for a grand finale, dressed as other Womble characters, including MacWomble and a couple of Guardsmen Wombles, using costumes left over from when we had marched fourteen Guardsmen Wombles past the Queen Mother as part of her one hundredth birthday parade. This would fill the stage with colourful Womble characters as a perfect grand finale.

The Tower Bridge studio facility we used for the Glastonbury rehearsals was also popular with other bands. Bobby Gillespie's Primal Scream were rehearsing in the next studio to us. At one point, a roadie of theirs approached me and explained that they were all Wombles fans and would it be okay to pop in and watch a bit of our rehearsal? Knowing we could never be photographed – even by fellow professionals – without our Womble heads on, I was delighted to agree to them popping in and seeing a few songs with our heads on, playing fully live, as a kind of dress rehearsal. When we were ready, in they came and we went through 'Remember You're a Womble' and a couple of other songs. Bobby apparently even filmed it.

The day of our Glastonbury appearance was a gloriously hot summer day – 82 degrees Fahrenheit in the shade – even before the added heat and exertion of jumping about in a Womble costume. Our staff gave out thousands of free Womble masks to the audience. Glastonbury organisers have a 'crowd-o-meter', and they told us we had pulled the biggest crowd on any stage, including the main Pyramid Stage, for our Sunday afternoon spot. Thousands of people had hiked through mud to get to us. I still often meet people, whether in the industry or just punters, who say, 'Oh yes, I was there for that.'

It was such a blast.

After the show, as the stalwart team were all clearing away, I sat with my costume hanging loosely around my waist, talking to my mother and drinking bottle after bottle of water, recovering for a good hour. Then we all drove back from Glastonbury to Ewshot Hall, where Julianne had cooked us a big tuna casserole and we sat on the sunny southern terrace and looked out across the Hampshire countryside, chatting about our exhilarating experience. Performing that gig was one of the happiest hours of my life. That's why when, in interviews, I'm asked – and of course I *always* am – whether I regret the Wombles, I always respond with an emphatic 'no'. How could I possibly have lived my life without the joyful experiences it has afforded me and which I have been able to give to others? And could I *really*, happily leave the world *not* having written 'Tobermory's Music Machine' or 'Wellington Goes to Waterloo'?

The Wombles' rights acquisition of 2011 set off a chain of events which, combined with the simultaneous ending of my management and production relationship with Katie Melua, led to another scary and let's just say 'character-developing' period of stress and hardship. Julianne would no doubt laugh and insist that 'I don't want my character developing any more' if she heard me say that.

The acquisition had led to a protracted and ultimately negative period of trying to raise the considerable budget to make a new series. In fact, I directed three new fifteen-minute TV episodes voiced by the late Bernard Cribbins as Great Uncle Bulgaria and our dear friend Ray Winstone as Tobermory, which will now, sadly, never be shown. I had allowed a close friend effectively to become my de facto business manager in matters Wombles. It all went sadly, terribly wrong. Suffice to say that I would have been better off not buying the overall character rights at all. I am now back owning just the music and pop group rights and, as before, other people own the non-musical character rights. It's all in the past now, but I do notice from time to time what is happening and because I am still publicly regarded as the 'Womble Man', I have an uneasy feeling that whatever they do with the non-band characters, people will think I am responsible for those decisions.

New Challenges

If you think of life as a succession of hills and valleys, the combination of the simultaneous Wombles debacle and the ending of my relationship with Katie Melua after such heavy outgoings, combined with a few other unfortunate but substantial business events, led us to our very own version of the 'dismal and desolate valley' of Lewis Carroll's Snark. In 2017 we found ourselves no longer in the sunny uplands like the rabbits of Watership Down; indeed, the 'View From a Hill' across Hampshire and our cherished central London home were replaced by a more modest, perhaps more *'normal'* existence in Wimbledon. Yes, sunny Wimbledon! People always presumed we lived in Wimbledon and now, by pure chance, we do!

The roof had fallen in on our world. It's a hell of a shock to the system when you've been living an extraordinarily special, albeit occasionally precarious lifestyle for most of your career. Philosophy kicks in at such times and the opportunity to see life from a different, less comfortable, perhaps more 'real' angle, once again presented itself as a non-negotiable fact rather than an optional opportunity. In my case, I really think my arduous training in the Lake District and in Dartmoor with the Army Cadets and long-distance cycling while in my teens in the Yorkshire Dales were good psychological preparation. I've never been any good at football or skill-sports, but I excelled at anything requiring endurance and pure doggedness. I do believe these early life experiences affect one's resilience.

In *The Hunting of the Snark*, the Beaver and the Butcher become the best of friends while being attacked by a common enemy, the Jubjub bird. Even though Julianne and I already *were* the best of friends, the shared perils of our newly challenging situation brought us even closer together than we had ever been. Once again, life and art converge. Nevertheless, at that time, I did go through another period of deep clinical depression and utter despair. The only other time I'd encountered serious clinical depression before had been after the closing of *The Hunting of the Snark* in 1991, which, being circumstantial, improved as the circumstances changed for the better. But this time, the shock was greater because the material loss and personal devastation to us was greater, leaving us, initially, homeless but for the generosity of hospitable friends; and all the worse because it was the result of a combination of my own swashbuckling foolishness, but also – and this is the different part – devious behaviour by others around us. I literally stared blankly at the ceiling for weeks and was under the care of a clinical psychiatrist. Mentally, I was on the floor.

Suffice to say there *were* dark, hopeless times, but gradually, they have gone. I hope that anybody reading this who is having a similar experience will take heart from that. My favourite line from *Sexy Beast* – the movie in which Julianne starred – is when Ian

McShane's character, while planning to rob a seemingly impregnable bank, says, 'Where there's a will, there's a way – *and there IS a fucking way!*'

It was scary though; out in the big wild world, starting again from scratch. I found that adrenaline-driven wish to get back in the thick of things was happening all over again, just as I had felt when I was starting out at the age of eighteen, impatient to get success, and then again on return from the boat voyage, and then *again* after Snark in the West End, and I guess also after my near-fatal car accident. I saw this renewed ambition as a useful top-up to my ongoing life-energy, and it has proven very helpful.

I was pleased therefore when, in 2018, I was asked to arrange and co-produce an album – *The Road to Utopia* – for the ubiquitous psych-rock band, Hawkwind. The band worked in Dave Brock's studio in a converted milking shed down in the West Country, where I visited and rehearsed with them. I even joined the band for one gig – on keyboards at the Citadel Festival in west London. Dave persuaded his old mate Eric Clapton to do a solo on one of the tracks and I recorded him at Mark Knopfler's studio in Chiswick. Essentially, Hawkwind put down the rhythm tracks at their studio and I overdubbed the orchestra at AIR Studios and mixed it at my place. The cover art featured a painting of the band playing cricket and the scoreboard bore the legend 'HAWKWIND IN TO BATT'.

Dave Brock and I had a little tiff about a tweet – nothing important at all, really – but he took umbrage and had the art people take the second 'T' off so that it just read 'HAWKWIND IN TO BAT', which I thought was a bit childish – and rather odd – considering we had a symphonic tour of the UK coming up, playing venues like the Sage in Gateshead and the Palladium in London.

THE SHAPE OF THINGS TO COME

We still went ahead with the tour, during which I conducted a thirty-piece orchestra, situated on stage with the band. I so much enjoyed those crazy gigs, even though there was now this underlying tension between myself and Dave. Arthur Brown joined us to create further happy havoc on stage; it was like being transported back to the psychedelic days of 1968 when, coincidentally, Hawkwind and I had both been signed to Liberty Records.

* * *

Along with all the wonderful benefits of the new communications technology, the floodgates have been opened and *everybody* has 'an album out' nowadays. Even without a label. That's fantastic in one way but has created confusion not only for music business colleagues but also for audiences because creators are now all part of a crowd. It's good for 'everyone' to be allowed into the space, but it's harder to get noticed.

Just before the 2020 lockdown, I met a fascinating young French artist and businessman called Jean-Charles Capelli, who seemed to match my own energy and diversity of ambition. We formed a new company to handle some joint enterprises and created a three-pronged project around our album, involving a video game, a novel and a comic/graphic novel. We were anxious that the project should have a solid literary base, which we achieved by commissioning a dark but funny 50,000-word novella by my friend, the award-winning writer David Quantick. The album – *Songs from Croix-Noire* – spans psychedelia, rock, ballads and all stations in between. We're immensely proud of this multi-faceted creation, but we don't see it as a vertical take-off shot at the charts, more the establishment of an Intellectual Property that will hopefully last for years and grow slowly but surely.

THE CLOSEST THING TO CRAZY

A few years ago I acquired a state-of-the-art Macintosh and Logic studio set-up to replace my late, lamented Ewshot Hall mega-studio with its big Neve desk and high-provenance valve compressors and microphones. I have amassed a range of superb orchestral and rhythm instrument samples. Almost always, I use real musicians for records – but it's also just a great boon to have the ability to create an album, or any music, at home with my own equipment, should I want or need to. Incidentally, my daughter Hayley – now an established and respected bass player living in LA (touring and playing with a range of stars from Conan Gray to Kylie Minogue) – was with us during lockdown and I had the unexpected pleasure of her being available to play on some of my recordings.

'Lockdown' was also a useful time to spend working on another pleasure: painting clothing, particularly jackets. I use acrylics and fabric medium, and have been doing it since the '70s when I needed a special-looking jacket for *Seaside Special*, continuing on and off ever since. I painted a very ambitious jacket quite recently for an appearance on the BBC quiz show *Pointless Celebrities*, hosted by my friend Alexander Armstrong. I've won it twice now, so I have two 'coveted' Pointless trophies to my name! I also recently issued a limited-edition collection of my art pieces and greetings cards via my website.

In the last few years I've been pleased to have been hired to provide string arrangements and conduct them on an interesting range of new pop material. Tracks by stars Mimi Webb, Olly Murs, a new American band called the Scarlet Opera on Universal and with a core of hip young producers based in LA – so I'm officially cool again. Yuck! I hate being cool.

THE SHAPE OF THINGS TO COME

Onwards

I wouldn't change anything about my life – the range of activities, the panic, the pace, the variety, the ups, the downs. I'm so lucky to keep being given the chance to be fulfilled by the work I do. To have worked with so many fascinating and talented characters in so many genres using my own mixture of passions and energies has been a blessing.

Somebody asked me to list all my new projects the other day. Two new musicals fully written and one, not yet finished, called *Railway Hotel*. The latter is inspired by my maternal grandfather, Arthur, who, having left my granny, was shot dead by his young mistress in a Hampstead flat in 1941. It's a hoot! A solo album of all new songs; a book of my art pieces; my ninth symphony. I've decided not to write the first eight; to me it invariably seems that people's ninth symphonies are their best.

I am completely aware that life is finite and that the pure quantity of my plans for the future might be a touch optimistic. But why change the habits of a lifetime? One day, I will, to quote my own lyrics from the Snark, 'vanish away like midnight smoke'. When that day comes, if I don't have a work in progress or if I'm not engaged in some thrilling, outlandish, probably very costly unfinished project, I'll be very annoyed indeed.

For now, though, I'm as excited as hell!

Acknowledgements

Firstly I'd like to thank everyone who advised me that it would be wiser to call the theatre critics bastards rather than cunts. It was funnier with cunts but some people just hate that word, so I haven't used it. On a more serious note, my special thanks to Pete Selby for inviting me to contribute my book to his brilliant and brave imprint, Nine Eight, and for his structural edit. Also thanks to Pete for honestly telling me what he thought even when he was clearly wrong. Sometimes it felt as if we were in that scene in *Women in Love* where Oliver Reed and Alan Bates engage in a naked wrestling match. I forget who won that but I think they remained the best of friends afterwards. Thank you, David Quantick, for your creative editing work after starting out just reading it as a pal. Much gratitude also to my good friends Suzanne Hawley and Pete Paphides just for reading and commenting at various stages along the way. Huge thanks to Sue Harris, my long-standing publicist (via her firm Republic Media), for temporarily taking up the challenge and being a skilful and trusted 'no-nonsense' finessing editor. Sue, it was your perseverance and talent that got it over the line. Thanks to copy editor Jane Donovan and proofreader Victoria Denne, who both gave it the sensible once-over but also prodded with useful questions and suggestions about things that hadn't occurred to me during the twenty years since I began writing this book, and to James Lilford for his vital supervising role as editor for Nine Eight. To David Green – I am so grateful to you for your patient and enthusiastic indexing expertise.

Thanks also to all the artists and musicians, executives, media folks, crew and other pals I've worked with on my life's journey to date, and particularly to Pete Rutland, my long-serving executive assistant and production manager, who has, for many years, been the faithful and indispensable Sancho Panza to my Don Quixote.

Of course, apart from other family members who put up with my quirks and obsessions, I'd specially like to thank my wife Julianne, who has made many sacrifices for me and who works so hard and sincerely in everything she does for so many people. For want of a better analogy of my own, I'll steal lyricist Larry Henley's words from one of the all-time classics he's written. She really is the wind beneath my wings.

For more information, please visit:
www.mikebatt.com

And follow:
X: @Mike_Batt
Instagram: @batt_mike
Facebook: facebook.com/mikebattmusic
TikTok: @real_mike_batt

Index

4' 33" (silent composition) 262–5
9/11 World Trade Center attack (2001) 259

'A One Minute Silence' 262–5
ABBA 70, 72–3, 86, 199
Abbacadabra (musical) 199
Abbey Road Studios 57, 194, 213, 220, 239, 243, 244
   mobile recording unit 217–18
ABC Studios, Sydney 165–6
Acapulco 156–7
Actors' Equity Australia 167, 168
Adam, Ian 205
AIR Studios
   Lyndhurst Hall 237–8, 292, 314
   Montserrat 145–6, 149–51, 153
   Oxford Circus 91, 177, 178
Alex (video producer) 256
Alexander, Jae 226
Alice's Adventures in Wonderland 187, 232
All for a Song (Dickson) 158–9
Allott, Nick 227–8

A&M Records 59–60, 122
Americana, The (hotel), New York 58
Amsterdam Chamber Orchestra 133–4
Andersson, Benny 72–3, 144, 189–90
Annotated Snark, The (Gardner) 183
Antigua 143–4, 151, 153
Armstrong, Alexander 316
Army Cadets 17
'As Long As the Moon Can Shine' 192
ASCAP (American Society of Composers, Authors, and Publishers) 57
Asher, Dick 63, 65, 73, 79, 90, 95–6, 173–4
Ashurst, Mr (headmaster) 17
Astaire, Fred 79–80
Australian Broadcasting Commission (ABC) 159, 161, 168
Autopilot *see Rapid Eye Movements*

Baden-Powell House, South Kensington 246, 263–4
'Ballerina, Prima Donna' 180
'Banana Rock' 79

Barbican 185, 188, 189–90
Bardell, Wayne 40
Barnett, John 130–31, 137
Barnett, Larry 130
BASCA (British Academy of Songwriters, Composers and Authors) 97, 98
Batt, Dick (brother) 6, 15
Batt, Elaine (*née* Jennings; mother)
   background 4–5, 11
   and Mike's childhood 6–7, 8–9
   pressures Mike to marry 48
   Womble costumes 65, 69, 76, 85, 87, 109, 309
   Christmas in Tenerife 141
   fancy dress bat costume 192
   on John Cage copyright affair 263
   in China 284
   death 303
Batt, Hayley (daughter) 218–19, 233, 235, 238, 316
Batt, John (brother) 5, 8, 9, 77–8
Batt, Julianne (*née* White; 'Jules')
   auditions for *Zero Zero* 168–9
   early relationship with Mike 170, 173–6, 180, 181
   acting career 173, 176, 178, 181, 184
   Queen Sod speech 184
   marriage to Mike 181, 192
   with George and Olivia Harrison 202–3
   birth of son Luke 211, 218
   part in *Brookside* 212
   birth of daughter Hayley 218–19
   shattered by *Snark* reviews 229
   heads for Australia with children 233
   returns to England 238
   with Mike after car crash 4
   stagecraft/styling role 255, 256, 259
   on Paul Walters 268
   dines with the Queen 298
   and Katie Melua 301–2, 304
   entertains at Ewshot Hall 311
   bond with Mike 313
Batt, Luke (son) 211–12, 218, 219, 233, 235, 238, 302–3
BATT, MIKE
Early years (1949–67):
   family background 4–5, 317
   birth 5
   early childhood 6–11
   schooling 6, 8, 11, 17–18
   writes first rhyme 31
   learns to play accordion 9–10
   interest in classical music 10–11
   early teenage years 11–15
   bedroom piano 11–12, 25
   musical influences 12–13
   pub pianist 13
   joins first band (Phase Four) 13
   forms duo with Alan Renton 13–14
   first experiences with girls 14–15
   in Army Cadets 17
   career ambitions 17, 18
   A-level results 17–18
Early music career (1967–70):
   strip club organist 18–19
   seeks opening in music business 19–22
   Decca test 20
   responds to new talent ad 21
   signs to Liberty 21–2

INDEX

'top line' work 23, 49
arranges Family album 24–8
girlfriend Michele Green 25, 29–30
first recording sessions as artist 28–9
head of A&R 29, 33–7, 40–41, 44–5
produces Big Joe Williams album 36–7
joins Hapshash and the Coloured Coat 37–40
early relationship with Wendy 42–5, 47
breaks up with Michele 44
marriage to Wendy 48

1970s:
lives on houseboat 48–9
birth of daughter Samantha 48
turns freelance 49
orchestral album series 49–52, 91
forms Batt-Songs Ltd 52
married life 52–3
signs to DJM 53
jingles and TV commercials music 53
Wombles theme song 54–5
Wombles adventure (*see* Wombles)
dispute with Musicians' Union 56–7
royalties cheque 56, 57
Big Revolt project 55–6, 57–61
first trip to US 58–60
negotiates contract with CBS 63–4, 73–4, 90
birth of daughter Robin 69
married life 74–5, 84, 117
growing disillusionment with Wombles 86, 89–90
works with Steeleye Span 90–92
career as solo artist 93, 95–7
'Summertime City' 95–7

Schizophonia 99, 100
'Bright Eyes' 101–8, 115–17, 120, 243, 284
Caravans soundtrack 111–13
Tarot Suite 114–15
party at Rod Stewart's place 119
produces Kursaal Flyers 120–22
Elkie Brooks recording session 122–3

1980s:
marital strains 123–4
contemplates adventure break with family 123, 130
three-album deal with CBS 128–9
two-album deal with Chrysalis 129
purchases the *Braemar* 129
works with Hollies 131
at Wisseloord 132–4, 136–7, 144, 159
Waves 133–4
breaks into Gaddafi's yacht 134–5
Rapid Eye Movements 129, 137
Braemar voyage (*see Braemar*)
with Paul McCartney in Montserrat 146–51
at recording of 'Ebony and Ivory' 149–51
Six Days in Berlin 142, 143, 151–3
with Rod Stewart in LA 157–8
produces Barbara Dickson album 158–9
ABC commission 159, 161
Zero Zero (*see Zero Zero*)
break-up of marriage 43, 163–4, 167
affair with Julie Murphy 165–7, 169, 170
first meets Julianne White 168–9

1980s: *(cont.)*
    early relationship with Julianne 170, 173–6, 180
    returns to England 173–4
    acrimonious divorce 173–4, 176, 182
    weekend with Julianne 175–6
    heartache hits 175, 176–9
    fling with ballerina 180
    re-unites with Julianne 181
    Snark project (*see* Hunting of the Snark, The)
    conducts LSO at Barbican 185
    marriage to Julianne 181, 192
    with George Harrison 193, 202–4
    'Phantom of the Opera' 200–201, 204–6, 207
    relations with Andrew Lloyd Webber 199–202, 204, 206–8
    birth of son Luke 211–12, 218
    makes new albums 213–14
    birth of daughter Hayley 218–19
    Dreamstone overtures 219–20

1990s:
    financial difficulties 233–4
    post-*Snark* exile and depression 234–6
    new creative projects 236–7
    works with David Essex 237–8
    Vanessa-Mae 239–42, 245
    enjoys success again 242–3
    works with Gary Wilmot 243–4
    puts together Bond 246–9

2000–present:
    the Planets (band) 253–6, 258–66
    car crash and neck injury 3–4, 257–8, 261
    John Cage copyright affair 262–5
    founds Dramatico 270
    scouts for new solo artist 268–9
    Katie Melua (*see* Melua, Katie)
    at Buckingham Palace 296–9, 303
    Wombles gig at Glastonbury (2011) 308–11
    appointed LVO 303
    Wombles' rights acquisition debacle 308, 311–12
    moves to Wimbledon 312
    dark, hopeless times 312–13
    starts from scratch 314
    works with Hawkwind 314–15
    launches *Croix-Noire* 315
    recent activities and new projects 316–17
    reflects on life and future 317

Homes:
    Warwick Road flat, Earl's Court 47
    houseboat at West Byfleet 48–9
    first home in Surbiton 52–3, 56, 71, 75
    Langley Avenue, Surbiton 73–5, 118, 174
    Wardour Street flat, Soho 179–80, 181
    Hyde Park Square, Bayswater 182, 214, 234, 237, 245, 251
    Ewshot Hall, Hampshire (*see* Ewshot Hall)
    Central Park West, New York 287
    Wimbledon home 312

Character and characteristics:
    cars 52–3, 74–5, 85, 122
    character xi
    as conductor 25–7, 32–3, 104–6, 113, 128, 152–3, 165–6, 185, 214–18, 221, 237

INDEX

credibility as musician 64, 70, 96, 99–100, 195
deadlines 49–50, 57–8, 79, 122, 131, 162, 188–9, 225
dress and appearance 6, 38, 40, 152, 316
drive and ambition 314, 315
drugs 119–20, 133
fascination with words 31–2
finances 47, 52–3, 56, 60, 61, 74–5, 188, 212, 233–4, 251, 253, 289
grandchildren 142
kinetic projection art 98, 169, 224, 232
musical education 32
musical style 58, 99, 115, 136, 152, 270
pianos 11–12, 25, 49, 118, 142, 296–7
resilience 313
reviews and articles about 69, 92, 144, 229–30, 235
risk-taking in business 117–18, 304
singing voice 13, 28
sound equipment 240–41, 316
Batt, Norman Frederick (father)
  background 4–5
  employment 5, 6, 8, 11
  and Mike's childhood 6–7, 8–9, 10
  at Hamble River Sailing Club 15
  and Mike's career plans 18
  Christmas in Tenerife 141
  death 295
Batt, Paula (sister) 6, 11, 174, 176, 178
Batt, Robin (daughter)
  birth 69
  upbringing 84
  schooling and social life at sea 140, 141, 158
  with Linda McCartney 151
  character 141
  break-up of parents' marriage 43, 163–4, 174, 183
  daughters 142
Batt, Samantha (daughter)
  birth and infancy 48
  upbringing 84
  schooling and social life at sea 140, 141, 158
  with Linda McCartney 151
  character 141
  break-up of parents' marriage 43, 163, 174, 183
  daughter 142
Batt, Wendy (*née* Lucas; first wife)
  in Wendy and the Raconteurs 41–2
  appearance 41
  Mike first meets 42–3
  character and temperament 43
  early relationship with Mike 44–5, 47
  marriage 48
  birth of children 48, 69
  at Batt-Songs Ltd 52
  married life 52–3, 74–5, 84, 117
  manages Mad Hatters 97
  socialises 112, 119
  marital strains 123–4
  aboard *Braemar* 140, 141
  infidelities 164
  friction over *Zero Zero* 163, 167
  break-up of marriage 43, 163–4, 167
  returns to London 167
  acrimonious divorce 173–4, 176, 182

Batt-Songs Ltd, Mayfair 52
Batts Corner, Totton 5
Bavariafilms Studios, Munich 110
Baverstock, Jack 20
BBC Radio 1 66, 116, 279
BBC Radio 2 117, 267–8, 275, 278, 279, 286, 296
Beatles 12, 19, 38, 39, 40
Beel, Amanda 277
Belle Vue Grammar School, Bradford 8
Bendall, Haydn 244, 245
Beresford, Elisabeth 53, 69, 75–6, 84
Berlin 151–3
Berlin Opera Orchestra 152–3
Berry, Chuck 13
'Better Than a Dream' 220
Betteridge, David 114
Big Revolt, The 55–6, 57–61, 115
Birch, Will 121–2
Bird, Laurie 104
Black, Cyril 41
Black, Don 199
Blackburn, Tony 66, 77
'Blame It on the Moon' 273
Blasko, Sarah 287
Blunstone, Colin 115
BMG Records 304
Bolan, Marc 59
Bombay Palace (restaurant), Bayswater 245
Bond (string quartet) 246–9
Bonzo Dog Doo-Dah Band 36
Boult, Sir Adrian, *A Handbook on the Technique of Conducting* 217
Boulton, Arthur 269

Bowen, Tim 128
Bowen, Will 224, 225
Boyd, Pattie 39
Boyle, Katie 72
Bradford 8–9
Braemar (motor yacht)
   construction and history 127–8
   costs 129–30
   sea trial 130
   crew 130, 137, 138, 140–41
   brought back from Monte Carlo 130–31, 133
   refit and repair work 131
   family accommodation 142
   sea-going qualities 137–8
   leaves Scheveningen harbour 137
   held up in Cherbourg 138
   stranded in Brest 139–40
   sails for Tenerife 140
   Atlantic crossing 142
   at Antigua 143–4, 151, 153
   at Montserrat 145–6, 147–9, 151, 153
   through Panama Canal 155–6
   repaired in Acapulco 156
   dolphin spectacle 156–7
   reaches Los Angeles 157
   Pacific crossing 159–60, 162
   restocks at Hawaii 159
   radio communications 160–61
   at Fiji 162
   in Sydney 162–3, 167
   final onward journey 167
   Mike's reflections on voyage ix–x, 124, 153, 163–4

INDEX

Brest 139–40
Bridge, Andrew 226
'Bright Eyes' 101–8, 115–17, 120, 243, 284
Brightman, Sarah 200, 201, 204–6
BRIT School, Croydon 269, 271, 282
British Phonographic Industry (BPI) 97, 269, 307
Brock, Dave 314–15
Brooks, Elkie 122–3
Brown, Arthur 315
Bruni, Carla 287
Bruno, Frank 220
Buckingham Palace 296–9, 303
Burnett, T Bone 291
Bush, Mel 237, 241, 245–8
Bushehri, Mehdi 110–12

Cage, John, copyright affair 262–5
'Call Off the Search' 270, 273
Camden, Anthony 184–5, 214–15
Canned Heat, 'Going Up the Country' 34
'Can't Lie No More' 131
Capelli, Jean-Charles 315
Captain Sensible 195, 208
'Caravan Song' ix, 111, 113–14, 123–4, 213
Caravans (album) 114
Caravans (film) 100, 110–13
Caro Emerald 287
Carroll, Lewis 119, 232
    'The Hunting of the Snark' ix, x, 183, 187–8, 189
Cassidy, Eva, 'Over the Rainbow' 267–8

Cassidy, Maurice 236
Cattini, Clem 72, 100
Cazenove, Christopher 189
CBS
    turns down *Big Revolt* 58–9
    negotiates contract with Mike 63–4, 73–4, 90
    and first Womble single 64–5, 67, 68
    ABBA 73
    attempts to break Wombles in States 81–2
    'Summertime City' release 95–6
    'Bright Eyes' 102, 103–7, 115–16
    kills off 'Caravan Song' 114
    and Kursaal Flyers 121
    three-album deal with Mike 128–9
    Hansa Studio in Berlin 152–3
    Barbara Dickson album 158–9
    Zero Zero project 161
    anti-fraternisation rules 166–7
    dispute over 'Snark' album 192, 195, 196, 208
Chambers, Guy 292
Channel 4 TV 181
Channel Tunnel: opening (1994) 295–6
Channon, Liz 53
Chapman, Roger 23, 24, 115, 124
Chappell (music publishers) 52
'Chase, The' (Family) 24
Cherbourg 138
Chess (musical) 144, 190
'Children of the Sky' ix–x, 182–3, 189
Christy, Lauren 292
Chronicles of Don't Be So Ridiculous Valley, The (book) 236

Chrysalis Records 90, 129, 137
Cilla (TV series) 66–7
Clapton, Eric 274, 314
Clarke, Allan 131
Classic FM 261–2
Classical BRIT Awards (2002) 265
'Classical Gas' (Williams) 240
Classical Graffiti (Planets) 260, 261–2, 263, 265
'Closest Thing to Crazy, The' 236, 273–4, 275, 278, 279, 284, 289, 296
Cohen, Kip 58–9
Collins, Vic 121
Colm Wilkinson: Stage Heroes (album) 213–14
conducting music 214–18
Connolly, Billy 208, 220
'Contradanza' 246
Cooper, Ray 100, 112, 193
copyright 262–5
Counsell, Eos 246
Crawford, Michael 206, 207
'Crawling Up a Hill' (Mayall) 14
Creedence Clearwater Revival, 'Proud Mary' 34
Cregan, Jim 118–19, 141, 142, 143, 157–8, 274, 283
Cress, Curt 151–2
Cribbins, Bernard 66, 311–12
Croix-Noire (art project) 315
CTS Studios, Wembley 111–12, 190–91

Daddo, Cameron 222
Daltrey, Roger 193, 208
'Dancing Towards Disaster' 195
Davis, Clive 58, 63

de Heer, Karen 173
Dearie, Blossom 21–2
Decca Records 19–20, 55
Deep Purple 61, 261
'Derek' (delivery skipper) 138
Dick James Music (DJM) 22, 51, 53
Dickson, Barbara 113–14, 158–9
dolphin spectacle, Acapulco harbour 156–7
Dorward, Neil 257–8, 261
Douglas, Graeme 121
Downie, Penny 229
Dramatico
  founded 270
  record label 182, 273, 275–6, 279
  expansion 286–7
  roster of artists 287
  management and welfare role 287, 301
  damaged trading position 288–9
  investment in Katie 278, 279, 304
Dreamstone, The (TV series) 219–20
Dreamstone overtures 217, 219–20
drugs 119–20, 133
'Dublin Overture, The' 237
Dudgeon, Gus 36
Dunne, Michael 278
Dylan, Bob 204

Earl's Court 47, 218
Eastbourne 6
Eastway, John 165
'Ebony and Ivory' (McCartney) 149–51
Ecker, Haylie 247
Edinburgh, Duke of *see* Philip, Prince
Edwards, Tony 61
Elizabeth, Queen Mother 310

INDEX

Elizabeth II, Queen 295–6, 297–9, 303
Emanuel, David and Elizabeth 192
Emery, Stuart 277
EMI Classics 241, 254, 255, 260, 265
EMI Studios, Sydney 166
Essex, David 85, 180, 182, 201, 221, 237
   'A Winter's Tale' 176, 177
   Cover Shot 237–8
Eurovision Song Contest 72–3, 134, 135
Evans, Bill 22
'Eve of Destruction' 48
Everett, Kenny 225–6
Ewshot Hall (country house), Hampshire
   Mike buys 251–2
   renovation work 252
   breathtaking views 253, 311
   base for Planets documentary 254–6
   Mike convalesces at 258
   studio 262, 270, 274, 278, 303, 316
   Katie auditions and performs at 269–70, 272
   recording sessions 274, 285, 289, 302–3
   Mike leaves 312
'Exercise is Good for You (Laziness is Not)' 64, 66–7

'Fading Yellow' 28, 29
'Fairyland' (Findon) 48
Fältskog, Agnetha 72–3, 86
Family, *Music in a Doll's House* 23–8
'Faraway Voice' (Melua) 269, 271, 273
Featherstone, Lisa 283
Ferris, Neil 116–17
Fiennes, Magnus 248
Fiji 162

FilmFair Productions, London 53, 54, 76, 77
Filmtrax record label 213
Findon, Ben 48
Finn, Mickey 39, 59
Fisher, Roy 35
Fleming, Paddy 68, 72
Fletcher, Guy 243
Flett, Doug 243
'Flood, The' 292, 293
Flounders, Terry 76, 77
Fowler, Simon 276–7
Friar Park, Henley 193, 202–3

Gaddafi, Colonel Muammar 134–5
Gallagher, Rory 115–16
Gardner, Martin, *The Annotated Snark* 183
Garfunkel, Art 102–5, 107–8, 120, 190, 191
Gates, Martin and Sue 219
Gatun Lake 155–6
Geno Washington's Ram Jam Band 12
Giddings, John 208
Gielgud, Sir John 190–91
Gilbert, John 23–4
Gillan, Ian 61
Gillespie, Bobby 310
Gillinson, Clive 214–15
Glastonbury Festival (2011) 308–11
Glazer, Jonathan 184
Glover, Dominic 283
Goddard, Liza 178–9
Goedicke, Kurt-Hans 216
Gore Hill Studios, Sydney 168–9
Grainge, Lucian 281

Grappelli, Stéphane 190, 191
Green, Derek 122
Green, Michele 25, 30, 42, 44
'Green Man' (XTC) 244
Grosvenor House, London 98, 99
Groundhogs, *Scratching the Surface* 35–6
Grylls, Bear 298, 299
Guatemala 156
Gurrumul 287

Halpern, Sir Ralph 77–8
Halsband, Michael 276, 277
Hamble River Sailing Club 15
Hands, Terry 221
Hansa Studio, Berlin 152–3
Hanson, John 76, 77
Hapshash and the Coloured Coat 37–40
   Western Flier 38, 39–40
Harker, Roland 103
Harley, Steve 180, 185, 204–6, 207
Harries, Tim 274
Harris, Sue 277, 280, 281, 287, 301
Harrison, George 193, 202–4
   Cloud Nine 204
Harrison, Olivia 193, 202–4
Hart, Tim 90–91
Hawaii 159
Hawkwind 120, 314–15
Hayes, Jamie 226
Hayes, Martin 226
Hayes, Tubby 26, 27
Hayward, Justin 208
   Classic Blue 213
Hazlehurst, Ronnie 72
Henbest, 'Happy' 138, 140

Hendrix, Jimi 12
Hewson, Richard 28
Highclere School of Dancing, Winchester 14
Hill, Andy 245
Hill, Jonathan 255, 260
Hill, Ken 200, 201–2
Holland, Bill 272
Hollies 131, 234
Holst, Gustav, 'The Planets' suite 217–18
Holzman, Jac 59
Hopkin, Mary 41
houseboating 48–9
Hubley, John 101–2, 104, 108
Hunting of the Snark, The (musical)
   inspiration 187–8
   writing ix–x, 182–3, 188–9
   autobiographical aspects ix–xi, 163–4, 183, 313
   financing 188, 190, 212, 220–21, 223, 224
   Barbican concert (1984) 188, 189–90
   album 190–92, 192–3, 194, 195–7, 208
   CBS/Sony dispute 192, 195, 196, 208
   Royal Albert Hall production (1987) 208, 209, 212
   TV recording 209, 221
   Australian productions (1990) 221–2
   West End show (1991) 190, 220–21, 224–8, 231
   reception 228–30, 231
   fundraising efforts 230–31
   closure of show 231
   dissolution of Snark company 231, 234
   Mike's reflections and thoughts 231–2

INDEX

Hurdle, Les 72, 100
Hurll, Michael 95
Hurt, Donna 194
Hurt, John 193, 194–5, 213–14
Hyatt House, Los Angeles 59, 60

'I Can't Own Her' (XTC) 244
'I Feel Like Buddy Holly' 178–9
'I See Wonderful Things in You' 29
'I Watch You Sleeping' 211–12
'I Will Be There' 303
Idle Race 36
'If the Lights Go Out' 131
'If You Were a Sailboat' 288, 290
Imagination Limited (company) 223–4, 228
'Imbecile' 115
Ivor Novello Awards 97–9, 223

Janvrin, Sir Robin 296
Jeffries, Lionel 109
Jennings, Arthur (Mike's grandfather) 317
Jennings, Elaine *see* Batt, Elaine
Jermyn, John (7th Marquess of Bristol) 128, 130
John, Elton 22, 53
John Cage copyright affair 262–5
Johnson, Bob 90–91
Jones, Beverley 254, 260
Jones, Brian 37
Jones, Paul 189
'Jungle Bridge' 227–8
Jupp, Mike 219

Karan, Chris 112
Katselas, Lisa 235
Keen, Alan 21–2, 23, 24
Kelly, Jo Ann 36
Kemp, Rick 91
Kenny, Paul 173
Kenwright, Bill 87, 89
Keshavarzian, Mahnaz (Ms Kesh) 218–19
kinetic projection art 98, 169, 224, 232
Knight, Peter 90, 91–2
Kremlin concert, Katie Melua 294
Kruk, Michael 254, 260
Kursaal Flyers 120–22

Lac-Hong Phi 260
'Lady of the Dawn' 115, 267
Laine, Denny 148
Land, David 179–80
Langham Hilton, London 277
Lansdowne Studios, Holland Park 91, 121, 131
Lapp, Theo 255
Larsen, Jorgen 143, 247
Lauder, Andrew 34, 35, 40
Leahy, Dick 20
Leaver, John 222, 223
Leaver, Sally 222
Lemmy 47–8
Lennon, John, death 140, 146–7
Lennon, Julian 208
Levy, Michael 20
Lewis, Linda 118–19, 141, 142, 143, 157, 185
Liberty Records 21–3, 28–9, 33–7, 40–41, 44, 49

Lieberson, Goddard 102, 103–7, 108
'Lilac Wine' (Brooks) 122–3
'Little Does She Know' (Kursaal Flyers) 121–2
Liverpool Institute for Performing Arts 151
Lloyd Webber, Andrew 144, 199–202, 204, 206–8
Logan, Johnny 135
Loggins, Dan 63–4, 65, 68, 73
London Philharmonic Orchestra 48, 111–12, 113, 213
London Symphony Orchestra (LSO) 78–9, 101, 184–5, 188, 189, 191, 212, 214–15, 216, 243
Lord, Jon 61
Loretto, Andrew 231
Los Angeles 59–60, 157–8, 195, 220, 291
'Losing Your Way in the Rain' 115
Love, Jackie 222
'Love Makes You Crazy' 181
Lyndhurst Hall, Hampstead 237–8, 292, 314
Lyngstad, Anni-Frid 86, 199
Lynne, Jeff 36, 204
Lyttleton, Richard 254, 255

Mackintosh, Cameron 190, 199–200, 220, 224–5, 228, 230, 234
Mackintosh, Robert 211
Mad Hatters (backing band) 97, 136
Magnet Records 20
Margaret, Princess 297
Marquee Studios, Soho 35, 38

Martin, George 145–6, 148, 150
'Mary Goes Round' 28, 29
Maskery, Chris 279
Mason, Dave 25, 27
Mason, Steve 275
Matthew-Walker, Robert 217–18
May, Brian 294–5
Maya and Nandy 289–90
Mayhew, Michael 38, 39, 40
McCallum, David 225
McCann, Barry 255, 261
McCarron, Anday 235
McCartney, Linda 147, 150, 151
McCartney, Paul 39, 146–51
McCormick, Neil 288
McDonald, Roger 4, 256–7, 258
McGann, Mark 225
McKinnon, Dr Jake 219
McLaren, Malcolm 152
McPhee, Tony (TS) 35, 38
McPherson, Stewart 220–21
Meadmore, Robert 287
Mechanical Copyright Protection Society 263
'Mellowing Grey' (Family) 26
Melody Maker 28
Melua, Katie
    background 269
    discovered 269–70
    as singer/songwriter 270–71, 282, 283–4
    'look' 271, 276
    industry meetings 272–3
    recording deal 273
    distribution deal 275

INDEX

marketing/TV advertising 276–82, 285–6, 288–9, 293
Royal Variety Performance 280–81
success 276, 282, 286
as manufactured pop star 282
touring 283, 284, 293–4
fails to break through in US 283, 287
perceived as 'middle-of-the-road' act 287–8
interview with Neil McCormick 288
performs at Buckingham Palace 296–7, 303
nearly duets with Prince 289–90
songwriting sessions 291–2
loss of fanbase 293, 304
and Brian fucking May 294–5
welfare 287, 301
nervous breakdown 301
bond with Mike 302
marriage to James Toseland 302
signs with BMG Records 304
later life and career 304–5
'Call Off the Search' 270, 273
'The Closest Thing to Crazy' 236, 273–4, 275, 278, 279, 284, 289, 296
'The Flood' 292, 293
'I Will Be There' 303
'Nine Million Bicycles' 284–5, 286, 289–90
Call Off the Search 273–4, 279, 281–2
The House 291, 292–3
Ketevan 213, 302–3, 304
Pictures 288–9
Piece by Piece 285–6
Secret Symphony 302

Melua, Zurab 302
Men Who March Away (musical) 235–6
Mercury Records 237, 238
Metric Music 21, 22
Michael, George 20
Michell, Keith 222
Michener, James A., *Caravans* 110–11
Midem conference, Cannes 51, 52
'Midnight Smoke' 191
Mike Batt Orchestra 51, 91
Miliband, David 298
Miller, Ruth 260
Mills, Heather 151
Mills, Richard 231
miming, on *Top of the Pops* 93
'Minuetto Allegretto' 79
Montserrat 145–6, 147–51, 153
Moore, Sir Patrick 261
Morley, Angela 101
Morley, Sheridan 228, 230
Moss, Jerry 59–60
'Mr Poem' 21, 28, 29, 91
Mud 88, 89
Murphy, Julie 165–7, 169, 170
Murray, Charles Shaar 92
Murs, Olly 316
Music Bank Studios, London 309–10
Music in a Doll's House (Family) 23–8
'Music of the Night' 207
music producer, role 92
music publishing etiquette, in theatre 202, 206
Musicians' Union 33, 51, 56–7, 93–4
'Myths and Legends of King Merton Womble, The' 78–9, 214

Nash, Robin 68
National Symphony Orchestra of Ireland 236
Nationwide (TV programme) 89
Nelson's Dockyard, Antigua 143, 144, 153
New Edition (dance group) 95, 96
New Musical Express 21, 82, 92
New Seekers 60
New York 58–9, 81–2, 259, 276, 287
Nicholson, Pamela (Vanessa-Mae's mother) 239, 242, 245–6
Nightingale, Annie 77
'Nine Million Bicycles' 284–5, 286, 289–90
Novakowski, Kazak 9–10
Nowels, Rick 292

Oberstein, Maurice 96, 116
'Oh What a Circus' (Essex) 201
'Old Songs, New Songs' (Family) 24, 26–7
Olympic Studios, Barnes 25–7, 79, 214
Opportunity Knocks (TV talent show) 41
Orbison, Roy 204
  'It's Over' 15
Orbit, William 292–3
Osbourne, Ozzy 220
Osbourne, Sharon 220

Pacific Ocean 156, 159–60, 162
Panama Canal 155–6
Pan's People 85, 96, 97
Paradise Club, Southampton 18–19
Parkinson, Doug 222
Parkinson, Michael 221–2, 267
Partridge, Andy 244–5

Paton, Maureen 228, 235
Pebble Mill at One (TV programme) 67
Pegrum, Nigel 91
Performing Rights Society (PRS) 56, 57, 97, 262, 307
Perkins, Carl 146, 148–9
Peter Symonds' School, Winchester 11, 17–18
Peters, Nick 277
Peters Edition (publishers) 263–4
Petty, Tom 204
Phantom of the Opera, The 199–202, 204–6, 207
Phase Four (band) 13
Philharmania (album) 48
Philip, Prince, Duke of Edinburgh 295, 296, 297
Philips Records, Bayswater 20
Pilavachi, Costa 247, 272
Pinewood Studios 109
Pinnacle (Indie distributor) 275, 278, 279, 286
pirate radio 21
Planets (band)
  formed 253–5
  EMI record deal 255
  rehearsals 256, 258–9
  photo shoot in Segovia 256, 258
  debut concert 259–60
  support band for Deep Purple 261
  John Cage dispute 261–5
  appearance at Classical BRIT Awards (2002) 265
  disbanded 265–6
  Classical Graffiti 260, 261–2, 263, 265

INDEX

'Please Don't Fall in Love' 175, 178
Pointless Celebrities (TV quiz show) 316
Police (band) 133, 136–7
Pooh Corner (houseboat) 48
Popovich, Steve 81
Portland Hospital, Westminster 211
Portrait (orchestral album series) 49–52, 91
Previn, André 215
Priestley, J.B. 8
Primal Scream 310
Prince 288, 289–90
Prince Edward Theatre, London 224–5, 231
Prior, Maddy 90–91
Pugsley, Ben 260, 262
punk 121, 152
Purple Records 61

Quantick, David 315
Quast, Philip 222, 225, 234
Queen Mary (hotel), Los Angeles 157, 158–9
Quo Vadis (restaurant), Soho 181

'Railway Hotel' 100, 213, 267
Railway Hotel (unfinished musical) 317
Ramsden, Michael 38, 39
Rapid Eye Movements (double album) 129, 137
Really Useful Group (company) 206
Rees, Tony 58, 61
Reid, Stuart and Patsy 52
Reisdorff, Bob 28, 29, 91
'Remember You're a Womble' 71–2, 73, 79, 310

'rent' records 54–5
Renton, Andy 13–14, 38, 69
Revolution Club, Mayfair 44
Rice, Condoleezza 297–8
Rice, Tim 144, 176–7, 189–90, 201, 206
Rich, Bill 130
Richard, Cliff 175, 178, 193
Riddle, Nicholas 263–4
'Ride to Agadir, The' 100
Rippon Lea (mansion), Melbourne 192
Rivers, Tony 189
Robertson, Kate 308
Robertson, Marcus 308
Robertson, Max 76, 77, 82–4
Robinson, Jo-Anne 226
Roemer, Richard 58, 59
Rogers, Frank 55
Rolling Stones 12, 208
Ronnie Scott's jazz club, Soho 22
Rosen, Martin 100–101, 103, 104, 105
Rothstein, Jack 72
Rowe, Dick 19, 55
Royal Albert Hall
    Bond's launch concert 246, 249
    Classical BRIT Awards (2002) 265
    Snark production (1987) 208, 209, 212
Royal Festival Hall 256, 259–60
'Royal Gold' commission 295
Royal Philharmonic Orchestra 217–18
Royal Shakespeare Company 221
Royal Variety Performance (TV show) 280–81
royalties 55, 56, 57
Ruffelle, Frances 211–12
'Run Like the Wind' 115, 124, 159

Russell, Paul 73–4, 90, 110, 128, 159, 161, 166, 192, 196, 197
Rutland, June 85, 87, 309
Rutland, Pete 277
Ryan, Paul and Barry 14

'Sailing Ships From Heaven' 213
St Barnabas' Junior School, Bradford 31
Sale, Steve 269, 270
Savigar, Kevin 157–8
Savoy restaurant, London 261
Scarlet Opera 316
Schirmer, Anne-Kathrin 260, 262
Schizophonia (album) 99, 100, 110, 114–15, 240
Schöen, Peter 136
Schubert's 'Symphony No. 9' 10–11, 214
Schwarzhaupt, Sandra 238–9
Seaside Special (TV show) 86, 95, 96, 195
Segovia, Spain 256–7, 258
Selwood, Clive 64, 65
'September Song' (Weill) 270
SEX (King's Road boutique) 152
Sexy Beast (film) 184, 313–14
Shapiro Bernstein (music publisher) 49, 50–51
Shelley, Peter 19–20, 179
Shuttleworth, Paul 121
Sinclair, Michael 123
Six Days in Berlin (album) 142, 143, 151–3
Skydel, Barbara 276
Slade 85
Slingsby, Chris 224
Smallman, Oliver 179
Smith, Don ('Doctor Death') 56–7, 93–4

Smith, Joe 59
'Snooker Song, The' 195
Society of Distinguished Songwriters 184
'Soldier's Song' 131, 213, 234
Somers, Daryl 222
Songs from Croix-Noire (album) 315
Songs of Love and War (album) 213
Songwriters' Guild (later BASCA) 97, 98
Sony 193, 194, 272–3
Soul Committee 34
Southampton 5, 13
Sparks (band) 93
Special Operations Executive 260
Spedding, Chris 72, 100, 103, 108, 152, 274
Spinetti, Henry 274, 283
Spot Studios, Mayfair 36–7
Stage, The (magazine) 235
Starblend Records 196–7, 208
Stardust, Alvin 20, 178–9
Starlight Express 199
State Orchestra of Victoria 217, 221
Steeleye Span 90–92, 93–4
  'All Around My Hat' 91, 92
Stephenson, Pamela 220
Stevens, Cat, *Matthew & Son* 28
Stewart, Mike 157
Stewart, Rod 118–19, 143, 157–8
Sting 133, 136–7
Stocks, Kathy 14–15
Stollman, Norman 116
stop-frame animation 54
Stringer, Rob 272–3
Stuttgart Philharmonic 217
'Summertime City' 95–7, 195

INDEX

'Superwomble' 79, 89, 93–4
Superwombling (album) 89, 214
'Surrender to the Sun' 159
Surrey Sound Studios, Leatherhead 136
Swap Shop (TV series) 117
Sydmonton Festival 202
Sydney 162–3, 165–9, 170, 173, 175–6, 222
Sydney Symphony Orchestra 159, 161, 165–6, 217
synthesisers 136

tarot cards xi, 115
Tarot Suite (album) 114–15, 124, 159, 240
'Tarota' 240
Taupin, Bernie 22
Tayler, Sally 181
Tenerife 140–41
'Terry' (*Snark* investor) 230–31
Thacker, Jeff 280–81
That Lady's Twins (school duo) 14
Theobald, Bernard 158–9
Thomas, Vaughan 53, 136
Thompson, Mike 91, 104
Thompson, Robin 91
Thoughts and Words (London duo) 34
'Tiger in the Night' 273
'Toccata and Fugue in D minor' (arr. Batt) 241
top line writing 23, 49
Top of the Pops
   Kursaal Flyers on 121
   remake and miming rules 93–4
   'Summertime City' performance 96–7
   Wombles on 68, 69, 70, 84–5, 89, 93–4

Torvill and Dean 209, 218
Toseland, James 302, 304
Traffic, 'Hole in My Shoe' 25
Traveling Wilburys 204
Trident Studios, Soho 38
Tripp, Eddie 38
Troggs 53
Tug of War (McCartney) 146

UK Records 121
Ulvaeus, Björn 72–3, 144, 189–90
'Uncle Bertie' (seaside entertainer) 6
United Artists 44, 49
Universal Records 59, 247, 272, 283
Ure, Midge 208

Vanessa-Mae 238–42, 245–6
Vietnam War 56
'View From a Hill, The' 253
vinyl for records, shortage 66
Vulcan (Womble-like dog) 297

Wakeman, Rick 78–9
Walker, Sir David 296–7, 299
Walters, Paul 267–8, 274–5, 279
'War Song of the Urpneys, The' 220
Warbey, Yvonne 160
Waters, John 222
Watership Down (film) 100–101, 117
   see also 'Bright Eyes'
Watership Down (TV series): soundtrack and album 217, 247, 253
Watford Town Hall 217–18
Watson, Graeme 169
Waves (album) 133–4

Waymouth, Nigel 38, 39, 40
Wayne, Jeff, *The War of the Worlds* 196
Webb, Mimi 316
Webster, Bourby 246
Wellington Hospital, St John's Wood 211, 218–19, 257
Wendy and the Raconteurs 41–2
Wessex Studios, Highbury 28, 51, 55, 72, 91, 103–8
Westerhoff, Gay-Yee 246
Westwood, Vivienne 152
Wexler, Jerry 59
'Whatever You Believe' 232, 236
'When Flags Fly Together' commission 295–6
White, Julianne *see* Batt, Julianne
Whitfield Street studios 64
Whitney, John (Charlie) 24
Who, *Tommy* 60
Wilkinson, Colm 202, 213–14, 236
Williams, Big Joe, *Hand Me Down My Old Walking Stick* 36–7
Williams, Deniece 195, 208
Williams, Elmo 100, 110–12, 157
Williams, Ray 21, 22
Williams, Salima 4, 257, 258, 260
Williams, Stacy 110
Williamson, Malcolm 101
Wilmot, Gary, *Gary Wilmot – The Album* 243–4
Wilson, Al 34–5
Winchester 11, 14, 30
'Winds of Change, The' 134
Winehouse, Amy 282
Winstone, Ray 184, 311–12

'Winter's Tale, A' 176–7
Winwood, Muff 192, 195, 196, 272–3
Wisseloord Studios, Hilversum 132–4, 136–7, 144, 159
Withers, Gary 223–4, 230
Witt, Katarina 114
Wogan, Terry: Radio 2 breakfast show 267–8, 275, 278, 279, 296
'Womble Shuffle, The' 79
Wombles
  advertising campaign (2001) 253, 278
  characters 53–4
  costumes 65, 69, 76, 78, 81–2, 85, 87, 109, 309
  film *(Wombling Free)* 109
  Mike's reflections on 70, 307, 311
  merchandising 76–8
  as national phenomenon 70, 75
  origins 53
  pop group (*see* Wombles, the)
  promotion and image-building 66, 69, 70
  rights 54, 76, 86–7, 308, 311–12
  song lyrics 82–4
  stage musical disaster 86–9
  theme song 54–5
  TV series (1973) 53–4, 63
  TV series (2015) 311–12
Wombles, the (pop group)
  formed 68–9
  members 69, 100
  first single 63, 64–5, 66–8, 69, 71, 79
  first album 55, 63–4, 78
  on BBC's *Cilla* 66–7

338

INDEX

on *Top of the Pops* 68, 69, 70, 84–5, 89, 93–4
second single 71–2, 73, 79
chart success 67, 69, 78, 79
interval act at Eurovision (1974) 72
merchandising 77–8
Music Week Award (1974) 78
other songs and albums 78–9, 82, 88, 89
in America 81–2, 309
credibility 87–8
falling record sales 89
'Womble Mania' period 92–3
Steeleye Span stand-in for 93–4
at Glastonbury (2011) 308–11
Wombles, The (TV series, 1973) 53–4, 63
Wombles, The (TV series, 2015) 311–12
Wombles Copyright Holdings Limited 308
Wombles Limited 76–8, 82–4, 86–8, 90, 109
'Wombles on Parade' 82
Wombling Free (film) 109
'Wombling Merry Christmas' 79, 88
'Wombling Song, The' 54–5, 63, 64–5, 66–8, 69, 71, 79
Wombling Songs (album) 55, 63–4, 78
'Wombling Summer Party' 79
'Wombling White Tie and Tails' 79–80, 89, 109

Wonder, Stevie 70, 146, 149–51
Wood, Ivor 53–4
World Trade Center attack (2001) 259
Wright, Chris 129
Wright, Finbar 236–7
Wright, Jack 151
writer's block 193

XTC, *Apple Venus Volume 1* 244

Yates, Brian 272
Yates, Paula 144
Yetnikoff, Walter 95–6
Yoga for Health (TV series), music for 56–7

Zero Zero (musical fantasia)
  commissioned 159, 161
  concept 161
  writing 161–2
  production 165, 167
  battle with unions 163, 167–8
  auditions 168–9
  filming of TV Special 169
  airs on Channel 4 181
  reception 181–2
  re-released on Dramatico 182
Zhadi, Dr (Iranian film investor) 110–12
Zieman, Josh 287